BACON NATION

BACON NATION

125 IRRESISTIBLE RECIPES

PETER KAMINSKY & MARIE RAMA

Photography by Lucy Schaeffer

WORKMAN PUBLISHING

NEW YORK

Library of Congress Cataloging-in-Publication Data is available.

ISBN 978-0-7611-6582-8

Cover design: Raquel Jaramillo
Interior design: Sarah Smith
Author photo of Peter Kaminsky by Melinda McIlwain
Author photo of Marie Rama by Melissa Lucier
Photography by Lucy Schaeffer
Food stylist: Jamie Kimm
Prop stylist: Sara Abalan
Illustrations on pages 57 and 116 by James Williamson
Additional photography by fotolia: p. 14 Aaron Amat, p. 27 Tim Glass, p. 36 myfotolia88, p. 38 Klsbear, p. 51 vj, p. 190 design56

Workman books are available at special discounts when purchased in bulk for premiums and sales promotions as well as for fund-raising or educational use. Special editions or book excerpts also can be created to specification. For details, contact the Special Sales Director at the address below, or send an email to specialmarkets@workman.com.

Workman Publishing Company, Inc.
225 Varick Street
New York, NY 10014-4381
workman.com

Printed in the United States of America
First printing April 2013

10 9 8 7 6 5 4 3 2 1

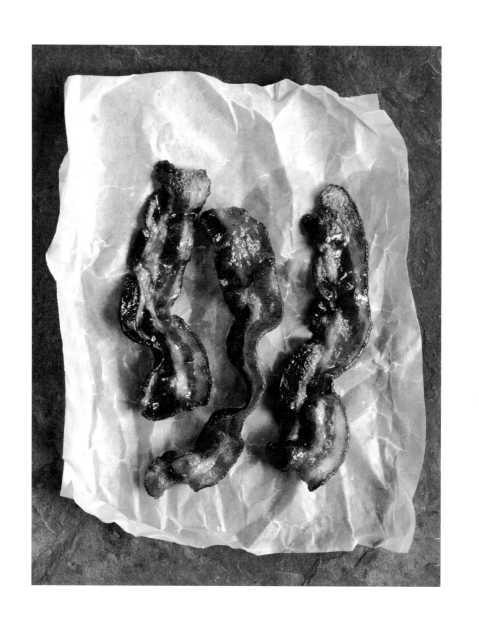

ACKNOWLEDGMENTS:

Thanks and appreciation go to:

Our editor Suzanne Rafer for believing in us and making our book better and more bacony.

Our agent, Mark Reiter, for the original bacon bracket that started it all and (since he's married to one of us) for taste-testing each recipe and always saying, "Yes, bacon!"

Our graphic team: Sarah Smith for a beautiful design, and Lucy Schaeffer, Jamie Kimm, and Sara Abalan for photographs that make us all hungry.

At Workman: Lisa Hollander, Anne Kerman, Melissa Lucier, Kate Karol, Selina Meere, Jessica Wiener, Bob Miller, Walter Weintz, Page Edmunds, and David Schiller. And to Peter Workman for supporting this book from the very beginning.

For technical and worldly wisdom: Nicholas Rama, Bill Schreiber, Pamela Johnson, Allan Benton, Sam Edwards III, Rick Lowry, Tanya L. Nueske, Ronny and Beth Drennan, Andrew Thielen, and the Sloan sisters of Swiss Meats and Sausage Company.

Special shout-outs to: Molly Kay Frandson for helping on the "therewillbebacon.com" blog; Workman's own Susan Bolotin for rolling up her sleeves to try out the Butternut Squash and Bacon Galette, and Chef Robert Wiedmaier for walking us carefully through his bacon-laced Coq Au Vin.

CONTENTS:

Blessed by Bacon

This is a book by bacon lovers for bacon lovers. When it comes to bacon, there are just two kinds of people in the world: those who adore bacon and those who have never eaten it. We definitely belong to the first group of people. And as for all those people who haven't tried bacon, say, vegetarians or folks who don't eat pork for religious reasons, while they may not eat bacon, that's not to say that they wouldn't love it if they did. They would.

To our way of thinking, bacon is the equal of pricey Périgord truffles, sybaritic Spanish saffron, and conspicuously consumed Caspian caviar. And, with bacon, just as we do before adding these more luxurious groceries to a recipe, we ask ourselves, "How much does it take to add just the right amount of flavor and texture?" As resourceful chefs have long known, a little bacon can turn a dish from blah to beautiful. Crumbled into a green salad, wrapped around a succulent shrimp, thrown into a pot of bubbling beans, or laid over a breast of spring chicken while it roasts in the oven, bacon takes good food and makes it fun.

There's a good and a bad side to the ability of bacon to improve food. You want to taste the bacon but you also want to know what else is in the dish so that the bacon subtly enhances rather than taking over. Bacon is not just smoky flavor or crispy texture. It is a complex ingredient. Great bacon starts with porky meatiness, an example of the supersavory flavor known as *umami* (from the Japanese word for "yummy") that we find so satiating. Its saltiness—just like table salt— pushes forward the other flavors in a recipe. Curing, aging, and cooking bacon brings out hundreds of delicious flavor compounds.

And then there is crunchiness. For the last half million years or so—ever since the discovery of fire, when we started preparing meat by cooking it and creating a perfectly charred crust—humans have craved crunchiness. There is nothing more cracklingly crunchy than a perfectly cooked piece of bacon. It satisfies.

As you know from food television, there are loads of places where people wolf down mega-calorie recipes made with unremarkable ingredients smothered with gobs of gloppy cheese and mucho bacon. It almost doesn't matter if your favorite double-wide TV host orders a cheeseburger, pizza, club sandwich, chef's salad, or a three-thousand-calorie bowl of *poutine;* it all tastes pretty much the same. Bacon and cheese overload isn't fair to your ingredients or your waistline and it's a downright diss to the full-flavored majesty of great bacon and superb cheese. You won't find any of those overkill recipes in this book.

Part of the current bacon craze is due, no doubt, to a social phenomenon that you might call "Good Nutrition Fatigue." There are so many experts giving us so many warnings about what's wrong with our diet that it makes you want to say "Get off my back" and curl up with a plate of Texas Wieners, followed by a pint of OREO chip ice cream, and a quart of Jim Beam.

Bacon obsession has become a way to proclaim our independence from the food police who would have us eat a diet mostly made with boiled lentils and mashed yeast. No doubt this explains the availability of such products as bacon-scented air fresheners, bacon jelly beans, bacon strip adhesive bandages; or how about the puzzlingly named Tactical Bacon. It's a "weapons grade" can of bacon designed for video game addicts. It's online sales testimonial offers this bit of strangeness: *"The zombies have fought long and hard, but the tide is seeming to finally turn. . . . we have been surviving on bacon. That is why we are strong; that is why we'll win."*

Kind of wacko? Yes. But what such products reveal is that we have a real pro-bacon movement happening in this country. We're all for it. But we are also for respecting bacon as a delicious invention that can elevate instead of dominate other foods. Rather than treating bacon as an ingredient of last resort to rescue an uninteresting recipe or run-of-the-mill ingredients, this book puts bacon in a place of honor as a true gastronomic star. As we found in the course of writing this book, bacon goes with just about everything. More than that, everything is better with bacon.

CHAPTER 1

PIG+SALT +SMOKE = BACON

Buy the Best Bacon: It Makes a Difference

"**W**hy pay a little more for good bacon?" we are often asked. "Doesn't all bacon taste pretty much the same?"

Yes and no. Like a bottle of regular table wine versus a prized vintage, bacon produced with the best ingredients will taste better. While it's true that bacon made with cheap ingredients from unremarkable pork will probably taste okay— hey, salt, sugar, meat, and fat could make a pair of sneakers fairly palatable—we have found that when you can get it, bacon from artisanal producers, and especially bacon from premium free-range pork, is the way to go. It's not just snob appeal. Your taste buds won't lie to you.

More and more supermarkets now carry really fine bacon. Some brands, like Niman Ranch or Benton's, are available in many parts of the country. There are now thousands of farmers' markets where you will often find local farmers who raise their own pigs and cure their own bacon. Their production won't be huge, and they are probably not known by more than the patrons of one or two markets, but how much do you need to make you happy? Latching on to one farmer who makes a really good product is like having your own private producer. Usually a lot more care goes into these small-production bacons than you can ever find with a big name brand.

We tried bacon from a number of quality producers when testing the recipes for this book and we recommend the ones you'll find on pages 289 to 297 without reservation. We'd be the first to admit, however, that if we really wanted to make something with bacon and all that was available was the nondescript supermarket stuff, we'd go ahead and cook with it. Even second-tier bacon has big flavor and "crispability." Still, all things being equal, when we can, we go for the good stuff.

While we sometimes specify using a thick-cut rather than a regular-cut bacon in our recipes, we don't as a rule call for a more specific bacon, such as cherrywood-smoked or a cracked black pepper bacon. You can assume that the more common applewood- or hickory-smoked bacon will work in the dish you are making. That said, today's bacon producers, big and small, are having a wonderful time adding cinnamon, black pepper, jalapeño peppers, maple syrup, garlic, and other spices and flavorings to their bacon or using cherrywood and even wood from old whiskey barrels to create bacons with different flavors and aromas.

WHAT'S IN A LABEL?

As in many things where the USDA is involved, bacon labeling can be confusing. You may see bacons that are labeled uncured. This is a little misleading. In terms of the real world all bacon is cured—that is, it is treated with salt and sometimes sugar to help preserve the fresh pork. Bacon is also smoked. All smoked products have naturally produced nitrates that act as a preservative. Bacon that is labeled cured has had more nitrates added. Generally we prefer the so-called uncured bacon because it is more natural and has fewer possible adverse effects on one's health.

Then there is the question of whether bacon is wet- or dry-cured. Wet-cured bacon is brined. Dry-cured is rubbed with salt and sometimes sugar and pepper. They are both good methods. We prefer the flavor and texture of dry-cured bacon, but it's purely a matter of taste.

Cooking Bacon

You don't need the skills of an *Iron Chef* contestant to cook bacon properly, but it does take some care. Hot spots on your skillet can produce bacon that is gristly and fatty on the ends and overcooked in the middle. Too hot and the bacon burns. Not hot enough and it is limp and oily. Thick-cut bacon needs to cook at a slightly lower temperature than thin-cut bacon. Here are some guidelines to getting the most flavor and best texture from your bacon. We say guidelines instead of rules because everybody's pan and stove are a little different, and bacon, just like any other ingredient, always varies.

You'll need to adjust the heat according to the type and heaviness of your pan or pot. A heavy cast-iron skillet works very well for sautéing bacon slices or cut-up pieces of bacon on the stovetop. A Dutch oven is our choice for stovetop-to-oven cooking. In our recipes, we use only an estimate of the time it takes to brown the bacon; your browning time will depend on the type of pan you are using, the intensity of the heat, the amount of bacon in the pan, the thickness and brand of the bacon, and other variables. But it's not hard to figure all this out after you've cooked some bacon once or twice. As a general guideline, bacon slices of a regular thickness will take from 6 to 10 minutes to cook starting in an unheated skillet, while bacon slices cut into small (1/4- to 1/2-inch) pieces will brown and crisp in 5 to 8 minutes. Of course, thick-cut bacon will take a little longer—from 7 to 12 minutes or more, depending on the thickness. So, our best advice is to monitor the cooking of bacon carefully, adjusting the heat and using your eyes to determine when it's done to your liking.

How Done Do You Like Your Bacon?

How fully cooked and browned you like your bacon slices is up to you. Some folks tell us they like the taste and texture that comes with moderate cooking so they fry the slices only until the fat is still soft and chewable. Others find that result dreadful. They prefer cooking the bacon until most of the fat is rendered and the bacon is crisp with a firm bite. Then there are those—and we are not among them—who like their bacon slightly to fully burnt without a trace of fat remaining so that it just about shatters when you bite into it.

We're not going to tell you how much to cook your bacon when you serve it alongside eggs or waffles, but we urge you to follow our directions when our recipes call for cooking cut-up pieces of bacon. Usually, the browned bacon pieces will go from the pan or skillet into the oven where they will cook longer. A lighter skillet browning ensures that some of the bacon fat, a main catalyst of flavor, will be released into the completed dish.

Panfrying Bacon Slices

Many people are impatient and cook bacon too quickly. We get the best results by cooking our bacon over medium heat so that it gently sizzles. Frying slices of bacon in a skillet requires some monitoring, so don't walk away until the slices are done the way you like them. No doubt you will need to adjust the heat to keep the right sizzle. We usually turn the bacon and move it around in the skillet at least once before the slices are fully cooked. Use metal tongs to turn the bacon and to transfer the slices to a paper towel-lined plate to absorb the excess grease.

Panfrying Diced Bacon

Most of the recipes in our book call for you to brown $1/4$- to $1/2$-inch pieces of bacon in a skillet or saucepan, rather than browning individual slices. The reason is a simple one: The bacon cooks more evenly. When bacon slices are first cut into small pieces or diced, we've found that it is easier to brown them uniformly and render the bacon fat without burning the meat.

Begin by setting the skillet, pot, saucepan, or Dutch oven over medium heat; add the cut-up pieces of bacon and adjust the heat up or down as necessary, stirring occasionally as the bacon cooks. As with full slices, you want enough heat to produce a gentle sizzling sound. Thicker-cut bacon requires a medium to medium-low heat to render the fat thoroughly without overbrowning the meat.

To prevent any splattering grease from hitting you when you stir the bacon pieces, use a long-handled utensil, such as a long-handled spoon or a Chinese bamboo skimmer. You might consider purchasing an inexpensive splatter guard to cover the skillet and cut down on bacon splattering your stovetop, your clothes, and you.

Baking Bacon

If you are cooking breakfast for a crowd or you need more slices than you can fit in a large skillet, oven baking is just fine. Baking bacon produces evenly browned slices. To bake bacon, position a rack in the center of the oven and preheat the oven to 400°F. Line a large broiler pan with aluminum foil, shiny side down. Set the broiler rack in the pan and arrange the slices of bacon on the rack without touching each other. Cook the bacon until golden brown, 11 to 15 minutes. The cooking time will depend on the thickness of the bacon slices. To ensure even browning, about halfway through the cooking time rotate the pan 180 degrees. When done, using metal tongs, transfer the bacon to paper towels to drain.

Microwaving Bacon

Before we tried cooking bacon in the microwave, we thought it was a horrible idea. Taking a lovely preindustrial food and nuking it seemed like sacrilege. Wrong: When you microwave bacon there's no greasy skillet or stovetop splatter to clean up and the bacon turns out fine. To microwave bacon, place five raw bacon slices in a single layer between pieces of paper towel on a microwave-safe plate. Microwave on high power for 45 seconds to 1 minute per slice, or about 5 minutes total. The bacon should be slightly crisp with the fat almost fully rendered. If you want the bacon to be more cooked, microwave it for 30 seconds to 1 minute longer. Cooking times will vary according to the power of your appliance,

SLICING BACON SLICES INTO UNIFORM PIECES

The best way to cut sliced bacon quickly into ¼- to ½-inch uniform pieces is to stack several slices on a cutting board (preferably a plastic board that can be washed with soap and water to eliminate any residual bacon fat). Then, using a sharp chef's knife, cut the slices crosswise into pieces of the desired width. Don't separate the pieces yet. Finally, while the bacon is still stacked, use the knife to make one or two lengthwise cuts down the middle of the stack, depending on how big you want the pieces.

so check for doneness after about 4 minutes. Wear an oven mitt to remove the plate from the microwave; it will be very hot. Then use metal tongs to transfer the bacon to a serving dish. Don't use this method for cooking bacon if the recipe calls for saving the bacon drippings; you won't have any.

Draining Bacon

Unless we tell you otherwise, get rid of the excess grease from cooked bacon by transferring it from the skillet or pan to a plate lined with paper towels. If the slices look exceptionally greasy blot them with more paper towels. We like using long-handled tongs to remove whole slices of bacon from the pan, while a slotted spoon works well for cut-up cooked pieces.

Ain't Nothin' Good Without the Grease

Bacon fat is rich in flavor and we never hesitate to recommend using it when we can if the recipe calls for fat in which to brown or sauté other foods. Many of us grew up in households where our moms or grandmothers kept a coffee can of bacon fat at the back of the kitchen stove. The fat was used and replenished almost daily for making dishes like fried eggs, boiled green beans, or skillet corn bread. Since then the discovery that animal fats contain high levels of cholesterol has—we would say misguidedly—altered our cooking and eating habits. Fat has calories, to be sure, but whether or not it affects cholesterol very much is a far from settled question. Fat is a vital component in a healthy diet, just not loads of it all the time. A healthier lifestyle doesn't mean we need to exclude moderate amounts of wonderfully flavored animal fats like bacon drippings, duck fat, chicken fat, or butter from our diets. If you choose to shy away from using bacon drippings, you can usually substitute an equal amount of vegetable oil for the fat called for in the recipe. Though we don't believe the dish will taste as good. We have intentionally created recipes that rely totally or partially on bacon fat for flavor, but at the same time we have worked carefully to strike a balance and appeal to health-minded cooks by ensuring that no recipe is overloaded with excessive fat.

Because the fat content of bacon varies from one producer to the next, you may fry up some pieces of bacon for a specific recipe in our book and find that the bacon has rendered too little fat. Not to worry; simply add a little olive or vegetable oil to make up the amount called for in the recipe. Likewise if your bacon renders too much fat, pour it off and either discard the amount you don't need or save the excess for another dish. And if it makes you feel nutritionally moral, you can always trim off and discard excess fat from the ends of the bacon slices before you cook them.

A quick perusal of Internet food websites shows us that cooking with bacon grease is still very much alive today. Here are some of the most popular uses we found for bacon drippings to enrich our own everyday cooking. We have just scratched the surface here. Experiment on your own whenever you need to cook with fat.

- Pop popcorn in bacon fat.

- Make Caesar salad dressing with bacon drippings in place of the olive oil.

- Fry chicken using four parts peanut oil and one part bacon fat.

- Add about 1 tablespoon of bacon fat per pound to raw hamburger, ground turkey, or venison meat before frying or grilling the patties.

- Fry liver and onions in bacon fat.

- Use bacon fat to make gravies and roux.

- Sauté onions, carrots, and/or garlic in bacon fat for vegetable soups.

- Use bacon fat to cook refried beans and sunny-side-up eggs.

- Stir 1 to 2 tablespoons of bacon fat into pots of boiling white beans, polenta, grits, or rice.

- Sauté sliced brussels sprouts in bacon fat.

- Add bacon fat when boiling water to cook or blanch green beans.

- When baking russet potatoes, coat the skin with bacon fat before putting the potatoes in the oven.

CHURNING THE BACON

When cooking cut-up pieces of bacon in a skillet, there's a point at which the bacon will turn quickly from a nicely browned stage to bacon that's slightly burnt or even fully burnt, and that's when it becomes inedible for most of us. To produce evenly browned pieces of bacon, here's what we do: About a minute before the bacon is fully browned, use a slotted spoon or a Chinese bamboo skimmer to turn the bacon pieces over a few times, or as we like to call it, churn the bacon in the hot fat. You want the pieces of bacon to keep sizzling and browning, but by churning the pieces in the drippings, you expose all of the sides to the fat, getting a nice, even browning without burning.

≋ Cook hash browns in bacon fat.

≋ Sauté chopped Swiss chard and other hearty winter greens in bacon fat.

≋ Fry sliced tomatoes in bacon drippings (great on sandwiches).

≋ Use bacon fat when making skillet corn bread; you'll get a crunchier crust.

≋ Substitute a tablespoon of bacon fat for other fats in single-crust pies.

Straining the Drippings

Many of our recipes call for bacon drippings. It's hard to be accurate when you try to pour, say, 2 tablespoons of bacon fat from a hot and heavy skillet. It's equally difficult to avoid pouring off the bitter, burnt brown bits that are left behind after you cook bacon. The way to get clear drippings that are easily measured is to transfer the drippings into a heatproof one-cup bowl (a coffee mug also works). Then, pour off the required amount of fat. The brown bits will have sunk to the bottom of the bowl or cup. Or, strain the drippings through a layer of cheesecloth set over a small bowl. (Some of our friends tell us they like the flavor of those browned bacon bits in the bottom of the skillet. In this case, don't bother to strain the fat.)

Thick or Thin?

Most bacon is sold presliced. It varies in thickness from thin (twenty-eight to thirty-two slices per pound) to regular (sixteen to twenty slices in a pound) to thick (ten to fourteen slices per pound). Slab bacon is sold in one piece and still has its rind, a thick, light-brown layer of pig skin that covers the top of the slab of bacon. The rind is usually removed before cooking. You can cut slab bacon into whatever size strips or pieces you desire. We especially like it for making lardons—thick strips that are perfect for stews and soups—because lardons release the bacon fat and flavor more gradually than thin strips or smaller pieces of bacon.

Most of our recipes use bacon of regular thickness. If you find that yours is thinly sliced and the recipe calls for using five regular slices, you will want to increase the number of slices you use to six or even seven. Or, if the bacon is relatively thick, use one slice less. However, as lovers of bacon we find it's always best to err on the side of too much rather than too little bacon: In fact, to our way of thinking it's really not erring at all.

A Matter of Taste

There are all kinds of flavored bacons on the market today. We encourage you to try these different bacons. For the most part we've written our recipes calling for unflavored hickory- or apple-wood-smoked bacon, but go ahead and experiment.

Storing Bacon

Bacon was originally created as a way to extend the length of time fresh pork could be kept. But that doesn't mean forever. Store bacon in the coldest part of the refrigerator. Always check the use-by date, although you can usually go a few days past the date without fear. Cook and eat the bacon within a week after opening the package. If it develops mold or smells rancid, heave it.

You can freeze bacon in its unopened package for up to one month. If you don't want to thaw a whole package, then wrap small amounts of bacon, say, two to six slices, tightly in plastic wrap and store them in the freezer in airtight freezer bags. All frozen bacon should be thawed before cooking. Soak the freezer bag in warm water for about 10 minutes to quickly defrost the frozen slices.

Recipes Optional

The most important thing that we hope you can take from this book is that bacon is an ingredient whose only limits are the cook's imagination. Just like salt, or pepper, or rosemary, or butter, bacon is something to turn to when dreaming up a recipe—which is to say, you don't always need our recipes or anybody's recipes. Many of our favorites started with us looking at what was on the kitchen shelves and in the fridge and then making something up on the basis of what we had on hand.

To put this assertion to the test, let's have a look around our kitchen and see what we can improvise. We have some pasta on the shelf, some fresh vegetables, and maybe a fresh herb like thyme or oregano. We have tomatoes—fresh and canned—but we're not of the school of pasta-sauce makers that says it always has to be a red sauce where tomatoes dominate. At the same time, we are not in the mood for a creamy or super-cheesy sauce. So we settle on vegetables, our goal being a dish that has as much vegetable as pasta, which is the best way we know to keep enjoying pasta without loading up on carbs.

Once we put pasta, say, linguine or perciatelli, on to cook, we chop and sauté some bacon and set it aside. (All the amounts will depend on how many people we're serving.) We dice an onion and cook it in the bacon drippings, with a little

MAKING LARDONS

Remove the rind from a slab of bacon. Cut the bacon slab crosswise into slices about a ½-inch thick. Stack two slices and cut them lengthwise into ½-inch-wide strips. Finally, cut the strips crosswise into lardons about 1 inch long.

olive oil if it's needed, until it's softened. Then we throw in garlic, grated fresh ginger, red pepper flakes, coarsely diced zucchini and bell pepper, and maybe some fresh thyme or oregano. When the vegetables are soft and tender (but not overcooked), we add the cooked bacon, along with a few cherry tomatoes cut in half. To this skillet sauce of mostly vegetables, we add the cooked, drained pasta, along with a little bit of the boiling pasta water. Finally, if it's needed, we add just enough olive oil to the sauce to moisten the pasta. Freshly grated cheese and freshly ground black pepper provide the finishing touches. So there you have it, a simple dish made from no recipe at all, with bacon adding its qualities of salt, meat, smokiness, and fat.

And While We're at It, Some More Ideas

Here are some other "nonrecipe" recipes that make good use of bacon. The list could go on and on, but you'll get the picture. Once you start thinking of bacon as a recipe ingredient, you'll find endless delicious ways to enhance your everyday meals.

- For a quick appetizer, roll handmade balls of goat cheese, flavored with chopped fresh basil or thyme, in finely chopped pieces of black pepper-flavored bacon.

- Wrap thin slices of raw bacon around bread sticks or asparagus spears and bake them in a 350°F oven until the bacon is crisp and brown, about 25 minutes.

- Use 2 to 3 tablespoons of bacon drippings, instead of butter or vegetable oil, to pop popcorn and then toss cooked diced pieces of bacon into the popped popcorn.

- Compose a salad of mixed greens dressed with a mayonnaise and mustard vinaigrette. Then toss in ripe cherry tomatoes, 1-inch pieces of cooked bacon, and toasted croutons. Enjoy your deconstructed BLT!

- Add cooked, diced bacon to your favorite mayonnaise-based or German potato salad and use some of the bacon drippings as a substitute for some of the fat in the dressing for either salad.

- Add crumbled cooked bacon, diced garlic, and chopped scallions to cooked lentils or dried beans and toss with a balsamic vinegar dressing for a healthy salad.

- Add browned, diced bacon to chicken salad recipes along with chopped green apples, celery, and sweetened dried cranberries.

- Toss ½-inch pieces of cooked bacon into thick soups, such as pea or cream of broccoli or even Manhattan clam chowder.

- Add cooked, diced bacon to scrambled eggs, omelets, and quiches.

- Top open-faced grilled cheese sandwiches with cooked slices of bacon, then broil them until the bacon is warmed through and the cheese is thoroughly melted.

- Sprinkle cooked, crumbled bacon on top of open-faced grilled cheese sandwiches along with toasted sunflower seeds and raisins.

- Place three slices of cooked bacon on top of a slice of toasted multigrain bread spread with a super-chunky peanut butter. Top with a second toasted slice of bread, cut the sandwich in half, and serve.

- Spread a flour tortilla with our Bacon Aioli (page 125), then layer two to three slices of smoked or pepper-flavored turkey, sliced avocado, and red onion on top. Wrap up the tortilla and eat.

- Instead of sausage, top your favorite pizza with 1-inch-long slices of lightly browned bacon before baking.

- Sprinkle 1-inch pieces of uncooked bacon over a roasting pan filled with 1-inch cauliflower florets, sliced red onion, and 2 to 3 cloves of garlic. Drizzle extra-virgin olive oil on top, sprinkle the cauliflower with curry powder and freshly ground black pepper to taste, and bake it in a 375°F oven until the cauliflower is tender, about 30 minutes.

- Add cooked ¼-inch pieces of bacon and cloves of roasted garlic to mashed potatoes.

- Add cooked ¼-inch pieces of bacon to stuffed twice-baked potatoes.

TAKE A PEEK

Testing dozens of different types of bacon has shown us that one of the major differences between brands of bacon is the proportion of meat to fat in a slice. Most producers give you a "peek flap" on the back of the package that allows you to view an individual slice without opening the package. The fat-to-meat ratio can vary even from one package to the next. So always peek before you buy.

≈≈≈ Add cooked ½-inch pieces of bacon to creamed spinach, using some of the bacon fat to make the creamy sauce.

≈≈≈ Sprinkle a mixture of cooked, crumbled bacon, chopped fresh herbs, and bread crumbs on top of baked or grilled ½-inch-thick slices of summer tomatoes or Vidalia onions and bake or grill them until the topping is golden brown.

≈≈≈ Sprinkle cooked pieces of bacon on grilled summer vegetables and toss them with an herb vinaigrette.

≈≈≈ Use bacon as a finishing touch for such cooked vegetables as broccoli, green beans, and summer squash. Cook diced bacon, save the bacon drippings, and drain the cooked bacon on paper towels. Heat the bacon drippings in a large skillet, add some chopped onion or shallots, and cook them until lightly browned. Then, add the cooked vegetables, cover the skillet, and cook until the vegetables are warmed through. Stir in the drained bacon and let everything cook for a minute or so. Season the vegetables with salt and pepper to taste and serve.

≈≈≈ Add cooked, diced pieces of bacon and some bacon fat to biscuit and quick bread batters, substituting an equal measure of the bacon drippings for whatever other fat is called for in the recipe, then bake as directed.

≈≈≈ Add cooked, diced bacon to pancake batter or sprinkle the browned bacon pieces over pancakes before drizzling maple syrup on top.

HOLD THE SALT

Bacon is salty—so, in making any recipe with bacon, our recommendation is to wait until the later stages of cooking before seasoning the dish with salt. Remember: You can always add saltiness but you can't remove it. Some producers (such as Oscar Mayer) now make a lower-sodium bacon that is quite good for bacon fans looking to reduce their sodium intake.

STARTERS, APPETIZERS & SWIZZLERS

Crispy Polenta Bites with
Sun-Dried Tomato Spread,
page 24

IN THIS CHAPTER...

To begin a meal you want something

that both stimulates your appetite yet satisfies your hunger . . . at least a little bit. The accent here is on "a little bit" because you also want the deliciousness of the meal to come through. Bacon, with its deep flavor and its saltiness, crunch, and fat is the perfect seasoning for other ingredients. Many of the chefs we spoke with in the course of writing our book said they use bacon when they want an ingredient that subtly alters the flavor of a dish so that people will say, "I taste something here that's different but I can't name it. What is that secret flavor?"

The secret is quite often bacon. Why, for example, would you want to tinker with a classic recipe like Sicilian caponata as we did on page 29? You'd think that dish made with olives, capers, and eggplant, would have flavor to spare. Our philosophy is there's no such thing as too much flavor. Bacon makes this delicious recipe divine. As an accent to such old standbys as cheese straws, salted nuts, stuffed artichokes, and baked clams, bacon adds its own delectable dimension.

Some of these appetizers can also be served as light suppers or only need a tossed salad to become a complete dinner. Our Bacon and Butternut Squash Galette is a wonderful party appetizer, but if you are looking for a meal that is light and very tasty, you'll be satisfied with a slice or two for lunch. Actually after a spin in the microwave it also makes a fine breakfast of leftovers. The Glazed Chipotle Meatballs or the Bacon and Tomato-Stuffed Artichokes are, likewise, good main courses, too.

Bacon is a crazy-good edible wrapper for foods like shrimp, scallops, chicken livers, stuffed dates, and asparagus. Bottom line, if you can mix it with bacon, you will improve it with bacon.

BACON SWIZZLE STICK

Makes 1 swizzle stick, can be multiplied as desired

Most swizzle sticks do one thing well: They swizzle. One evening, we invited our friend Richard Bonomo over to enjoy a cocktail and taste a few of our newly tested bacon recipes. Richard, a chemist and avid cook, helped us find a way to make a bacon swizzle stick hold its spiral shape by wrapping it in a paper towel before popping it in the microwave. Sometimes it really helps to have a scientist in the kitchen. The swizzle sticks are great with Bloody Marys, martinis, and planter's punch. Keep experimenting; it's fun.

1 slice medium-thick bacon (see Note)

Arrange a slice of bacon diagonally on top of a piece of paper towel. Holding the slice of bacon at each end, twist the slice in opposite directions into a tight spiral. Fold the paper towel in half over the twisted bacon slice so that the towel's opposite corners meet. Then, starting at the fold, roll the paper towel under the palms of your hands around the bacon into a tube. Microwave the bacon in its rolled paper towel on high power until it is firm and shaped like a swizzle stick, about 1 minute and 15 seconds. Because microwave ovens vary in power, check for doneness after about 1 minute. Unroll the paper towel and let the swizzle stick cool before using it as a garnish for your favorite Bloody or Virgin Mary.

NOTE: To make more than one bacon swizzle stick at a time increase the microwave time by about 1 minute for each additional slice of bacon. The length of microwaving time will depend on the power of your microwave oven.

BACON CHEESE STRAWS

Makes 14 cheese straws

History doesn't record the genius who came up with the idea of baking cheese into crisps, but our guess is it was someone in the Deep South in the days before refrigeration when cheese wouldn't keep very long. Cheese straws are the ideal predinner finger food—crunchy and salty, with just enough fat to keep the hunger pangs at bay. Some old-time recipes call for cheddar cheese, but with the puff pastry we use here we found in our testing that using cheddar can make the final result soggy. We love the concentrated umami punch in Parmesan, which gets even stronger and more satisfying when you add bacon. Cheese straws are great with beer, or Champagne, or martinis, or come to think of it, just about any cocktail.

You might ask why you would want to spend the time making cheese straws when the supermarket probably has pretty good commercial ones. Fair enough, but you can't buy bacony cheese straws like these.

6 slices bacon, diced

1 teaspoon your choice of hot sauce

1 sheet frozen puff pastry, preferably Pepperidge Farm, thawed at room temperature for 10 to 15 minutes

¾ cup (3 ounces) freshly grated Parmesan cheese

Scant ¼ teaspoon salt

1 Place racks in the upper-middle and lower-middle positions in the oven and preheat the oven to 425°F. Line 2 large baking sheets with parchment paper and set them aside.

2 Cook the bacon in a large skillet over medium heat until lightly browned and most of the fat is rendered, 5 to 8 minutes, stirring often and adjusting the heat as necessary. Using a slotted spoon, transfer the bacon to a paper towel-lined plate to drain. Place the bacon in a small mixing bowl and toss it with the hot sauce.

3 Place the puff pastry on a piece of parchment paper and sprinkle the pastry with half of the Parmesan cheese, half of the bacon and hot sauce mixture, and ⅛ teaspoon of salt. Place a second piece of parchment paper over the cheese and bacon. Using a rolling pin, press the cheese and bacon into the puff pastry by rolling back and forth several times over the pastry. Keeping the parchment paper in place, carefully flip the puff pastry over so the cheese and bacon side faces down. Remove the parchment paper from the top of the pastry and sprinkle the remaining Parmesan cheese, bacon mixture, and ⅛ teaspoon of salt over it. Cover the pastry again with the parchment

paper. Using the rolling pin, press the cheese and bacon into the pastry. Measure the puff pastry and then roll it out, as necessary, to form a 10½-inch square.

4 Remove the parchment paper from the top of the puff pastry and, using a pizza cutter or a sharp knife, cut the pastry into fourteen ¾-inch-wide strips. Holding a strip of pastry at each end, twist the ends in opposite directions into a spiral and place the pastry strip on a parchment-lined baking sheet. Repeat with the remaining pastry, arranging the cheese pastry strips about 1 inch apart and placing 7 on each prepared baking sheet.

5 Bake the pastry strips until they are puffed and golden brown, about 10 minutes, switching the positions of the baking sheets from the top to bottom racks after 5 minutes. Transfer the baked cheese straws to a wire rack to cool for about 5 minutes before serving. The cheese straws are best eaten the day they are made.

Cheese straws are an ideal predinner finger food.

SPICED NUTS with Bacon

Makes about 2 cups

The combination of crunch, sweetness, salt, and meatiness is irresistible to most folks. Add the nuance of aromatic spices and seasonings and you get pleasing notes and accents that make this simple recipe complex on the palate.

Glazing the nuts before combining them with the spice mix keeps them super-crunchy, never soft and soggy. Using bacon instead of butter produces a brawny flavor that stands up to a cold dark beer or a peaty single malt Scotch or fine old bourbon. We are partial to the combination of walnuts and cashews, but feel free to use whatever nuts you like, so long as they are raw and unsalted.

5 slices thick-cut bacon, cut into ½-inch pieces

1 cup unsalted raw cashews

1 cup unsalted raw walnuts or pecans

1 tablespoon granulated sugar

3 packed teaspoons light or dark brown sugar

½ teaspoon kosher salt

¾ teaspoon curry powder

½ teaspoon ground cumin

¼ teaspoon ground cinnamon

⅛ teaspoon cayenne pepper

1 Position a rack in the center of the oven and preheat the oven to 350°F.

2 Cook the bacon in a medium-size skillet over medium heat until lightly browned and most of the fat is rendered, 5 to 8 minutes, stirring often and adjusting the heat as necessary. Using a slotted spoon, transfer the bacon to a paper towel-lined plate to drain, setting aside 1 tablespoon of bacon fat in the skillet.

3 Line a large shallow rimmed baking sheet with parchment paper and scatter all of the nuts on it in a single layer. Bake the nuts until they begin to brown, about 5 minutes, then

rotate the baking sheet 180 degrees so the back of the baking sheet faces the front of the oven and bake the nuts until fragrant and slightly darker in color, about 5 minutes longer. Transfer the baking sheet to a wire rack and let the nuts cool.

4 While the nuts cool, combine the granulated sugar, 1 teaspoon of the brown sugar, and the salt, curry powder, cumin, cinnamon, and cayenne pepper in a medium-size mixing bowl. Set the spice mixture aside.

5 Add 2 tablespoons of water and the remaining 2 teaspoons of brown sugar to the

skillet with the reserved bacon fat. Let come to a boil over medium heat, whisking constantly. Stir in the nuts, setting aside the lined baking sheet. Add the drained bacon and cook, stirring constantly, until the nuts are glossy and the liquid has evaporated, about 1½ minutes.

6 Add the glazed nut mixture to the bowl with the spice mixture and toss well to coat. Transfer the nut mixture back to the parchment paper-lined baking sheet to cool completely. When cool, the nut mixture can be stored in an airtight container for up to 4 days.

CRISPY POLENTA BITES
with Sun-Dried Tomato Spread

Makes 48 polenta triangles

From Marie: "As a third-generation Italian American, I often crave polenta. Seeing it on restaurant menus with an expensive price attached to it always amuses me. In the northwest corner of Italy, in the mountains of Aosta where my grandparents came from, it was eaten daily as peasant food."

In this recipe, bacon, scallions, garlic, and smoky chipotle peppers infuse the polenta. Once it's cooked, the mixture is chilled, baked, and cut into crispy triangles with soft centers. They make tasty appetizer morsels by themselves, or you can top them with sun-dried tomatoes. Turn the polenta bites into a side dish by partnering them with a hearty bowl of beef or chicken stew, a tossed salad, your favorite bowl of chili—well, just about anything. If you're a polenta fan, you might never eat it again without adding some bacon to the bubbling pot.

Olive oil or vegetable oil cooking spray

4 slices thick-cut bacon, cut into
¼- to ½-inch pieces

2 scallions, both white and green parts,
finely chopped

3 large cloves garlic, minced

Salt

1 cup quick-cooking polenta

¼ chipotle pepper, packed in adobo
sauce, seeded and chopped

Freshly ground black pepper

Sun-Dried Tomato Spread
(optional; recipe follows)

1 Line the bottom of a 13- by 9-inch baking dish (Pyrex is fine) with parchment paper and coat the paper lightly with olive oil or vegetable oil cooking spray. Set the baking dish aside.

2 Cook the bacon in a large skillet over medium heat until it starts to brown and the fat begins to render, 3 to 5 minutes, stirring occasionally. Add the scallions and garlic and cook, stirring occasionally, until the bacon is lightly browned, the fat is rendered, and the scallions soften, 2 to 3 minutes. Set the scallion mixture aside.

3 Place 4 cups of water in a heavy-bottomed 4-quart saucepan, cover the pan, and bring to a boil. Add 1 teaspoon of salt, reduce the heat to low, then add the polenta to the water in a

very slow and steady stream while stirring with a wire whisk. Cook the polenta until it is soft and smooth, 4 to 5 minutes, whisking it often to eliminate any lumps. Remove the pan from the heat. Stir in the scallion and bacon mixture and the chipotle pepper. Taste for seasoning, adding more salt as necessary and black pepper to taste.

4 Pour the polenta into the prepared baking dish and refrigerate it, uncovered, until firm, about 1 hour. The polenta can be prepared up to this point and refrigerated overnight before cutting it into triangles and baking it the next day.

5 About 30 minutes before serving, position racks in the center and lower third of the oven and preheat the oven to 450°F. Line 2 baking sheets with aluminum foil and coat each lightly with olive oil or vegetable oil cooking spray.

6 When the polenta is firm, using the tip of a paring knife, slice it into 24 rectangles, then slice the rectangles into 48 triangles. Transfer the polenta triangles to the prepared baking sheets, arranging them about 1 inch apart.

7 Bake the polenta triangles until they are crisp and lightly browned, about 20 minutes, switching the positions of the baking sheets from the top rack to the bottom rack after 10 minutes.

8 Transfer the baked polenta triangles to a large serving platter and serve immediately topped with a small amount of the Sun-Dried Tomato Spread, if desired.

SUN-DRIED TOMATO SPREAD

Makes about ²/₃ cup

This spread works as a tasty condiment for a grilled burger or a piece of grilled white fish as well as a topping for the crisp polenta bites. Use a fruity, good-quality extra-virgin olive oil to enhance the flavor of the sundried tomatoes.

> 4 ounces (about ²/₃ cup) oil-packed sun-dried tomatoes, drained
>
> 2 to 3 tablespoons extra-virgin olive oil
>
> 2 teaspoons balsamic vinegar
>
> 3 tablespoons chopped fresh basil
>
> 1 tablespoon finely chopped red onion

Place the sun-dried tomatoes in a mini food processor or in a blender. Add 2 tablespoons of the olive oil and the balsamic vinegar and basil. Process until fairly smooth but still a little coarsely chopped. If the mixture is dry, add some or all of the remaining 1 tablespoon of olive oil. Spoon the sun-dried tomato mixture into a small bowl and add the red onion. Cover the tomato spread and refrigerate it until ready to use. You can prepare the spread several hours or even a day before you plan to use it. Let the spread return to room temperature before serving.

CHEERS FOR CHIPOTLE

We think of chipotles as Mexico's version of sun-dried tomatoes: a versatile ingredient that can be added to many recipes. Chipotle peppers are smoked jalapeños, so be sure to remove the seeds carefully as they are quite hot. Chipotles add a fiery smokiness to such dishes as chili, tomato sauce, or an omelet, and for that reason they work well with smoky bacon. Chipotles are often sold marinated in adobo, a sauce of tomatoes, vinegar, garlic, and spices. You can buy canned versions in specialty food stores that carry Mexican foods, or you can purchase them online. After opening a can of chipotles, you can freeze any leftover peppers in an airtight container for up to six months.

BACON JAM

Makes about ½ cup

I f anyone were to rank recipes by how much flavor you get compared to how much time they take to make, we think this one would be in the running for Most Flavor Per Minute. Bacon Jam combines almost all the flavor giants into one dish: saltiness, meatiness, sweetness, peppery heat, bright acidity, and fruitiness. It makes a wonderful condiment for hamburgers or grilled steak. It's great with cream cheese on a toasted bagel. And the next time you serve an appetizer platter of assorted cheeses, be sure to include a bowl of Bacon Jam. Your guests will love a spoonful of it atop a slice of goat cheese or Brie. The recipe is really no more than a road map that you should feel free to adjust according to your taste. We like it hot and spicy but it's delicious without jalapeños. When serving the jam with spareribs or grilled chicken, try rosemary instead of ginger. Bourbon has just the right amount of sweet, smooth smokiness that complements bacon so well, although a really peaty Scotch is worth a try, too.

½ pound (8 to 9 slices) applewood- or cherrywood-smoked bacon, sliced crosswise into ½-inch-wide pieces

1 medium-size shallot, diced (about ¼ cup)

1 teaspoon seeded and chopped jalapeño pepper

¼ cup packed light brown sugar

¼ cup apple cider vinegar

2 tablespoons fresh orange juice

2 tablespoons bourbon

3 pieces peeled fresh ginger, each about the size and thickness of a quarter

1 bay leaf

½ teaspoon honey

Freshly ground black pepper

Crackers and assorted cheeses (optional), for serving

1 Cook the bacon in a large skillet over medium heat until browned and crisp and the fat is rendered, 7 to 10 minutes, stirring often and adjusting the heat as necessary. Using a slotted spoon, transfer the bacon to a paper towel-lined plate to drain, reserving 1 to 2 tablespoons of the bacon fat in the skillet.

2 Add the shallot and jalapeño to the skillet and cook over medium-low heat until the shallot is softened, about 2 minutes, stirring often and scraping up the brown bits from the bottom of the skillet. Return the bacon to the skillet and add the brown sugar, cider vinegar, orange juice, bourbon, ginger, and bay leaf. Cover the skillet and let come to a boil, then reduce the heat and let simmer gently, uncovered, until most of the liquid has evaporated, 10 to 15 minutes, stirring occasionally.

3 Remove and discard the bay leaf. Transfer the bacon mixture to a mini food processor and pulse until the bacon is finely diced but not pureed, 10 to 15 times, pausing several times to scrape down the side of the bowl.

4 Place the Bacon Jam in a small bowl and stir in the honey and a couple of grindings of black pepper. Serve with crackers and assorted cheeses, if desired. The jam can be refrigerated, covered, for up to 1 week.

CAPONATA

Makes about 3 cups

Caponata is a flavor bomb of sweet, sour, and savory vegetables, spices, and seasonings. Although it's traditionally served as an appetizer, when you are stuck for something to eat with steak or grilled chicken or as a light lunch with a few crackers, you may find, as we do, that this Sicilian/Neapolitan eggplant stew becomes one of your go-to recipes. You might wonder how your palate can make room for bacon amid the strong flavors of raisins, tomatoes, eggplant, fennel, olives, vinegar, and red pepper flakes. One taste, though, and you'll remember: There's always room for some bacon.

Eggplant soaks up copious amounts of oil when it's sautéed in a pan. To avoid an overly oily caponata, we first roast the eggplant in the oven, using only 2 tablespoons of olive oil. Then we use about 2 tablespoons of bacon drippings to sauté the onion, fennel, red pepper, garlic, and tomatoes. Many caponata recipes call for celery, but we prefer fennel, which has the same crunch plus a hint of licorice that punches up the sweetness in the caramelized vegetables.

1 large eggplant (about 1¼ pounds), cut into ½-inch cubes (about 6 cups)	3 ripe plum tomatoes (about ¾ pound), cored and chopped
2 tablespoons extra-virgin olive oil	2 tablespoons tomato paste
½ teaspoon kosher salt	4½ teaspoons packed light brown sugar
5 slices bacon, cut into ½-inch pieces	¼ cup red wine vinegar
1 medium-size yellow onion, chopped	¼ teaspoon crushed red pepper flakes
¾ cup diced fennel or celery	¼ cup minced fresh flat-leaf parsley leaves
½ cup red bell pepper, stemmed, seeded, and diced	¼ cup diced oil-packed black olives
2 large cloves garlic, minced	3 tablespoons golden raisins
	Table salt

1 Preheat the oven to 400°F. Line a baking sheet with parchment paper.

2 Place the eggplant in a large mixing bowl.

Add the olive oil and toss to mix, then sprinkle the kosher salt on top. Arrange the eggplant in a single layer on the prepared baking sheet. Bake the eggplant until tender, about 20 minutes.

3 While the eggplant cooks, cook the bacon in a large, deep-sided skillet or a saucepan over medium heat until it is lightly browned and most of the fat is rendered, 5 to 8 minutes, stirring often and adjusting the heat as necessary. Add the onion, fennel or celery, red bell pepper, and garlic and cook, stirring occasionally, until the vegetables are lightly browned at the edges, 8 to 10 minutes. Add the tomatoes and the baked eggplant. Cover the skillet and continue cooking over medium heat until the tomatoes soften a little, 3 to 4 minutes.

4 Mix the tomato paste with 2 tablespoons of water and stir it into the skillet. Stir in the brown sugar, wine vinegar, crushed red pepper flakes, parsley, olives, and raisins. Reduce the heat to medium-low and let simmer, partially covered, stirring occasionally, until the caponata is thickened and the flavors are fully blended, about 8 minutes.

5 Taste for seasoning, adding table salt as necessary. Refrigerate the caponata for at least 4 hours or overnight if possible. Let the caponata return to room temperature before serving. The caponata can be refrigerated, covered, for 4 to 5 days.

GLAZED CHIPOTLE MEATBALLS
Makes 32 to 36 meatballs

When people show up hungry, meatballs disappear in a hurry. This is a good thing. It means you have served something that puts everyone in a satisfied frame of mind. The bacon contributes a salty meatiness and succulence to the meatballs, the chipotle peppers offer smoky heat, and the sweet and tart combination of brown sugar, tomato, and lime juice in the glaze for the meatballs adds depth. Savory, meaty, and with a flavor that might be overly strong in a main course, these bite-size meatballs go beautifully with cocktails or beer.

⅔ cup dry homemade fine bread crumbs
(see page 32)

⅓ cup milk

6 slices bacon, diced

2 tablespoons tomato paste

1 tablespoon fresh lime juice

2 packed teaspoons light or dark brown
sugar

Salt

1 small onion, finely chopped
(about ⅔ cup)

3 large cloves garlic, finely chopped

2 teaspoons ground cumin

1 teaspoon dried oregano

1 teaspoon ground cinnamon

¾ pound ground pork

½ pound ground beef

1 large egg, lightly beaten

¼ cup chopped fresh cilantro

2 canned chipotle peppers, packed
in adobo sauce, seeded and finely
chopped (about 1 tablespoon)

1 Combine the bread crumbs and milk in a large mixing bowl. Set the bread crumb mixture aside.

2 Cook the bacon in a large skillet over medium heat until lightly browned and most of the fat is rendered, 5 to 8 minutes, stirring often and adjusting the heat as necessary. Using a slotted spoon, transfer the bacon to a paper towel-lined plate to drain, reserving the bacon fat in the skillet. Spoon 1 tablespoon of the bacon fat into a small bowl. Add the tomato paste, lime juice, brown sugar, and a pinch of salt and stir to combine. Set this glaze aside for brushing on the meatballs before baking.

3 Preheat the oven to 400°F.

4 Heat the remaining bacon fat in the skillet over medium heat. Add the onion and garlic and cook, stirring occasionally, until the onion is softened and lightly browned, 4 to 5 minutes. Add the cumin, oregano, and cinnamon

and cook, stirring, until fragrant, about 30 seconds. Add 2 tablespoons of water and cook briefly until the water has evaporated, scraping up any brown bits from the bottom of the skillet. Add the contents of the skillet to the bread crumb mixture followed by the pork, beef, egg, cilantro, chipotle peppers, drained bacon, and a scant ½ teaspoon (or to taste) of salt. Mix well.

5 Lightly grease a large rimmed baking sheet. Using your hands, roll a heaping tablespoon of the meatball mixture into a small ball. Place the meatball on the prepared baking sheet. Repeat with the remaining meatball mixture, spacing the meatballs about 1 inch apart. Brush the top of each meatball with the reserved glaze. Bake the meatballs until cooked through, about 12 minutes. Serve the meatballs hot.

MAKING AND TOASTING
FRESH BREAD CRUMBS

To make fresh bread crumbs, break slightly stale country white or Italian bread into 1- to 2-inch
pieces or chunks. Place the pieces of bread in a food processor or blender and pulse until the
crumbs are of the desired degree of coarseness. Untoasted bread crumbs can be stored in a
sealed freezer bag or airtight plastic container in the freezer for up to six months. Toast them just
before using.

To toast bread crumbs, preheat the oven to 350°F. Spread the bread crumbs out on a rimmed
baking sheet and toast them in the oven until lightly browned, 5 to 10 minutes. Watch the bread
crumbs carefully so they don't overbrown and burn. Or, put the bread crumbs in a dry skillet over
medium heat and cook them until golden, 4 to 5 minutes, tossing the crumbs and shaking the
skillet occasionally to prevent them from burning.

POACHED SHRIMP with Red Onions

Serves 6

French chefs, who have the time, the skills, and most important, the staff, like to create flavorful but complicated poached fish stocks using the ground-up shells of lobsters, mussels, shrimp, and clams. For the rest of us, who don't have the resources of these master chefs, we have found that adding just shrimp shells as part of a quick homemade stock lays a pretty solid foundation for poaching shrimp. We also found that tossing a thick slice of bacon into the poaching liquid produces a pleasant creamy smokiness for the poached and chilled shrimp. We like serving these poached shrimp as a prologue to a dinner of several courses; it's a light appetizer that welcomes the heavier main courses that follow. Served with a salad, the shrimp make a light meal.

1 pound extra-large shrimp (21 to 24 per pound), deveined in their shells (see box below)

¼ cup dry white wine

¼ cup white wine vinegar

¼ cup extra-virgin olive oil

1 slice thick-cut bacon, cut into 2 inch pieces

2 large cloves garlic, peeled and lightly crushed with the flat side of a chef's knife

5 black peppercorns

2 bay leaves

Salt

4 to 5 very thin red onion slices

Hot sauce of your choice

1 Remove the shells from the shrimp and place the shells in a large skillet with the white wine, wine vinegar, olive oil, bacon, garlic, peppercorns, bay leaves, and a pinch of salt. Add 1 cup of water. Cover the skillet and bring the mixture to a boil over high heat. Then, reduce the heat as necessary and let the poaching liquid simmer until the flavors blend, about 5 minutes.

2 Add the shrimp and cook over medium-low heat, covered, until the shrimp are opaque and no longer translucent, 2 to 3 minutes. (Turn the shrimp over in the poaching liquid once or twice to help them cook evenly but don't let the shrimp overcook or they will toughen.) Using tongs or a slotted spoon, transfer the shrimp to a medium-size bowl, reserving the poaching liquid in the skillet. Cover the shrimp loosely with plastic wrap and refrigerate them.

3 Bring the poaching liquid to a boil, then reduce the heat as necessary and let simmer until the liquid is reduced to 1 to 1¼ cups. Strain the poaching liquid and discard the solids. Refrigerate the poaching liquid until chilled, about 1 hour. Pour the chilled poaching liquid over the shrimp, add the red onion, and stir to mix. Let the shrimp marinate in the refrigerator, covered, for a few hours, or overnight if you have the time, turning the shrimp in the marinade once or twice.

4 Before serving, season the shrimp with salt and hot sauce to taste, tossing the shrimp again in the marinade. Transfer the shrimp from the marinade to a serving platter, scatter the red onion slices on top, and spoon some of the marinade over all.

SHRIMP SIZE ADVISORY

Supermarkets don't have uniform names for shrimp. One pound of large shrimp in one store is one pound of jumbo shrimp in another. When shopping for shrimp, it's best to ignore the size listed on the label and instead purchase the shrimp according to how many are in a pound. Colossal shrimp come ten to fifteen per pound. Jumbo shrimp have a count of sixteen to twenty per pound. Extra-large shrimp are likely to come twenty-one to twenty-four per pound. Large shrimp will have a count of twenty-five to thirty per pound. And medium-size shrimp will have a count of thirty-one to thirty-five per pound.

BACON-WRAPPED SHRIMP
with Scallions and Ginger

Makes 12; serves 6 as an appetizer

There are oodles of recipes that call for wrapping whole shrimp in slices of bacon before broiling, baking, grilling, or microwaving them. Often these recipes never live up to the promise of the ingredients. The shrimp, especially farm-raised frozen shrimp, may be overpowered by the bacon. To perk up the shrimp we have added a traditional Asian marinade of scallions, ginger, garlic, soy sauce, and brown sugar. The bacon is crisp on the outside with moist, flavorful shrimp inside.

2 scallions, both white and green parts, thinly sliced

1 tablespoon light soy sauce

2 teaspoons finely chopped peeled fresh ginger

1 packed teaspoon light or dark brown sugar

1 large clove garlic, minced

⅛ teaspoon cayenne pepper, or more to taste

12 jumbo shrimp (16 to 20 per pound), peeled (leaving the tail on) and deveined (see Notes)

4 slices bacon (see Notes)

1 Combine the scallions, soy sauce, ginger, brown sugar, garlic, and cayenne pepper in a medium-size mixing bowl. Taste for seasoning, adding more cayenne as necessary. Add the shrimp, toss to coat in the mixture, and let stand for 15 to 20 minutes.

2 Cut each slice of bacon crosswise into 3 equal pieces.

3 Position a rack in the lower third of the oven and preheat the oven to 450°F. Cover the bottom of a large roasting pan completely with aluminum foil.

4 Remove a shrimp from the marinade. Working on a flat surface, press pieces of scallion, garlic, and ginger from the marinade onto the sides of the shrimp. Wrap a piece of bacon around the shrimp, securing it with a wooden toothpick. Repeat with the remaining shrimp.

5 Arrange the bacon-wrapped shrimp on the aluminum foil-lined roasting pan so that they are not touching and bake them until the shrimp begin to firm up and the bacon begins to brown and render its fat, 5 to 6 minutes. Remove the roasting pan from the oven and, using long-handled tongs, carefully turn the shrimp over. Return the pan to the oven and bake the shrimp until they are cooked through and the bacon is lightly browned, 3 to 5 minutes longer. Serve the shrimp immediately.

NOTES: Larger shrimp (ten to fifteen per pound) also work well for this dish. If your bacon is fatty, be sure to cut off the excess fat at the ends of each slice before wrapping the shrimp.

To make this recipe on the grill, instead of holding the bacon in place with toothpicks, thread the bacon-wrapped shrimp a few inches apart on metal skewers and grill them on the grill's food grate set over a bed of medium-hot coals for 3 to 5 minutes per side.

TREAT GINGERLY

We have an unabashed culinary love for fresh ginger. Pungent, clean, crisp, tangy, spicy, warm, bright, intense: Ginger has all these qualities and few limitations as an ingredient. It's one that partners so well with all the taste factors—smokiness, saltiness, meatiness, and a slight sweetness—found in bacon. Ginger brightens a dish like succotash and can punctuate maple syrup and pancakes, ice cream, and cookies. Its effect is most pronounced when it is shredded raw into a salad dressing or marinade. Ginger softens a bit when combined with garlic in oil—a mix essential to so many Chinese stir-fries. From Japan through China and India to Africa and the Caribbean, you'll find ginger in stews, soups, teas, beers, cookies, and sauces. A great drink on a hot day is fresh ginger lemonade, made by simply adding grated ginger to that quintessentially American mixture of fresh lemon juice, water, and sugar. If you're not a gingerphile, simply leave it out or reduce the amount we call for in our recipes. But we've found in our testing that fresh ginger works exceptionally well with bacon.

CLAMS CASINO

Makes 24 stuffed clams

According to legend, Clams Casino was first created in 1917 in Rhode Island at the Narragansett Pier Casino for a society lady who wanted a unique dish for her dinner guests. Good story but, like most food legends, probably not true. "Dishes are not invented; they evolve," maintains the scholarly food journal *Gastronomica*. We tend to agree, especially when there are two ingredients—clams and bacon—that seem to cry out for each other.

While this dish has many variations, especially in good old-fashioned red sauce restaurants, its signature ingredients are still clams, bell pepper, butter, bread crumbs, and bacon. In our version we use bacon as an ingredient twice—once as a fat for sautéing and again in the topping. Instead of painstakingly (and often painfully) shucking clams, we steam them in a little white wine and water just until their shells start to open. We omitted the strong seasoners called for in a lot of Clams Casino recipes, for example Tabasco or Worcestershire sauce. You'll find that our seasonings don't get in the way of the intoxicating combination of clams and bacon.

3 slices thick-cut bacon, cut into ½-inch pieces (see box, page 45)

About 2 tablespoons (¼ stick) unsalted butter

¼ cup plus 2 tablespoons diced green bell pepper

¼ cup plus 2 tablespoons diced fennel

2 medium-size shallots, diced

2 large cloves garlic, minced

½ cup toasted coarsely ground homemade bread crumbs (see page 32)

2 tablespoons chopped fresh flat-leaf parsley

Grated zest from half a medium-size lemon, plus 1 lemon (optional), cut into 6 wedges

Freshly ground black pepper

⅔ cup dry white wine

24 littleneck clams in their shells (each 2 inches or less in diameter), well scrubbed (see box, page 38)

1 Cook the bacon in a medium-size skillet over medium heat until the bacon is browned but not too crisp and most of the fat is rendered, 5 to 7 minutes, stirring often and adjusting the heat as necessary. Using a slotted spoon, transfer the bacon to a paper towel-lined plate to drain, reserving the bacon fat in the skillet. You should have about 2 tablespoons of fat. If necessary, pour off enough fat or add enough butter to the skillet to measure 2 tablespoons.

2 Heat the bacon fat in the skillet over medium heat. Add 2 tablespoons butter, green bell pepper, fennel, and shallots and cook, stirring occasionally, until the vegetables are softened, 4 to 5 minutes. Add the garlic and cook until fragrant, about 1 minute. Transfer the mixture to a small bowl and stir in the drained bacon, bread crumbs, parsley, and lemon zest. Season with black pepper to taste and set the mixture aside.

3 Position a rack in the center of the oven and preheat the oven to 475°F.

4 Add the white wine and ⅔ cup of water to a large deep saucepan or other heavy-bottomed pot big enough to hold all of the clams (a pasta pot works fine). Cover the pot and let the liquid come to a boil over high heat. Add the clams, cover the pot again, and let the liquid return to a gentle boil. Steam the clams just until they begin to open, about 5 minutes, depending on the size of the clams. Watch the clams carefully; if you cook them too long they will become tough (the length of time the clams will take to cook depends upon the size of the clams and the pot). Using tongs, transfer the clams from the pot to a large bowl just as they start to open. Discard any clams that do not open after about 8 minutes.

5 Let the clams cool slightly and then, working over the bowl to catch the juice, carefully twist off and discard the top shells while retaining as much juice as possible in the bottom shells. Set the reserved clam juice aside. Using a paring knife, sever the 2 muscles that attach the clams to each side of their bottom shells. Then, arrange the clams, in their shells, on a large rimmed baking sheet.

6 Add 2 tablespoons of the reserved clam juice to the bacon and bread crumb mixture. Top each clam with an equal portion of the topping, mounding it slightly. Bake the clams until they are heated through and the topping is crisp and brown, 9 to 10 minutes. Transfer the clams to a platter and, if desired, garnish them with the sliced lemon wedges. Serve immediately.

CLAMMING UP

Clams should not be stored for more than a day in your refrigerator after you have purchased them. When you get the clams home, unwrap them from their packaging so they can breathe and remain alive until you cook them. To clean clams, soak them for about 20 minutes in fresh water to cover. As clams breathe they filter water, pushing salt and sand out of their shells. After soaking the clams, you'll be tempted to turn them all out at once into a colander to drain. Don't. You might accidentally crack their shells or pour the salt and gritty sand back over them. Instead, use tongs to lift them individually out of the water and into a bowl or the cooking pot.

BACON AND TOMATO-STUFFED ARTICHOKES

Serves 2

Stuffed turkey, stuffed eggplant, stuffed pork roast, and—in this case—stuffed artichokes are all more fun than unstuffed. We realize that the world is divided into two kinds of cooks: those who don't mind prepping artichokes and those who find it a major pain. This recipe won't change your mind on that burning culinary divide. But if you love the way that artichokes provide a mild, slightly nutty, smooth-textured base for other flavors (we sure do), you will find your labor well rewarded. We recommend using large, sweet vine-ripened cherry tomatoes in the stuffing.

FOR THE ARTICHOKES

2 large artichokes

Salt

3 slices thick-cut bacon, diced

2 large shallots, diced

8 large, ripe cherry tomatoes, cut in quarters

1 large clove garlic, minced

¼ cup coarsely ground homemade bread crumbs (see page 32)

3 tablespoons chopped fresh flat-leaf parsley

2 tablespoons toasted pine nuts (see page 264), coarsely chopped

Grated zest of half a medium-size lemon

Freshly ground black pepper

2 teaspoons fresh lemon juice

About 4 teaspoons extra-virgin olive oil

FOR THE OLIVE OIL AND LEMON DRESSING

4 teaspoons extra-virgin olive oil

2 teaspoons fresh lemon juice

Salt and freshly ground black pepper

1 Prepare the artichokes: Trim the artichokes so that their stems are flush with their bottoms. Cut off and discard the top third from each artichoke and, using kitchen shears, cut off the tips of the remaining leaves. Place the trimmed artichokes in a saucepan, bottom side down, so they fit snugly against the side of the pan. Add enough water to barely cover the artichokes, salt the water lightly, cover the pan, and bring to a boil. Let the artichokes simmer, partially covered, until partially cooked, about 20 minutes.

2 Meanwhile, preheat the oven to 375°F.

3 Cook the bacon in a medium-size skillet over medium heat until very lightly browned, 3 to 5 minutes, stirring often and adjusting the heat as necessary. Add the shallots, stirring to coat them in the bacon fat, and cook until the shallots soften, 3 to 4 minutes. Add the cherry tomatoes and garlic and cook, stirring, until the garlic is fragrant and the tomatoes soften, about 2 minutes. Stir in the bread crumbs, parsley, pine nuts, and lemon zest until well combined. Season the stuffing with salt and pepper to taste. Set the stuffing aside.

4 Remove the artichokes from the pan and turn them upside down on a plate to drain. When cool enough to handle, place the artichokes top side up in an 8-inch-square baking dish. Gently pull the leaves outward from the center of each artichoke so they open slightly. Remove the small purple-tipped leaves in the center above the choke. Using a spoon or melon baller, remove and discard the fibrous choke from each artichoke. Sprinkle 1 teaspoon of lemon juice into the cavity of each artichoke and then evenly distribute the stuffing between the 2 artichokes, placing it in the cavities and between the outer leaves. Brush the outer leaves of each artichoke with 1 to 2 teaspoons of olive oil to lightly coat.

5 Add enough water to the baking dish to come about one quarter of the way up the sides of the artichokes. Cover the baking dish with a large piece of aluminum foil and bake the artichokes until a leaf at the base of an artichoke comes out easily when pulled, 25 to 30 minutes. Using tongs or a slotted spoon, gently remove each artichoke from the baking dish so that the cooking water drains off; then place the stuffed artichokes on a serving dish or 2 individual plates.

6 Make the olive oil and lemon dressing: Whisk together the 4 teaspoons of olive oil and the 2 teaspoons of lemon juice in a small bowl. Drizzle the dressing over the outer leaves of each artichoke and season them lightly with salt and black pepper before serving.

CARAMELIZED ONION TART
with Goat Cheese and Lardons

Serves 6 to 8

Our thanks to *New York Times* food columnist and cookbook author David Tanis (*A Platter of Figs and Other Recipes*) for giving us a recipe for this lovely, rustic onion and bacon tart. You can adapt it to your own taste by adding or substituting a variety of ingredients. David champions the use of pitted green olives if you're a vegan, but we prefer the rich smokiness of bacon lardons. You could try adding ripe cherry tomato halves or substituting whole basil leaves for the thyme. We first tested the tart using only all-purpose white flour, as the original recipe calls for, and then added some graham flour in another test to give the dough some extra heft. The good news is it is delicious either way.

FOR THE TART DOUGH

1½ cups unbleached all-purpose flour, or 1 cup unbleached all-purpose flour and ½ cup graham flour, plus flour for rolling out the dough

1 teaspoon rapid-rising dry yeast, such as Fleischmann's (from one ¼-ounce package)

½ teaspoon kosher salt

Pinch of sugar

½ cup lukewarm water, heated to between 120° and 130°F

1 tablespoon unsalted butter, melted

1½ teaspoons extra-virgin olive oil

FOR THE ONION AND BACON TOPPING

1 tablespoon unsalted butter

1 tablespoon extra-virgin olive oil

3 large onions (about 1½ pounds total), sliced ⅛ inch thick, large rounds cut in half crosswise

Salt and freshly ground black pepper

1 tablespoon fresh thyme leaves

6 to 7 ounces slab bacon, rind removed (see page 57)

4 ounces goat cheese

3 tablespoons sour cream

1 Prepare the tart dough: Combine the flour, yeast, the ½ teaspoon of kosher salt, and the sugar in the metal bowl of a standing mixer.

2 Add the warm water, the 1 tablespoon of melted butter, and the 1½ teaspoons of olive oil and, using a wooden spoon, stir the dough into a ball. Using a bread-making hook, beat the dough on medium speed until a smooth dough forms, about 5 minutes. Cover the bowl with a damp towel or plastic wrap and let stand until doubled in size, about 1 hour.

3 Prepare the onion and bacon topping: Heat the 1 tablespoon of butter and 1 tablespoon of olive oil in a large skillet over medium-high heat. Add the onions and cook until evenly lightly browned, about 10 minutes, stirring and adjusting the heat as necessary. Season the onions with salt (lightly as the lardons add salt) and pepper to taste. Remove the skillet from the heat and stir in the thyme leaves.

4 Cut the slab of bacon into lardons by first cutting it crosswise into slices about ½ inch thick. Stack 2 slices and cut them lengthwise into ½-inch-thick strips. Finally, cut the strips crosswise into lardons about 1 inch long (see page 45). Place the lardons in a small saucepan and cover them with about ½ inch of water. Bring to a boil over high heat, then reduce the heat as necessary and let the lardons simmer, about 2 minutes. Drain the lardons and if desired trim off any excess fat. Set the lardons aside.

5 Position an oven rack in the center of the oven and preheat the oven to 375°F. Line a 12-by 17-inch baking sheet with parchment paper.

6 Lightly flour a work surface. Punch down the dough and knead it for about 1 minute on the work surface. Using a rolling pin, roll the dough into a rectangle about 11 by 14 inches. Transfer the dough to the parchment-lined baking sheet. If the dough shrinks after it's transferred, gently pull at its edges to create the desired rectangle and then pat it down onto the parchment paper to help it hold its shape.

7 Place the goat cheese and sour cream in a medium-size mixing bowl and mash them together. Dab teaspoons of the goat cheese mixture all over the surface of the dough, leaving a border of about ½ inch around the edge of the tart bare. Spread the onion mixture over the goat cheese. Scatter the lardons evenly over the top of the onions.

8 Bake the tart for about 15 minutes, then rotate the baking sheet 180 degrees so the back of the baking sheet faces the front of the oven. Continue baking the tart until the edges are browned, 10 to 15 minutes longer. Turn on the oven's broiling unit and broil the tart until the onions and lardons are lightly browned and the goat cheese is melted and hot, 2 to 3 minutes. Watch carefully so you don't overbrown or burn the edges of the tart under the heat of the broiler.

9 Using a pizza cutter or a sharp knife, cut the tart into 6 to 8 rectangles and serve immediately.

You can also add ripe cherry tomatoes if desired.

BACON AND BUTTERNUT SQUASH GALETTE

Serves 8 as a side dish

n the vegetable world, we think of butternut squash as a solid citizen: a food that serves as the dependable backbone of a recipe but becomes much more interesting when combined with deeply flavored ingredients. This savory tart is a quintessentially autumn dish. The last tomatoes of summer, the ripe squash of autumn, the heartiness of bacon, and the crispness of a flaky, free-form pie crust make for a fine lunch or supper on an October weekend—whether it's an Indian summer evening or a crisp afternoon when the fallen leaves want to be raked into piles that young children can't resist diving into. Here we provide two different, equally delicious ways to roll out and fold the pastry around the savory filling.

FOR THE PASTRY CRUST DOUGH

1¼ cups unbleached all-purpose flour, plus flour for rolling out the crust

8 tablespoons (1 stick) cold unsalted butter, cut into ½-inch pieces

1 tablespoon chopped fresh tarragon

¼ teaspoon salt

3 to 4 tablespoons ice-cold water

FOR THE GALETTE

5 slices thick-cut applewood-smoked bacon, cut into ½-inch dice

Olive oil, if necessary

1¾ pounds butternut squash, peeled, seeded, and cut into pieces 2-by-½-inch-thick inches long (4 to 4½ cups)

¼ teaspoon salt

Freshly ground black pepper

2 large leeks, white and pale green parts only, cut in half, well rinsed, and thinly sliced crosswise (about 1½ cups)

8 cherry tomatoes, cut in quarters

1 medium-size clove garlic, minced

1 large egg, lightly beaten

1 Make the pastry crust dough: Combine the flour, butter, tarragon, and ¼ teaspoon of salt in a food processor and pulse until the mixture resembles coarse cornmeal. Drizzle 3 tablespoons of the cold water evenly over the mixture and pulse until the dough holds together. If necessary, add more water, 1 teaspoon at a time, and pulse a few more times, just until the dough holds together. Remove the dough from the food processor and gently press it into a 5-inch disk. Wrap the disk of dough in plastic wrap and refrigerate it for at least 1 hour or as long as overnight.

2 Position a rack in the center of the oven and preheat the oven to 450°F.

3 While the dough chills, make the filling for the galette: Cook the bacon in a large skillet over medium heat until browned but not too crisp and most of the fat is rendered, 5 to 7 minutes, stirring often and adjusting the heat as necessary. Using a slotted spoon, transfer the bacon to a paper towel-lined plate to drain, reserving the bacon fat in the skillet. You should have about 2½ tablespoons of fat. If necessary, pour off enough fat or add enough olive oil to the skillet to measure 2½ tablespoons.

4 Place the squash on a large rimmed baking sheet. Drizzle 1 tablespoon of the bacon fat from the skillet over the squash. Sprinkle the ¼ teaspoon of salt over the squash and season it with pepper to taste, tossing the squash to coat it with the bacon fat. Spread the squash out in a single layer on the baking sheet and bake it until golden brown around the edges, 16 to 18 minutes, turning the pieces once after about 8 minutes. Remove the squash from the oven and reduce the oven temperature to 375°F.

5 Heat the remaining bacon fat in the skillet over medium heat. Add the leeks and cook, partially covered, stirring occasionally, until the leeks have softened and are lightly browned, about 5 minutes. Add the tomatoes and garlic and cook, partially covered, until the tomatoes and garlic have softened slightly, about 1 minute.

6 To assemble the galette, lightly flour a work surface. Using a lightly floured rolling pin, roll the pastry crust dough out into a very thin 12- to 13-inch round. Transfer the dough to a large ungreased nonstick baking sheet. Arrange the squash in an even layer in the center of the round of dough, leaving about a 1 to 1½-inch border of dough bare (see Note). Distribute the leek and tomato mixture evenly over the squash. Sprinkle the drained bacon evenly over the vegetables. Fold the border of dough toward the center of the galette so that the dough covers the outer rim of the filling. If the filling looks a little dry, drizzle the top with a little olive oil. Pleat and pinch the border of dough as necessary where the edges overlap. Brush the dough with the beaten egg (you don't need to use it all) and bake the galette until the crust is cooked through and golden at the edges, 30 to 35 minutes.

7 Place the baking sheet with the galette on a wire rack and let it cool for 10 minutes before slicing and serving.

COOKING THICK-CUT BACON

It's best to start cooking pieces of thick-cut bacon over medium heat and then, after about a minute of cooking, when the skillet is hot and the fat starts to render, lower the heat to medium-low to create a slight sizzling sound so the bacon browns gently without burning. Stir the bacon as often as necessary. A long-handled slotted spoon or a Chinese skimmer works well to toss the pieces in the bacon fat and ensure that all sides brown evenly. Bacons that are wet-cured will take a little longer to brown and cook than dry-cured bacons.

NOTE: As a variation, distribute the vegetable-bacon topping leaving a larger 2-inch border of dough. Fold the dough toward the center of the tart leaving a 3- to 4-inch-wide hole in the center. Then follow the remaining recipe as instructed.

NOT ALL BACONS ARE CREATED EQUAL

While all bacon has fat, not all bacon has the same amount of fat. A lot depends on the hog it came from: How old it was. How much it weighed. Whether it was free-range. What breed it was. Some bacon can be quite lean, and some can be exceptionally fatty. For that reason, when we recommend a certain number of slices of bacon, you should take that with—ahem—a grain of salt. Niman Ranch bacon, which we love, can sometimes be a little fatty. Oscar Mayer bacon, on the other hand, can be lean by comparison. You might want to trim some fat from the Niman Ranch bacon. Allan Benton's amazing bacon is like solidified smoke, so use it sparingly when cooking delicately flavored ingredients. If you like an extra-bacony taste, you could add another slice of bacon to any recipe. Use our recipes as a guideline, but let your own taste be the final judge of how much bacon you use. You'll find a guide to bacon producers starting on page 289.

CHAPTER 3

SOUPS: BACON IN A BOWL

Summer Vegetable
and Bacon Soup with
Tomato-Basil Pistou,
page 58

IN THIS CHAPTER...

Most good soups start with a great

stock, and in the process of creating our bacon stock, we discovered that adding bacon to any stock—homemade or store-bought—introduces a delightfully smoky, slightly creamy, and of course, salty accent that we think of as "bacon essence." Use bacon stock in place of traditional chicken, meat, fish, or vegetable stock in almost any soup recipe and you add flavor power and heartiness. Quite often we use slab bacon cut into small pieces for a toothsome bit of chew.

When thinking about what soup recipes we wanted in our book, we knew we wanted a couple that combined bacon and beans, hence Three "B" Soup (Bacon, Bean, and Bread) and Black Bean and Bacon Soup. The Three "B" soup is a party for fresh vegetables, with onion, potato, fennel or celery, butternut squash, tomatoes, carrots, and dark leafy green kale all in the soup pot. Nothing better shows the spirit of our book: You can cook with bacon and still make something appealingly nutritious. The same holds true for Summer Vegetable and Bacon Soup with Tomato-Basil Pistou, Minestrone with Bacon, and our Mushroom-Barley-Bacon Soup, which gets "healthed up" with a handful of fresh spinach just before serving. As for legumes, we would never prepare them without bacon. Even the plainest dried legume or bean becomes a creamy flavor bomb when infused with bacon.

ONION SOUP with Bacon, Red Wine, Cognac, and Baguette Croutons

Serves 6

n the days before the wonderful Les Halles market was torn down and moved to the outskirts of Paris, you could fall into a bar at two in the morning and order some Champagne and oysters and, if that didn't fill you up, a brawny onion soup topped with great cheese and a crouton would surely hold you until breakfast. Here is our homage. It just about explodes with flavor, thanks to bacon and more bacon.

4 slices thick-cut bacon, cut into ½-inch pieces

5 medium-size yellow onions, cut in half lengthwise and very thinly sliced

1 tablespoon unbleached all-purpose flour

8 cups Bacon-Flavored Stock (see box, page 51)

⅓ cup dry red wine

2 teaspoons fresh thyme leaves, or 1 teaspoon dried thyme

1 bay leaf

1 baguette

Freshly ground black pepper

About 2 tablespoons Cognac or other brandy

1½ to 2 cups (6 to 8 ounces) coarsely grated Gruyère, Emmentaler, or Comté cheese

1 Cook the bacon in a large Dutch oven or heavy soup pot over medium heat until browned and the fat is rendered, 5 to 10 minutes, stirring often and adjusting the heat as necessary. Using a slotted spoon, transfer the bacon to a paper towel-lined plate to drain.

2 Add the onions to the bacon fat in the pot, stirring to coat the onions well. Cook the onions over medium to medium-high heat until lightly browned, 20 to 25 minutes, stirring often. Adjust the heat so that the onions sizzle gently without browning too quickly and burning. Then, reduce the heat to medium-low

and cook the onions until they are very soft and deeply browned, 30 to 40 minutes longer, stirring often. As the onions cook, occasionally scrape up any brown bits from the bottom of the pot with a wooden spoon.

3 Stir in the flour and cook until it is lightly colored, about 1 minute. Stir in the drained bacon, Bacon-Flavored Stock, red wine, thyme, and bay leaf. Scrape the bottom of the pot with the wooden spoon again to loosen any brown bits. Increase the heat sufficiently to let the soup come to a boil. Then, reduce the heat as necessary and let the soup simmer, partially covered, until the flavors blend, 15 to 20 minutes, skimming any fat or foam that rises to the surface with a large spoon.

4 Meanwhile, preheat the oven to 400°F.

5 Depending on the size of the baguette and the size of the ramekins or soup crocks, you'll need 1 to 2 slices of baguette per bowl of soup. The slices should be able to support the cheese and prevent it from melting into the soup. Cut the baguette diagonally into ¾-inch-thick slices so that the slices will fit snuggly into each ramekin or soup crock. Arrange the slices of bread in a single layer on a baking sheet and bake them until golden at the edges, 8 to 10 minutes.

6 Remove the toasted baguette slices from the oven and, using an oven mitt, carefully position an oven rack about 6 inches from the broiler element. Preheat the broiler.

7 Place the ramekins or soup crocks on a large heavy baking sheet. Remove and discard the bay leaf from the soup. Season the soup with pepper to taste. Divide the soup evenly among the ramekins. Spoon about 1 teaspoon Cognac or brandy into each ramekin. Arrange 1 to 2 toasted baguette slices on top of each bowl of soup so that they fit snuggly over the soup like a lid. Spread the grated cheese over the baguette slices.

8 Place the baking sheet with the ramekins of soup on the oven rack and broil until the cheese is melted and bubbly. Watch carefully; depending on the heat of the broiler it should take between 90 seconds and 3 minutes for the cheese to melt. Serve the soup immediately while it is piping hot.

BACON-FLAVORED STOCK OR BROTH

A rich and flavorful stock is the key to any soup. Packaged stocks are, as a rule, pretty bland. Our solution is to save time without sacrificing flavor by simmering pieces of slab bacon along with a few soup vegetables in store-bought stock or broth. After only about 30 to 45 minutes, you have an outstanding base for onion or other soups. If you decide to make our Bacon-Flavored Stock, make it with a low-sodium stock or broth and hold off on adding salt until the end of the recipe as you may find the bacon adds a sufficient amount.

The terms stock and broth have become somewhat interchangeable. Stock technically means a liquid made from bones, meat, and seasonings, while broth is made from meat and seasonings, without the bones. You can use either stock or broth to make our soups, but to simplify the recipes and avoid confusing you, we call for stock in our ingredient lists.

BUTTERNUT SQUASH SOUP

Serves 5 to 6

How can you lose with something that combines the words *butter* and *nut*? It almost sells itself as it conjures up images of a fire in the hearth, football on the tube, and napping in an easy chair (preferably all happening simultaneously). We discovered that instead of cooking the squash in broth, as many recipes instruct you to do, roasting it first concentrates the sweetness and brings out the squash's smoky nuttiness. Voilà! Instead of being a mild-mannered platform for other flavors, the squash stands up to the power of bacon, garlic, and aromatic spices.

Vegetable oil cooking spray or vegetable oil, for oiling the roasting pan

1 butternut squash (about 2 pounds)

1 large russet potato (12 to 14 ounces), peeled and cut in quarters

5 slices thick-cut bacon

1 medium-size onion, chopped

2 large cloves garlic, minced

5 cups low-sodium chicken stock

1 can (14½ ounces) diced tomatoes

1 cinnamon stick (about 2½ inches long)

2 teaspoons ground cumin

½ teaspoon saffron threads

Salt and freshly ground black pepper

½ cup chopped fresh cilantro or flat-leaf parsley

1 Preheat the oven to 425°F. Spray a large roasting pan lightly with vegetable oil cooking spray or coat the pan lightly with vegetable oil.

2 Using a large heavy knife, cut the squash in half lengthwise. Scoop out and discard the seeds and fibers. Using a vegetable peeler, remove the skin from the squash, then cut it into 10 to 12 large chunks. Place the chunks of squash and the potato on the prepared roasting pan. Cut 2 of the bacon slices into thirds. Arrange the cut bacon pieces over the squash and potato. Loosely cover the pan with aluminum foil. Bake the squash and potato until they are barely fork-tender, about 30 minutes.

3 While the squash and potato bake, cut the remaining 3 slices of bacon into ½-inch pieces. Cook the bacon pieces in a soup pot or large Dutch oven over medium-high heat until they begin to brown and some of the fat is rendered, 2 to 3 minutes, stirring occasionally. Add the onion and cook until softened, about 4 minutes. Reduce the heat to medium, add the garlic, and cook until fragrant, about 1 minute. Add the chicken stock, tomatoes, cinnamon stick, cumin, and saffron threads, crumbling them over the soup. Cover the pot and increase the heat sufficiently to let the stock mixture come to a boil. Then, reduce the heat as necessary and let simmer until the flavors blend, about 20 minutes.

4 Let the baked squash and potato cool slightly, then cut them into 1/2-inch pieces. Finely chop the bacon that baked with the squash and potato. Add the squash, potato, and chopped bacon to the soup along with any liquid in the roasting pan. Add 1 cup of water and let simmer, partially covered, until the flavors blend, about 15 minutes. Remove and discard the cinnamon stick. Taste for seasoning, adding salt and pepper as necessary. Sprinkle the cilantro or parsley over the soup before serving.

BACON-FLAVORED STOCK

Makes 8 cups

While testing our onion soup, we found that when we used only store-bought beef stock the result was a little too strong and when we used only chicken stock the soup was a little too weak. But a combination of chicken and beef stock was just right and produced a full-flavored liquid that supported the richness of the caramelized onions. If you want to toss in other veggies, like a large leek, or add a handful of herbs, go right ahead. For a somewhat milder stock with more chicken flavor that will work well as a base for other soups in this chapter, omit the canned beef stock altogether and substitute all chicken stock or equal parts chicken stock and water.

3 whole cloves

1 onion, cut in half

5 cups low-sodium chicken stock

4 cups low-sodium beef stock

8 to 12 ounces slab bacon, with rind, cut into large chunks

2 carrots, trimmed, scrubbed, and cut into quarters

2 ribs celery

1 Stud the onion halves with the cloves. Place the chicken stock, beef stock, slab bacon, carrots, celery, and clove-studded onion halves in a large pot over high heat. Cover the pot and let the stock come to a boil. Then, reduce the heat as necessary and let the stock simmer, partially covered, until the liquid is reduced and the flavor is concentrated, about 45 minutes.

2 Strain the stock and discard the solids before using the stock for soup. (You can save the slab bacon, if you wish, to slice and add to omelets, salads, or other dishes.) You should have 8 cups of stock but, if you find that the liquid has evaporated to less than that, add a little water to make up the difference.

MINESTRONE with Bacon

Serves 6

Many different ingredients can be used to make minestrone. Some cooks add potatoes, others favor kidney beans over cannellini, and some prefer to skip the beans altogether. This minestrone recipe begins with a bacon-enhanced store-bought chicken stock that simmers about 30 minutes before the pasta, cabbage, and beans are added.

Because it calls for cabbage, ours is more of a winter version, but you could easily substitute such spring or summer vegetables as green beans or zucchini. Experiment with the recipe that follows, but be sure the finished soup is quite thick. You want that lovely mix of vegetables sitting up, not swimming, in the broth. You don't usually find tasty chunks of bacon floating in minestrone, but you will here.

This makes a big pot of soup, but the good news is it's fairly inexpensive and can be refrigerated or frozen to serve weeks later. Fresh oregano is added at two points in the cooking: the first time to infuse the broth; the second time, just before the soup has finished simmering. This second addition punches up the herb flavor, allowing it to come through when most needed. You'll note that here we chose to add the bacon rind to the broth for extra flavor and body.

12 ounces slab bacon, with rind

1 large onion, finely chopped

1 cup ½-inch pieces fennel

2 medium-size carrots, trimmed, peeled, and sliced crosswise into ¼-inch-thick rounds

2 large cloves garlic, finely chopped

1 can (14½ ounces) diced tomatoes

8 cups low-sodium chicken stock, or more, if necessary

1 tablespoon finely chopped fresh oregano

2 bay leaves

3 to 4 cups (about 6 ounces) coarsely chopped cored green cabbage (see Note)

1 can (15½ ounces) cannellini or red kidney beans (optional), rinsed and drained

⅔ cup small pasta, such as ditalini, farfalline, or small shells

Salt and freshly ground black pepper

Freshly grated Parmesan cheese

1 loaf crusty French bread, sliced and drizzled with extra-virgin olive oil

1 Using a sharp chef's knife, remove the rind from the slab bacon and set the rind aside. Cut the bacon slab into ½-inch cubes (see the facing page).

2 Place a soup pot or large Dutch oven over medium heat; add the bacon cubes, and cook until browned, 10 to 15 minutes, stirring occasionally. If the bacon starts to brown too quickly before the fat is rendered, reduce the heat. Using a slotted spoon, transfer the bacon cubes to a paper towel-lined plate to drain, setting aside 2 to 3 tablespoons of bacon fat in the pot. After the bacon has cooled, remove and discard any solid cubes of fat.

3 Add the onion, fennel, and carrots to the pot. Using a wooden spoon, stir the vegetables to coat them with the bacon fat and scrape up any brown bits from the bottom of the pot. Cook the vegetables over medium heat until they have softened but not browned, 7 to 8 minutes, stirring occasionally. Add the garlic and cook until fragrant, 1 to 2 minutes, stirring occasionally.

4 Stir in the tomatoes, browned bacon cubes, reserved bacon rind, and the chicken stock, 1½ teaspoons of the oregano, the bay leaves, and 1 cup of water. Cover the pot and increase the heat sufficiently to let the soup come to a boil. Then, reduce the heat as necessary and let the soup simmer, partially covered, until the bacon cubes are quite tender, about 30 minutes, occasionally skimming any fat or foam that rises to the surface with a large spoon. Remove and discard the bacon rind and bay leaves.

5 Stir in the cabbage and beans, if using. Cover the pot and let the soup come to a boil. Add the pasta, reduce the heat as necessary, and let the soup simmer, partially covered, until the pasta is al dente, 6 to 7 minutes, depending on the size of the pasta. Check the soup's consistency and, if desired, add ½ to 1 cup more water or chicken stock, if you have it.

6 Add the remaining 1½ teaspoons of oregano. Season the soup with salt and pepper to taste. Ladle the minestrone into individual serving bowls and serve it with Parmesan cheese and the slices of French bread. The soup can be refrigerated, covered, for up to 5 days or frozen in an airtight container for up to 6 months.

NOTE: If you buy a small head of cabbage and have leftovers after making the minestrone, slice the cabbage thinly and then sauté it with some chopped fresh ginger, some garlic, and two or three slices of coarsely chopped thick-cut bacon for a delicious side dish.

DEALING WITH THE RIND AND SLAB

To remove the rind from slab bacon, place the slab on a cutting board and insert the edge of a sharp chef's knife under the rind at one corner. Move the blade of the knife back and forth under the rind, holding the knife parallel to the cutting board and slicing just above the bacon meat from one end of the slab to the other. Once the rind has started to be separated from the meat, you can help the process along by using one hand to pull the rind away from the slab as you slice.

Cut the slab into cubes by first cutting it into slices ½ to ¾ inch thick. Stack two to three slices and cut them crosswise ¼ to ½ inch wide. If some of them seem too thick, cut them in half. Repeat wtih the remaining bacon slices.

When cooking slab bacon, while we cherish the flavor of rendered bacon drippings, most of us would prefer not to find solid cubes of bacon fat floating in our soup. After browning cubes of raw bacon cut from a slab, you will most likely end up with a few that are only fat with no meat. We recommend you remove and discard any solid cubes of bacon fat that remain in the skillet or pan after browning.

SUMMER VEGETABLE AND BACON SOUP with Tomato-Basil Pistou

Serves 4 to 5

By default, we usually think of bacon as a way to add extra heft to already hearty soups, but the truth is that more delicate recipes can also be transformed by bacon. Here's a delicious soup, loaded with fresh vegetables, so you can feel nutritionally "moral" with each slurp. Finishing it with a pistou of basil, tomatoes, and floral olive oil makes it even lighter. The puree of tomatoes and garlic creates the satisfying mouthfeel of cream . . . with no cream.

5 slices bacon, cut into ¼-inch pieces

1 medium-size onion, diced

2 large carrots, trimmed, peeled, and sliced crosswise into ¼-inch-thick rounds

2 large cloves garlic, finely chopped

3 cups low-sodium chicken stock

1 medium-size baking potato, peeled and diced (about 1⅓ cups)

1 small zucchini, trimmed and diced (about 1⅓ cups)

2 large ripe tomatoes, cored, seeded, and chopped

½ cup coarsely chopped fresh basil

1 tablespoon extra-virgin olive oil

Salt and freshly ground black pepper

1 Cook the bacon in a medium-size saucepan or pot over medium heat until lightly browned and most of the fat is rendered, 5 to 8 minutes, stirring often and adjusting the heat as necessary. Using a slotted spoon, transfer the bacon to a paper towel-lined plate to drain, reserving the bacon fat in the pan.

2 Place the pan over medium heat, add the onion, and cook, stirring occasionally, until the onion has softened and lightly browned, 4 to 5 minutes.

3 Stir in the carrots and half of the garlic and cook until the garlic is fragrant, about 1 minute. Add the chicken stock and 2 cups of water. Cover the pan, increase the heat to high, and let come to a boil. Then, reduce the heat as necessary and let the stock mixture simmer, uncovered, until the carrots soften, about 5 minutes.

4 Add the potato, zucchini, half of the chopped tomatoes, and half of the drained bacon. Cover the pan, increase the heat to high, and let come to a boil. Then, reduce the heat as necessary and let the soup simmer, partially covered, until the potatoes are cooked and the flavors blend, about 20 minutes, skimming any fat or foam that rises to the surface with a large spoon.

5 While the soup cooks, combine the remaining garlic, the remaining chopped tomato, and the basil and olive oil in a blender or a mini food processor and process until smooth. Set the tomato-basil pistou aside.

6 When the soup is done, taste for seasoning, adding salt and pepper as necessary. Remove the soup from the heat and swirl the tomato-basil pistou into the pan. Ladle the soup into individual bowls, sprinkling each serving with the remaining pieces of bacon.

MUSHROOM-BARLEY-BACON SOUP

Serves 4 to 5

Mushroom barley soup, usually made with beef flanken, is one of the glories of kosher cuisine. In our nonkosher homage we add the flavors of bacon and dried porcini mushrooms to amp up the savory umami taste. The result is a supremely satiating soup. The woodiness of the sherry picks up the earthiness of the mushrooms. The barley has the slippery mouthfeel of pasta with the toothsome bite of real whole grain. We had some spinach in the fridge, tossed it in, and it worked great.

4 slices thick-cut bacon, cut into ¼-inch pieces

1 medium-size onion, finely chopped

1 pound cremini, baby portobellos, or white mushrooms, or any combination of them, stems trimmed, mushrooms wiped clean and sliced into ½-inch-thick pieces

½ ounce (about ¼ cup) dried porcini mushrooms, rinsed and finely chopped

2 large cloves garlic, finely chopped

5 tablespoons dry sherry

4 cups low-sodium beef stock

2 large carrots, trimmed, peeled, and chopped into ½-inch pieces

½ cup pearl barley, rinsed

1 bay leaf

Salt and freshly ground black pepper

2 teaspoons chopped fresh thyme leaves, or 1 teaspoon dried thyme

2 packed cups (about 2 ounces) rinsed chopped spinach

1 Cook the bacon in a soup pot or large saucepan over medium heat until browned but not too crisp and most of the fat is rendered, 5 to 7 minutes, stirring often and adjusting the heat as necessary. Add the onion and cook over medium-high heat until it begins to soften, about 5 minutes, stirring occasionally. Stir in the fresh and dried mushrooms and the garlic and cook until the mushrooms release their liquid, 5 to 6 minutes, stirring occasionally. Add 3 tablespoons of the sherry and let boil for about 1 minute to reduce the liquid slightly.

2 Stir in the beef stock, carrots, barley, bay leaf, and 3 cups of water. Cover the pot and let the soup come to a boil. Then, reduce the heat as necessary and let the soup simmer, partially covered, stirring occasionally, until the barley is barely tender, 35 to 40 minutes. Season with salt and pepper to taste.

3 Add the thyme and the remaining 2 tablespoons of sherry and let simmer until the flavors blend, about 3 minutes. Add the spinach, increase the heat to high, cover the pot, and cook the spinach until just wilted, about 1 minute. Remove and discard the bay leaf before serving the soup.

THREE "B" SOUP
(Bacon, Bean, and Bread)

Serves 6

These three Bs do not refer to the mélange of beans that often takes the place of culinary inspiration in bean soups. If one bean doesn't make your palate dance, why compound the crime? But bacon, used three ways, wakes up beans in this one-pot meal. The bacon fat rendered at the beginning of the cooking process is used to sauté the savory mix of onion, carrots, and fennel. Then, the slab of bacon imparts flavor to the cooking liquid during the 40 minutes it takes for the vegetables to simmer, and we add cubes of slab bacon so that tender pieces of pork float in the finished dish. If you are feeling *molto toscano,* look for Tuscan kale. Its tender blue-green leaves have a more elegant taste than its cousin, the more common curly kale. But either kind is acceptable.

3 cups cooked cannellini beans
　　(see page 63), or 2 cans
　　(15½ ounces each) cannellini beans,
　　rinsed and drained

8 ounces slab bacon, rind removed
　　(see page 57)

Olive oil, if necessary

2 medium-size carrots, trimmed, peeled,
　　and chopped

1 large onion, chopped (about 1½ cups)

1 cup chopped fennel or celery

3 medium-size cloves garlic, minced

2 cups peeled butternut squash,
　　cut into ½-inch cubes

1 medium-size waxy potato, peeled and
　　cut into ½-inch cubes (about 1 cup)

1½ cups peeled and seeded diced fresh
　　ripe tomato (about 2 large tomatoes)

3 cups low-sodium chicken stock

2 bay leaves

Freshly ground black pepper

Salt

1 small bunch kale, tough stems and
　　ribs removed and discarded, leaves
　　chopped into bite-size pieces and
　　rinsed (about 5 cups)

Garlic–Rosemary Oil Bread Slices
　　(recipe follows)

1 Place 1 cup of the cooked beans and ½ cup of water in a food processor and process until nearly smooth, 10 to 12 pulses. Set the pureed beans aside.

2 Cut the slab bacon crosswise into 2 equal pieces. Place the 2 pieces, fat side down, in a large deep saucepan or pot over medium heat and cook until the bacon begins to brown and some of the fat is rendered, about 5 minutes. Reduce the heat to medium-low and continue cooking the bacon until it is browned on all sides and has rendered about 2 tablespoons of fat, 20 to 25 minutes. If necessary pour off enough fat or add enough olive oil to the pan to measure 2 tablespoons.

3 Transfer the bacon to a plate and heat the bacon fat in the pan over medium heat until it shimmers, about 1 minute. Add the carrots, onion, and fennel or celery, stirring to coat the vegetables with the bacon fat. Cook until the onion softens, 8 to 10 minutes, stirring occasionally. Stir in the garlic and cook until fragrant, about 1 minute.

4 Return the bacon to the pan. Stir in the butternut squash, potato, tomatoes, pureed beans, chicken stock, bay leaves, and 2½ cups of water. Season with pepper to taste. Cover the pan and let come to a boil. Reduce the heat to medium-low and let simmer, partially covered, until the squash and potatoes soften, about 20 minutes, occasionally skimming any fat or foam that rises to the surface with a large spoon.

5 Stir the remaining whole beans into the pan and let simmer until the flavors blend, about 10 minutes. Remove both pieces of slab bacon from the pan. Cut one of the slabs into ¼- to ½-inch cubes and add the cubes to the soup. (You can save the other piece of bacon to eat with your morning eggs or to add to a skillet of stir-fried vegetables, if you wish.)

6 Taste for seasoning, adding salt and more pepper as necessary. The soup can be made up to this point and refrigerated, covered,

overnight. Reheat the soup over medium heat before proceeding. Stir in the kale and let simmer until the kale is tender but still a vibrant green, 10 to 15 minutes. Remove and discard the bay leaves before serving the soup with the Garlic–Rosemary Oil Bread Slices.

GARLIC-ROSEMARY OIL BREAD SLICES

Makes 6 to 8 slices

The savory infusion of garlic and rosemary on toasted crusty bread adds a wonderful accent to hearty soups.

½ cup extra-virgin olive oil

4 large cloves garlic, peeled and lightly crushed with the flat side of a chef's knife

2 sprigs fresh rosemary

6 to 8 thick slices country-style or crusty Tuscan-style bread

1 Heat a small skillet over medium heat, then add the olive oil and garlic. When the garlic turns a light brown, after about 1 minute, add the rosemary sprigs. Cook until the rosemary leaves become fragrant, about 1 minute, turning the rosemary sprigs in the oil a few times. Discard the garlic and rosemary. Set the garlic-rosemary oil aside.

2 Toast the slices of bread and brush each with about 1 tablespoon of the garlic-rosemary oil. Serve the slices of bread alongside bowls of soup for dunking.

BEANS: CANNED OR DRIED? LONG OR QUICK SOAKED?

Some cooks insist on using only quality dried beans in their soups. They soak them overnight before cooking them. Others use the quick-soak method, bringing a pot of water to a boil and letting the beans soak for an hour before draining the liquid and proceeding with the recipe. Both methods are intended to yield beans that are soft and creamy on the inside but firm enough to hold their shape. Adding ½ a teaspoon of baking soda to the soaking liquid is a chef's trick to tenderize dried beans. An equal number of great cooks and authors skip the soaking and preboiling and opt for canned beans.

It's up to you. In our Three "B" Soup, we found the flavor of the dish was not compromised by using good-quality canned cannellini beans, especially since a third of the beans are blended smooth in a food processor, adding a lovely creaminess to the final broth. If you're a purist, however, by all means use the dried beans and soak away. Here are two recommended soaking techniques, one quicker than the other.

Overnight bean soaking: Sort through the beans, picking out and discarding any pebbles or twigs. Rinse the beans under cold running water. Place the beans in a large soup or pasta pot. For every 1 pound of beans (about 2 cups), add 3 to 4 quarts of cold water to the pot. Let the beans stand at room temperature for at least 8 hours and up to 24 hours. Rinse and drain the beans before using, discarding the soaking liquid.

Quick-soak method: Sort through the beans, picking out and discarding any pebbles or twigs. Rinse the beans under cold running water. Place the beans in a large soup or pasta pot. For every 1 pound of beans (about 2 cups), add 2 quarts of boiling water and 1 tablespoon of salt to the pot. Cover the pot and let the beans soak for 1 hour at room temperature. Rinse and drain the beans before using, discarding the soaking liquid.

BLACK BEAN AND BACON SOUP

Serves 8

There is something less "beany" about black beans than the rest of the bean family. When black beans are properly prepared, their taste and texture is smoother and more savory. Caribbean people have taken black beans to heart (and hearth) and added layers of flavor. We find it's the bean soup that even bean soup avoiders finish with gusto. You'll note the use of jalapeño pepper. It really boosts and sharpens the flavors. Also, while the use of a *sofrito* (sautéed aromatic vegetables) is common in Latin cooking, we feel that the flavors get lost if you make your *sofrito* at the outset and let it cook into anonymity with the long-simmering beans. Instead we add it at the end so the flavors and textures are multidimensional.

Some black bean recipes call for thickening the soup with a paste of flour or cornstarch, but we opted instead for mashing a handful of cooked beans with a potato ricer and then returning them to the simmering soup to thicken it slightly.

FOR THE BEAN SOUP

12 ounces slab bacon, with rind	3 tablespoons tomato paste
1 tablespoon olive oil	1 medium-size onion, finely chopped
1 pound (2⅓ to 2½ cups) dried black beans, rinsed, drained, and picked over (see page 63)	2 large cloves garlic, finely chopped
	2 bay leaves
4 cups low-sodium chicken stock	Salt and freshly ground black pepper

FOR THE SOFRITO

Olive oil, if necessary	1 small jalapeño pepper, seeded and finely chopped
2 medium-size onions, finely chopped (about 2 cups)	4 large cloves garlic, finely chopped
2 large carrots, trimmed, peeled, and chopped into ¼- to ½-inch pieces	2 teaspoons dried oregano
1 red bell pepper, stemmed, seeded, and chopped	1 tablespoon ground cumin
	1¼ teaspoons dried thyme

Balsamic vinegar or fresh lime juice

Hot sauce of your choice

Sour cream

Chopped fresh cilantro leaves

1 Prepare the bean soup: Using a sharp chef's knife, remove the rind from the slab bacon and set the rind aside. Cut the bacon slab into ¼- to ½-inch cubes (see page 57).

2 Heat the 1 tablespoon of olive oil in a large skillet over medium heat. Add the bacon cubes and cook until lightly browned, 8 to 10 minutes, stirring occasionally and adjusting the heat as necessary. Remove and discard any solid cubes of bacon fat.

3 Using a slotted spoon, transfer the bacon pieces to a soup pot or large Dutch oven. Add the bacon rind to the soup pot. Set the skillet with the bacon fat aside to use for making the *sofrito*.

4 Add the beans, chicken stock, tomato paste, onion, garlic cloves, bay leaves, ½ teaspoon of salt, and 9 cups of water to the pot. Stir to blend the tomato paste into the liquid. Taste for seasoning, adding more salt and black pepper to taste. Let come to a boil, then reduce the heat as necessary and let the soup simmer, partially covered, until the beans are tender, about 1 hour and 20 minutes, stirring occasionally and skimming any fat or foam that rises to the surface with a large spoon.

5 Prepare the *sofrito:* While the beans cook, place the skillet with the bacon fat over medium heat. If the fat in the skillet is less than 1 tablespoon, add enough olive oil to measure 1 to 2 tablespoons. When the fat is hot, add the 2 onions and the carrots, red bell pepper, and jalapeño pepper and cook until the vegetables soften, 6 to 8 minutes. Stir in the garlic cloves, oregano, cumin, and thyme and cook until the garlic and herbs are fragrant, about 1 minute. Set the *sofrito* aside in the skillet.

6 After the beans are cooked, remove and discard the bacon rind and bay leaves. Using a slotted spoon, transfer about 1½ cups of beans to a small bowl (don't worry if you remove some of the bacon cubes as well; you can't avoid them). Mash the beans with a potato masher until smooth. Return the mashed bean mixture to the pot.

7 Place the skillet with the *sofrito* over high heat, add 1 cup of water, and let come just to a simmer, scraping up any brown bits from the bottom of the skillet. Add the *sofrito* mixture to the soup. Let the soup come to a boil, then reduce the heat as necessary and let the soup simmer, partially covered, until the flavors fully blend, about 20 minutes, stirring occasionally and skimming any fat or foam that rises to the surface of the soup with a large spoon.

8 Ladle the soup into individual bowls. If desired, add ½ teaspoon of balsamic vinegar or fresh lime juice to each bowl and serve the soup with hot sauce and small bowls of sour cream and chopped cilantro for those who want them. The soup can be refrigerated, covered, for up to 5 days or frozen in an airtight container for up to 6 months.

LENTIL AND BACON SOUP

Serves 6

t is not a law of nature that lentils have to be boring. They only seem that way because if you are like us, you often leave them in your pantry ignoring the fact that they are losing flavor until the day that you don't want to be bothered to go shopping and there's nothing else to make. Anything that is neglected for that long, whether it's a bag of lentils or a romantic relationship, is bound to lose some of its zip. But dried green lentils from the farmers' market or the imported French ones (*lentilles du Puy*) don't taste like paper towels and they plump up nicely. Wine, bacon, spices, tomatoes, and aromatic vegetables turn this basic legume into a rib-sticking restorative. If you have some sherry or port on hand, adding a couple of tablespoons to the cooking liquid can't hurt. Pour yourself a glass while you are at it.

8 ounces slab bacon, rind removed (see page 57)

1 large onion, finely chopped

2 large carrots, trimmed, peeled, and chopped

1½ cups French green lentils (lentilles du Puy), rinsed and picked over

1 teaspoon ground cumin

1 teaspoon ground coriander

Scant ¼ teaspoon cayenne pepper

Freshly ground black pepper

6 cups low-sodium chicken stock

½ cup dry white wine

2 tablespoons tomato paste

1 bay leaf

Salt (optional)

¼ cup minced fresh flat-leaf parsley

1 Cut 4 thin slices, each about 3 inches long and ¼ inch thick, from the slab of bacon. Cut the slices into ¼-inch pieces and set the rest of the slab of bacon aside.

2 Cook the bacon pieces in a large stockpot or Dutch oven over medium-low heat until lightly browned and some of the fat is rendered, 8 to 10 minutes, stirring occasionally and adjusting the heat as necessary.

3 Add the onion and carrots to the pot and cook over medium heat until the vegetables begin to soften, about 5 minutes, stirring occasionally. Stir in the lentils, cumin, coriander, and cayenne pepper and season with black pepper to taste. Cover the pot, reduce the heat to medium-low, and cook the lentils until they have softened slightly, 3 to 4 minutes. (This step allows the lentils and vegetables to soak up the flavor of the bacon drippings.)

4 Add the chicken stock, white wine, tomato paste, bay leaf, 2 cups of water, and the remaining slab of bacon. Cover the pot and let come to a boil. Then, reduce the heat as necessary and let the soup simmer, partially covered, until the lentils are tender but still hold their shape, about 30 minutes, skimming any fat or foam from the surface with a large spoon.

5 Discard the bay leaf and the slab of bacon. (Or, if you like, trim and discard the fat from the slab, then dice and return the bacon pieces to the soup.) Taste for seasoning, adding salt and more black pepper as necessary. If the soup seems too thick, add ¼ to ½ cup more water to thin it to the desired consistency. Ladle the soup into individual soup bowls and garnish it with the parsley. The soup can be refrigerated, covered, for up to 5 days.

BACON CURRY SPLIT PEA SOUP

Serves 4

No doubt you have noticed that whenever you ask for the soup of the day at a diner, invariably one of the choices is split pea soup. Well, too often this wonderful combination is overcooked, overpureed, and over-the-hill. Our soup is made with whole yellow split peas. Also, rather than mooshing the whole thing up in a food processor, we elected to keep the flavors and ingredients separate, distinct, and to our way of tasting, more interesting. The bacon and curry really shine forth. Sour cream smoothes out the soup and gives a long finish to each mouthful.

7½ cups low-sodium chicken stock

1¼ cups yellow split peas, rinsed and picked over

2 bay leaves

5 slices bacon, diced

Extra-virgin olive oil, if necessary

1 large onion, chopped

2 carrots, trimmed, peeled, and chopped

2 large cloves garlic, minced

2 teaspoons your choice of hot sauce, or more to taste

1¼ teaspoons curry powder

Freshly ground black pepper

2 tablespoons minced fresh flat-leaf parsley

¼ cup sour cream or crème fraîche

Homemade Bacon-Flavored Croutons (optional; recipe follows)

1 Combine the chicken stock, yellow split peas, and bay leaves in a large heavy pot. Cover the pot and let come to a boil over high heat. Then, reduce the heat as necessary and let the yellow peas simmer, partially covered, until softened, 50 minutes to 1 hour, stirring occasionally.

2 While the peas cook, cook the bacon in a large skillet over medium heat until browned and crisp, 6 to 9 minutes, stirring often and adjusting the heat as necessary. Using a slotted spoon, transfer the bacon to a paper towel-lined plate to drain, reserving 2 tablespoons of the bacon fat in the skillet. If necessary, add enough olive oil to the skillet to measure 2 tablespoons. Add the onion, carrots, and garlic to the skillet and cook over medium-high heat until the onion softens, 3 to 5 minutes, stirring occasionally.

3 Set aside 2 tablespoons of the bacon to garnish the soup. Add the rest of the bacon, the onion mixture, the hot sauce, and curry powder to the pot with the peas. Let the soup simmer, partially covered, until the flavors blend and the peas are fully cooked, stirring occasionally. Remove and discard the bay leaves. Season the

soup with black pepper to taste, adding more hot sauce as necessary. The soup can be made up to this point and refrigerated, covered, for up to 4 days.

4 Before serving, combine the parsley with the 2 tablespoons of reserved bacon. Ladle the soup into 4 individual bowls, dividing it evenly among them. Place a tablespoon of sour cream in the center of each serving and sprinkle it with the bacon and parsley garnish.

HOMEMADE BACON-FLAVORED CROUTONS

Some soups seem to call out for crunchy croutons, and the best bread for making them has a light and airy interior texture. A crusty country loaf or a baguette or a good-quality white sandwich bread works well. Of course, you can substitute olive oil or melted butter for the bacon

fat, if you wish, or if you don't have any bacon fat on hand to do the job. And if you have any leftover corn bread, you can substitute corn bread cubes for the white bread; they also make tasty soup croutons.

2 cups ½-inch bread cubes from good-quality white sandwich bread

3 tablespoons bacon fat

Pinch of salt

1 Position the oven rack in the center and preheat the oven to 350°F.

2 Combine the bread cubes and the bacon fat in a medium-size bowl and toss well to coat the cubes. Spread the cubes in an even layer on a rimmed baking sheet and bake until golden, 15 to 20 minutes, turning them twice with a large spoon. Spread out on the baking sheet and let cool, uncovered, at room temperature. If desired, the croutons can be stored in a covered container at room temperature for up to 24 hours.

CLAM CHOWDER
with Bacon-Tarragon Garnish

Serves 4

Mention the word *chowder* and people are pretty much disposed to like it even before they taste it. It's a word that makes you comfortable as it calls up images of the coast on a day when waves pile against the shore and sea mist sparkles in the air. Chowder fills you up, restores you, warms you on a cool day. This chowder, which we made when corn was at its ripest and sweetest, is deeply bacony. The fennel brings out the sweetness in all the ingredients. The clams, steamed in their shells at the last minute (actually make that the last 5 to 8 minutes), don't lose any of their fresh briny flavor.

20 littleneck clams
  (about 2 pounds; see page 38)

7 slices bacon

4 teaspoons chopped fresh tarragon
  (see Note)

1 leek, white part only, rinsed well and
  chopped

⅔ cup diced fennel or celery

2 tablespoons (¼ stick) unsalted butter

1 medium-size clove garlic, minced

I pound boiling potatoes, peeled and cut
  into ½-inch cubes

2 bottles (8 ounces each) clam juice

½ cup dry white wine

¼ teaspoon cayenne pepper

1 bay leaf

2 cups fresh corn kernels
  (from about 2 large ears)

1 cup whole milk

½ cup half-and-half

Freshly ground black pepper

1 Place the clams in a large bowl, cover them with cold water, and let them soak for about 20 minutes so they can release their sand and grit. After soaking and draining the clams, use a firm brush to scrub off any additional sand or barnacles that may cling to the shells.

2 Dice 3 of the slices of bacon. Add the diced bacon to a small skillet and cook over medium heat until browned and crisp, 5 to 6 minutes, stirring often and adjusting the heat as necessary. Using a slotted spoon, transfer the cooked bacon to a paper towel-lined plate to drain, then place it in a small bowl. Add the tarragon and stir to mix. Set the bacon-tarragon garnish aside.

3 Coarsely chop the remaining 4 slices of bacon. Heat a heavy 4- to 5-quart pot or saucepan over medium heat; add the chopped bacon, and cook until it is lightly browned but not crisp, about 5 minutes, stirring often and adjusting the heat as necessary.

4 Add the leek, fennel or celery, and 1 tablespoon of the butter to the pot. Cook until the vegetables have softened, about 5 minutes, stirring occasionally and scraping up any brown bits from the bottom of the pan. Stir in the garlic and cook until fragrant, about 1 minute. Add the potatoes, clam juice, white wine, cayenne pepper, and bay leaf. Increase the heat to high, and let come to a full boil, uncovered. Then, reduce the heat as necessary and let the chowder simmer until the potato has softened, about 7 minutes. Stir in the corn and let the chowder return to a boil.

5 Add the clams, cover the pot, then reduce the heat as necessary and let the chowder simmer until the clams have just opened, 5 to 8 minutes, depending on the size of the clams and the pot. Remove and discard the bay leaf and any clams that have not opened after about 8 minutes.

6 After the clams have opened, add the milk, half-and-half, and the remaining 1 tablespoon of butter to the chowder. Let cook until heated through, adjusting the heat so the chowder does not boil. Season the chowder to taste with black pepper. To serve, spoon the chowder into individual bowls and sprinkle each serving evenly with the bacon-tarragon garnish.

NOTE: If you prefer, substitute fresh chives for the tarragon.

LAKE HOUSE CLAM CHOWDER

Serves 4

I t was a hot day up at the lake. We wanted a chowder that screamed flavor but didn't rely on the rib-stickingness of the creamy New England version. We came up with a clam chowder that is packed with the distinctive flavors of clams, bacon, thyme, and tomato and with nary a dairy ingredient. Fennel and fresh herbs turned old-fashioned Manhattan clam chowder into a punchier, more contemporary recipe. The addition of crispy potatoes creates interesting body and texture. Why Lake House? Because that's where we make it.

2½ pounds littleneck clams
  (24 to 28 clams; see page 38)

8 ounces slab bacon, rind removed
  (see page 57)

1 large yellow onion, diced
  (about 2 cups)

⅔ cup chopped fennel, or 2 ribs celery,
  chopped

2 large cloves garlic, thinly sliced

1 pound small new potatoes
  (about 1 inch in diameter) or fingerling
  potatoes, sliced into ¼-inch–thick
  rounds (about 3 cups)

Sea salt

2 tablespoons vegetable oil

Freshly ground black pepper

1 large ripe tomato, cored and diced

1 bottle (8 ounces) clam juice

2 teaspoons fresh thyme leaves

Juice of 1 large lemon

½ cup chopped fresh flat-leaf parsley

1 Place the clams in a large bowl, cover them with cold water, and let them soak for about 20 minutes so they can release their sand and grit. After soaking and draining the clams, use a firm brush to scrub off any additional sand or barnacles that may cling to the shells.

2 While the clams soak, cut the bacon slab into ¼- to ½-inch cubes. Cook the bacon in a large heavy-bottomed skillet or saucepan over medium to low heat until crisp, about 15 minutes, stirring occasionally. Using a slotted spoon, transfer the bacon to a paper towel-lined plate to drain, reserving the bacon fat in the skillet. Discard any solid cubes of bacon fat that remain after browning.

3 Add the onion and fennel or celery to the skillet and cook over medium to medium-low heat until the vegetables are softened and translucent, 7 to 10 minutes, stirring occasionally and scraping up the brown bits from the bottom of the pan. Stir in the garlic and cook until fragrant, about 1 minute. Transfer the vegetables to a large pasta pot or stockpot. When the skillet has cooled, wipe it clean with paper towels.

4 Place the potatoes in a medium-size saucepan and add cold, lightly salted water to just cover. Cover the pan and let come to a boil. Then, reduce the heat as necessary and let the potatoes simmer, uncovered, until they are barely tender, 10 to 12 minutes. Drain the potatoes well in a colander and set them aside.

5 Place the wiped skillet over medium heat. Add the vegetable oil and heat it until it just begins to shimmer, about 30 seconds. Add the potatoes in a single layer and cook them until crisp and golden, 8 to 10 minutes, turning them once or twice. (If the skillet is not large enough, you might find it easier to brown the potatoes in 2 separate batches.) Transfer the potatoes to a paper towel-lined plate to absorb the excess fat, then season them with salt and pepper to taste.

6 Add the clams, drained bacon, tomato, clam juice, thyme, and $3\frac{1}{2}$ cups of water to the pot with the vegetables. Partially cover the pot, place it over medium heat, and let come to a simmer. Let the clams simmer just until they open, 5 to 8 minutes, depending on the size of the clams and the pot. Reduce the heat to low and add the lemon juice and parsley. Remove the chowder from the heat and discard any clams that have not opened after about 8 minutes.

7 Using a slotted spoon, divide the clams, bacon, and vegetables among 4 serving bowls. Distribute the potatoes equally among the bowls, then evenly ladle the chowder over each serving.

CHAPTER 4

SALADS: BACON AND CRUNCH

Mad Ave Salad,
page 79

IN THIS CHAPTER...

When you say the word *salad* often

the first thing that comes to mind is *crisp* or *crunchy*. The same goes for bacon, so it's not surprising that we, along with most of the salad-eating world, like to add some bacony punch to our salads. But the story of bacon and salad doesn't begin and end with crispy crunchiness. Bacon adds salt and smoky funk. A great summer beefsteak tomato has a hint of bacon in it (we are told by food scientists that ripe tomatoes, like bacon, have a good deal of umami).

In this chapter, we give our own twist to some salad standbys with bacon, such as the classic Cobb, and our homage to TV's *Mad Men* and iceberg lettuce—the Mad Ave Salad. We also go in for some warm-ingredient salads that can be served as a main course, including a beautifully clean-tasting scallop and edamame salad as well as a curried broccoli and bacon salad. Bottom line, crunch calls for more crunch and salads cry for bacon.

BACON, PEAR, AND HUMBOLDT FOG SALAD

Serves 4

E asy to assemble, this salad combines some of the most scrumptious foods on the planet on one plate—ripe Bosc pears, Humboldt Fog cheese, shallot, bacon, crinkly Bibb lettuce, and raspberries, all lightly dressed with a simple vinaigrette. You can find Humboldt Fog, an American goat cheese, in specialty food markets and at farmers' markets. If you don't have Humboldt Fog, substitute another good-quality goat cheese or even blue cheese. We prefer to oven-bake the bacon for this salad as we like the evenly browned slices baking produces.

6 slices bacon

3 tablespoons plus 1½ teaspoons
   extra-virgin olive oil

1 tablespoon plus 1½ teaspoons white
   wine vinegar

1 small shallot, finely chopped

Salt and freshly ground black pepper

2 ripe, but still firm, Bosc pears

5 to 6 ounces Bibb or Boston lettuce,
   rinsed well, dried, and torn into bite-
   size pieces (about 4 handfuls)

20 sprigs watercress, rinsed and dried

5 ounces Humboldt Fog or other
   good-quality goat cheese, at room
   temperature, sliced into 4 pieces

12 raspberries, or 4 large strawberries,
   stemmed and cut in half

1 Position a rack in the center of the oven and preheat the oven to 400°F.

2 Line a broiler pan with aluminum foil (the foil makes it easy to clean the pan after the bacon cooks). Place the broiler pan rack on the pan, over the foil, then arrange the bacon slices in a single layer on the rack. Bake the bacon until it is browned and most of the fat is rendered, 11 to 14 minutes (the exact baking time will depend on the thickness of the bacon). Transfer the bacon to a paper towel-lined plate to drain. When cool, break the bacon into 1-inch-long pieces.

3 Place the olive oil and wine vinegar in a small bowl or glass measuring cup and whisk them together. Add the shallot. Season the dressing with salt and pepper to taste and set it aside.

4 Using a paring knife, cut each pear in half lengthwise. Remove the core, the stem, and the blossom end, then cut the pears lengthwise into ¼-inch-thick slices.

5 Place the lettuce and watercress in a large bowl, add the dressing, and toss well.

6 Divide the salad greens equally among 4 individual salad plates. Arrange the pear slices, goat cheese, bacon pieces, and raspberries or strawberry halves on top of the salad greens, dividing them equally, and serve.

MAD AVE SALAD

Serves 4 to 6

Iceberg lettuce wedges with blue cheese dressing were just the thing to have with a porterhouse steak back in the heyday of Madison Avenue. Maybe three martinis as well. This retro combination made a comeback about the same time that the cable TV series *Mad Men* captured our imagination. And so did the idea of crunchy pieces of bacon, with blue cheese on a wedge of crisp lettuce nearly as cold as a real iceberg. We found this recipe to be so rich that it works both as a satisfying lunch for four diners or as a side-dish dinner salad for six. You choose.

8 slices bacon

½ cup mayonnaise

½ cup sour cream

3 to 4 tablespoons milk

2 to 2½ tablespoons apple cider vinegar

2 tablespoons minced fresh flat-leaf parsley

1 large clove garlic, minced

1 cup (4 ounces) coarsely crumbled blue cheese, such as Roquefort or Danish blue

Salt and freshly ground black pepper

1 large head iceberg lettuce

½ small red onion

2 hard-cooked eggs (see page 98), peeled and coarsely chopped

1 large ripe tomato, cut into wedges, about 1 inch thick

2 hard-cooked eggs, peeled and coarsely chopped

1 Cook the slices of bacon in a large skillet (cast-iron is best) over medium heat until browned and crisp on both sides, about 8 minutes, turning the slices occasionally and adjusting the heat to keep the bacon sizzling without burning or browning too rapidly. Don't

crowd the slices in the skillet; if necessary, cook the bacon in 2 separate batches. Using tongs, transfer the bacon to a paper towel-lined plate to drain, setting aside 1 tablespoon of the bacon fat in a small mixing bowl.

2 Add the mayonnaise, sour cream, 3 tablespoons of the milk, 2 tablespoons of the cider vinegar, and the parsley and garlic to the bacon fat in the bowl. Stir in ⅔ cup of the blue cheese. If desired, thin the dressing with the remaining 1 tablespoon of milk and 1½ teaspoons of cider vinegar. Season the dressing with salt and pepper to taste. Refrigerate the dressing, covered, for about 1 hour to allow the flavors to bloom.

3 Rinse the head of lettuce and, using paper towels, dry the outer leaves. Slice the head of lettuce through the stem end into 4 equal wedges or, if serving 6, cut the head in half through the stem end, then cut each half into 3 wedges. Use a paring knife to remove the tough core from each wedge. Season the lettuce wedges lightly with salt and pepper. Slice the red onion into very thin rings, then slice the rings in half.

4 Place the lettuce wedges on 4 or 6 large plates. Stir the dressing and spoon 2 to 3 tablespoons over the top of each lettuce wedge. Top the wedges with remaining ⅓ cup of blue cheese. Break the bacon into 2 to 3 inch pieces and add it to the salads, dividing it evenly. Sprinkle the chopped egg evenly over each serving and garnish each salad with the red onion and 1 or 2 tomato slices. Serve with any remaining dressing on the side.

CURRIED BROCCOLI SALAD
with Bacon

Serves 4

Inside every grown-up who likes broccoli there dwells a kid who couldn't stand it. One exception is when the broccoli is in this Midwestern covered-dish-dinner classic. We've enjoyed versions of the salad at holiday picnics and backyard barbecues, where it never fails to get eaten with gusto. Curry, a powerful seasoning in its own right, really ups the powerhouse flavor, especially with the bacon acting as heavy taste artillery.

4 slices thick-cut bacon, cut crosswise into ½-inch-wide pieces

Extra-virgin olive oil, if necessary

⅓ cup mayonnaise

1 tablespoon honey

1 tablespoon apple cider vinegar or white wine vinegar

¼ teaspoon curry powder

Salt and freshly ground black pepper

4 cups uncooked bite-size broccoli florets

¼ cup minced red onion

2 tablespoons raisins

2 tablespoons roasted, unsalted sunflower seeds

1 Cook the bacon in a medium-size skillet over medium heat until browned and crisp, 7 to 9 minutes, stirring often and adjusting the heat as necessary. Using a slotted spoon, transfer the bacon to a paper towel-lined plate to drain, setting aside 1 tablespoon of the bacon fat in a large bowl. If necessary, add enough olive oil to the bowl to measure 1 tablespoon.

2 Add the mayonnaise, honey, vinegar, and curry powder to the bacon fat in the bowl and whisk until the dressing is smooth. Season the dressing with salt and pepper to taste.

3 Add the broccoli and stir to coat the florets evenly with the dressing. Add the red onion, raisins, sunflower seeds, and drained bacon and stir to combine thoroughly. Taste for seasoning, adding more salt and pepper as necessary. If you have the time, refrigerate the salad for 2 hours before serving to allow the dressing to infuse the broccoli with its flavor.

FARRO AND BACON SALAD

Serves 6

arro is a traditional grain that's quite popular in Italy. Although some people call it hard wheat, spelt, emmer, or einkorn, to us it tastes like a hearty barley. High in fiber and protein, farro is nutty and slightly crunchy. It is a wonderful alternative to Arborio rice for risotto. Because it is so robust, farro can play in the same sandbox as bacon. We think of this whole-grain salad as our bacony version of tabouleh. Great with ribs and fried chicken; fine with a fish fry, too.

6 slices bacon, cut into ¼- to ½-inch pieces

3 whole cloves

1 medium-size onion, peeled and cut in half

1 cup farro

Salt

10 cherry tomatoes, cut in half

1 small cucumber, peeled, seeded, and cut into ½-inch pieces (about 1 cup)

1 cup cooked chickpeas (garbanzo beans), rinsed and drained, if canned

½ cup red onion, diced

½ cup chopped fresh flat-leaf parsley

2 teaspoons minced seeded jalapeño pepper

¼ cup plus 1 to 2 tablespoons extra-virgin olive oil

Juice of 1 large lemon

Grated zest of half a large lemon

1 large clove garlic, minced

½ teaspoon ground cumin

Freshly ground black pepper (optional)

1 Cook the bacon in a large skillet over medium heat until lightly browned and most of the fat is rendered, 5 to 8 minutes, stirring often and adjusting the heat as necessary. Using a slotted spoon, transfer the bacon to a paper towel-lined plate to drain, setting aside about 1 tablespoon of the bacon fat in a small bowl.

2 Stick the whole cloves into the onion halves and place the onion halves and 4 cups of water in a medium-size saucepan. Cover the pan and let come to a boil over high heat. Add

the farro, the reserved bacon fat, and a pinch of salt. Cover the pan, let come to a boil, then reduce the heat as necessary and let the farro simmer, partially covered, until it is medium-tender, 7 to 8 minutes. You want the farro to have a little bite, with a softened center; be careful not to overcook it. Drain the farro, discarding the onion and cloves, and let the farro cool.

3 As the farro cools, place the tomatoes, cucumber, chickpeas, red onion, parsley, and jalapeño pepper in a large mixing bowl or salad bowl. Place ¼ cup of the olive oil and the lemon juice and zest in a small mixing bowl and whisk to mix. Stir the garlic and cumin into the lemon dressing.

4 Stir the cooled farro into the tomato and cucumber mixture. Add the lemon dressing and the drained bacon and toss to combine. Add a little more olive oil, 1 tablespoon at a time, if the salad is too dry. Taste for seasoning, adding more salt and some black pepper, if desired. Let the farro salad stand at room temperature or refrigerate it for about 20 minutes to let the flavors blend before serving.

VARIATION:

You can substitute 1 cup of corn kernels for the chickpeas, if you wish. Or add about ¼ cup of fresh mint to the farro salad. And if you want the bacon to play a more prominent role, increase the number of slices from 6 to 8.

GREEN BEAN AND POTATO SALAD
with Cashews and Lardons

Serves 6 to 8

This salad makes people look up and take notice when you bring it to a potluck dinner or barbecue. It features crunchy, nutty bacon, and there's a touch of tang in the vinaigrette. If crunch is good (think oven-roasted cashews), then double crunch is better (bacon). When the green beans are summertime fresh, they are downright invigorating, and the creamy waxiness of fingerling potatoes gives a long finish to each mouthful.

FOR THE SALAD

Salt

1½ pounds thin green beans (haricots verts), trimmed and rinsed

1½ pounds fingerling potatoes (each about 1 inch in diameter), scrubbed and sliced ¼ inch thick

2 large cloves garlic, peeled and lightly crushed with the flat side of a chef's knife

3 sprigs fresh thyme

1 bay leaf

5 black peppercorns

1 cup unsalted cashews

½ cup diced red onion

8 ounces slab bacon, rind removed (see page 57)

FOR THE VINAIGRETTE

⅔ cup vegetable oil

¼ cup sherry vinegar

1½ teaspoons Dijon mustard

3 tablespoons chopped fresh mint

2 tablespoons chopped fresh flat-leaf parsley

1 large clove garlic, minced

Salt and freshly ground black pepper

1 Prepare the salad: Bring 5 to 6 cups of water to a boil in a large saucepan over high heat. Lightly salt the water, add the green beans, cover the pan, and let come to a boil. Remove the cover, then reduce the heat as necessary and let the green beans simmer until just tender, 3 to 5 minutes. Meanwhile, fill a large bowl with ice water.

2 Turn off the heat. Using tongs or a slotted

spoon, transfer the green beans to the bowl of ice water to cool. Set aside the green bean cooking water in the saucepan. When the green beans are cooled, drain them well in a colander and set aside.

3 Add the potatoes, garlic cloves, thyme sprigs, bay leaf, and peppercorns to the cooking water in the saucepan. Bring to a boil, then reduce the heat as necessary and let the potatoes simmer until they are just tender, 7 to 10 minutes. (Don't allow to overcook.) Drain the potatoes well in a colander, discarding the garlic, thyme, bay leaf, and peppercorns. Rinse the potatoes under cold water to cool them, then rinse them again and drain well. Transfer the potatoes to a large mixing bowl.

4 Position a rack in the center of the oven and preheat the oven to 350°F. Line a rimmed baking sheet with parchment paper.

5 Spread the cashews on the prepared baking sheet. Bake the cashews until lightly browned, 5 to 6 minutes. Remove the cashews from the oven, let them cool, then set them aside in a small bowl.

6 Add the drained green beans and the red onion to the mixing bowl with the potatoes and toss to combine. Refrigerate the green bean and potato mixture while preparing the lardons. The salad can be prepared up to this point and refrigerated, covered, for a couple of days before serving. If you are not serving the salad right away, store the toasted cashews separately in a covered container.

7 Cut the slab of bacon into lardons by first cutting it crosswise into slices about ½ inch

thick. Stack 2 slices and cut them lengthwise into ½-inch-wide strips. Finally, cut the strips crosswise into lardons about 1 inch long (see box on page 11). Place a medium-size skillet large enough to hold the lardons in a single layer over medium-high heat and add 3 tablespoons of water (this will prevent the lardons from browning too quickly and crisping as their fat renders). Add the lardons, reduce the heat to medium-low, and let the lardons cook and render their fat for about 25 minutes, turning the lardons as necessary to brown them on all sides. The lardons should brown and have soft centers, without becoming too crisp or dry. Transfer the lardons to a paper towel-lined plate to drain.

8 Make the salad dressing: Combine the vegetable oil, sherry vinegar, mustard, mint, and parsley in a mini food processor or blender. Pulse for a few seconds to combine. Add the minced garlic and pulse once more, just to combine. Pour enough of the dressing over the green bean and potato mixture to lightly coat the vegetables. Add the lardons and cashews to the salad and toss well. Taste for seasoning, adding salt and black pepper to taste (you may not need to add salt as the lardons are salty), and serve.

CURRIED COBB SALAD

Serves 4 to 5 as a main dish

The Cobb salad was, they say, invented in the glory days of Hollywood by Robert Cobb, owner of the famed celebrity hangout the Brown Derby. Bing Crosby, Fred Astaire, Jean Harlow, Lana Turner—the whole Hollywood pantheon fell in love with this beautifully composed version of a chef's salad. It featured bacon, blue cheese, hard-cooked eggs, greens, avocado, chicken, and tomatoes arranged in formal rows on a large platter, dressed with a lovely vinaigrette. We make our version of Cobb's salad with a mustardy curry dressing that has a tinge of honey for sweetness. The salad is easily changed according to what you like and how you plan to serve it. For example, impress guests at your next summer dinner party by substituting one pound of grilled or poached shellfish, such as shrimp, lobster, or scallops, for the chicken and toss some pungent watercress for the romaine lettuce leaves.

FOR THE CURRY DRESSING

⅔ cup extra-virgin olive oil

¼ cup apple cider vinegar

1 teaspoon honey

1 teaspoon Dijon mustard

¾ to 1 teaspoon hot curry powder, according to taste

Salt and freshly ground black pepper

2 tablespoons minced shallots

FOR THE COBB SALAD

8 slices bacon, cut into ½-inch pieces

2 skinless, boneless chicken breast halves (8 ounces each)

Salt and freshly ground black pepper

Juice of half a lemon

8 to 9 cups packed romaine leaves, bite-size pieces, rinsed and dried

⅓ cup packed fresh basil leaves, chopped

2 large ripe tomatoes, cored and diced

⅓ cup chopped red onion

2 avocados, pitted, peeled, and cut into ¼-inch-thick slices

2 large hard-cooked eggs (see page 98), peeled and coarsely chopped

¾ cup (3 ounces) crumbled Roquefort or other blue cheese

1 Make the curry dressing: Combine the olive oil, cider vinegar, honey, mustard, and curry powder in a blender and blend on medium speed for a few seconds until smooth and well combined. Season with salt and pepper to taste. Add the shallots and pulse 3 to 4 times to combine. Set the curry dressing aside.

2 Make the Cobb salad: Cook the bacon in a large skillet over medium heat until crisp and the fat is rendered, 7 to 9 minutes, stirring often and adjusting the heat as necessary. Using a slotted spoon, transfer the bacon to a paper towel-lined plate to drain. Pour the bacon fat into a small bowl and wipe the skillet clean with paper towels.

3 Place a chicken breast in a heavy-duty plastic bag or between 2 pieces of waxed paper and pound it with the flat side of a meat pounder or Chinese cleaver until it is about ½ inch thick. Repeat with the second chicken breast half.

4 Season the chicken with salt and pepper to taste. Heat 1 to 2 tablespoons of the reserved bacon fat in the skillet over medium-high heat until it's hot, about 30 seconds. Add the chicken and cook until golden brown, about 3 minutes per side, turning once.

5 Add the lemon juice and 3 tablespoons of water to the skillet, reduce the heat to medium-low, and let the chicken simmer, covered, until it is cooked through, 3 to 4 minutes, depending on the thickness of the chicken breasts. To test for doneness, use a paring knife to make a small incision into the thickest part of each chicken breast half. The meat should appear white with no trace of pink and the juices should run clear. Transfer the chicken to a carving board and let it cool for about 10 minutes before cutting it into ½- to 1-inch pieces.

6 Place the romaine and the basil in a large mixing bowl and toss it with about ¼ cup of the curry dressing, then spread the greens out on a large serving platter. Toss the chicken in the same bowl with 3 tablespoons of the dressing. Arrange the chicken on top of the greens in a single row. Add the tomatoes and red onion to the bowl and toss with 1 to 2 tablespoons of the dressing. Arrange the tomato and onion mixture in a row next to the chicken. Arrange the avocado slices and hard-cooked eggs in rows and drizzle the remaining dressing over them. Sprinkle the bacon and blue cheese evenly over the entire salad and serve.

BACON-WRAPPED ASPARAGUS
with Mixed Greens, Toasted Bread Cubes, and Soft-Cooked Eggs

Serves 4

Americans (and our cousins in the British Isles) are devoted to bacon and eggs. We are relative newcomers to the practice of wrapping vegetables in bacon as, for example, Sicilians do with their famous *cipollate con pancetta*—slices of bacon (or the more traditional pancetta) wrapped around spring onions or scallions. Combining the two ideas, a bacon-wrapped vegetable and eggs, seemed a fine way to create a lunch or dinner salad. So we tried it and it worked. For a more substantial meal, the salad is really nice with some freshly caught flounder dredged in cornmeal and panfried in bubbling brown butter.

FOR THE BREAD CUBES

2½ cups sourdough or rustic peasant bread cut into ½- to 1-inch cubes

1 tablespoon extra-virgin olive oil

¼ teaspoon minced fresh rosemary leaves

Salt and freshly ground black pepper

FOR THE SHERRY VINAIGRETTE

2 tablespoons sherry vinegar

½ teaspoon Dijon mustard

1 small clove garlic, minced

¼ cup extra-virgin olive oil

Salt and freshly ground black pepper

FOR THE BACON-WRAPPED ASPARAGUS AND THE SALAD

20 medium-thick to thick asparagus stalks, trimmed

8 slices bacon

Salt

4 cold large eggs

About 8 cups mixed salad greens

1 Prepare the bread cubes: Position a rack in the center of the oven and preheat the oven to 300°F.

2 Place the bread cubes on a rimmed baking sheet or broiler pan. Sprinkle the 1 tablespoon olive oil over the bread cubes and toss to coat.

Season the bread cubes with the rosemary and salt and pepper to taste and bake until just crisp, 8 to 10 minutes. The bread cubes should not be as dry or as crisply toasted as croutons. Set the cubes aside in a small bowl and increase the oven temperature to 350°F if you will be baking the bacon-wrapped asparagus.

3 Make the sherry vinaigrette: Whisk together the sherry vinegar, mustard, and garlic in a small bowl. Add the ¼ cup of olive oil in a steady stream, whisking constantly until it is well incorporated. Season the sherry vinaigrette with salt and pepper to taste. Set the vinaigrette aside. Or put all of the ingredients for the sherry vinaigrette in a small jar, cover it, and shake it vigorously just before serving.

4 Prepare the bacon-wrapped asparagus stalks and the salad: Hold 5 asparagus stalks together in a bunch and either wrap 2 slices of bacon around the middle of each bundle or, starting about 1 inch from the cut ends and working on the diagonal, wrap the bacon around the bunch, overlapping the slices slightly and leaving the tips of the asparagus stalks exposed. Repeat with the remaining asparagus stalks and bacon, making a total of 4 bundles.

5 Place the bacon-wrapped asparagus bundles on the rack of a broiler pan and bake them until the bacon is crisp and the asparagus is tender, 12 to 15 minutes, turning the bundles over once after about 6 minutes. Alternatively, you can cook the asparagus bundles in a large skillet over medium-low heat. Cover the skillet and cook the asparagus bundles until the bacon is browned all over and the asparagus stalks are crisp-tender, 12 to 15 minutes total, turning the bundles every 3 to 4 minutes.

6 While the asparagus bundles cook, bring a medium-size saucepan of lightly salted water to a boil. Put one of the cold eggs on a spoon and lower it carefully into the water so as not to break its shell. Repeat with the remaining eggs. Boil the eggs until the whites are set and the yolks are still slightly runny, exactly 6 minutes. Transfer the eggs to a strainer and rinse them under cold water. Fill the saucepan with cold water, add the eggs, and let them sit until you are ready to assemble the salad.

7 When the asparagus bundles are done, transfer them to a plate and cover them with aluminum foil to keep warm, reserving the bacon drippings in the broiler pan or skillet. To assemble the salad, carefully shell the eggs. Warm the bacon fat in the broiler pan or skillet over medium heat. Gently add the eggs to the pan and roll them in the drippings for just a few seconds to heat them a little and coat and color them lightly.

8 Whisk the sherry vinaigrette again or shake it to combine just before dressing the salad. Place the salad greens and bread cubes in a large bowl, drizzle 2 to 3 tablespoons of the vinaigrette over them, and toss well. Divide the salad among 4 individual dinner plates. Place a bundle of asparagus and an egg on each plate and drizzle as much of the remaining sherry vinaigrette as desired on top. Serve the salads immediately.

VARIATIONS:

〰️ Omit the eggs and substitute roasted beets and goat cheese.

〰️ Substitute ½ cup of toasted cashews or walnuts for the bread cubes.

〰️ Use a lemon dressing instead of the sherry vinaigrette.

〰️ Substitute grilled shrimp or thin slices of smoked salmon for the eggs and omit the bread cubes.

STUFFED TOMATOES with Bacon and Avocado-Serrano Chile Dressing

Serves 6

When you think "chicken salad," chances are you think of mayonnaise and diced celery. Mayonnaise adds moisture to chicken but often overwhelms its flavor. Instead, to moisten the chicken, here we add a ripe avocado blended with a little sour cream and some lime juice. Stuffing beautiful peak-of-summer tomatoes with chicken, bacon, and crunchy fennel instead of celery takes this tired old warhorse and puts some bounce in its canter. You can roast your own chicken for this dish or buy a whole roasted chicken. A 4-pound chicken will yield about the amount of meat you will need here.

6 slices bacon, cut crosswise into ¼- to ½-inch-wide pieces

1 ripe avocado, pitted, peeled, and coarsely chopped

5 tablespoons sour cream

¼ cup fresh lime juice

Grated zest of half a lime

1 large clove garlic, coarsely chopped

Salt and freshly ground black pepper

6 large ripe tomatoes (each 10 to 12 ounces)

4 cups coarsely shredded roasted chicken, homemade or store bought

¾ cup diced fennel

½ cup chopped red onion

½ cup chopped fresh cilantro

1¼ teaspoons seeded and chopped serrano pepper

1 Cook the bacon in a medium-size skillet over medium heat until lightly browned and most of the fat is rendered, 5 to 8 minutes, stirring often and adjusting the heat as necessary. Using a slotted spoon, transfer the bacon to a paper towel-lined plate to drain.

2 Combine the avocado, sour cream, lime juice, lime zest, and garlic in a blender and blend until smooth. Scrape the avocado dressing into a small mixing bowl. Season the

dressing with salt and black pepper to taste, cover the bowl with plastic wrap, and set it aside.

3 Cut a ½-inch-thick slice off the stem end of each tomato and discard the slices. Using a small paring knife or a melon baller, remove the inside of each tomato, leaving a shell about ½ inch thick. Spoon the tomato flesh into a wire-mesh strainer set over the sink to drain off as much of the juices as possible. Discard the seeds and chop the strained tomato flesh, transferring it to a large bowl.

4 Place the chicken, fennel, red onion, cilantro, serrano pepper, and drained bacon in the bowl with the chopped tomato. Add the avocado dressing and mix well to blend.

Season both the chicken salad and the inside of each tomato shell with salt and pepper to taste. Stuff each tomato with chicken salad, mounding the salad over the top.

BACON AND EDAMAME SALAD
with Sea Scallops

Serves 3 as a main dish, 4 as a first course

H ere is a dish we couldn't have imagined twenty years ago. Only Japanese food lovers in the know ate edamame (soybeans). An everyday café that served BLTs or bacon cheeseburgers was unlikely to serve these beans beloved of vegans and sushi eaters. But we are more adventuresome eaters today and this recipe offers our favorite way of preparing scallops, pairing them with edamame—which is both earthy and green—and then drives home the flavor with soy, ginger, and sesame oil.

We've made this salad with scallops that are seared in luscious bacon fat, but you can substitute pieces of tuna or omit the fish altogether and simply serve the edamame-bacon salad as a side dish all on its own.

4 slices bacon, cut crosswise into
½-inch-wide pieces

Extra-virgin olive oil, if necessary

8 to 9 large sea scallops (about ¾ to
1 pound) (see Note)

1 package (10 ounces) frozen shelled
edamame (about 2¼ cups)

1 cup lightly salted boiling water

1 teaspoon grated peeled fresh ginger

2 medium-size ripe tomatoes (about
¾ pound total), cored and chopped

2 medium-size scallions, both white
and green parts, chopped, or ⅓ cup
chopped red onion

2 tablespoons soy sauce

1 tablespoon Asian (dark) sesame oil

Salt and freshly ground black pepper

1 Cook the bacon in a large-size skillet over medium heat until lightly browned and most of the fat is rendered, 5 to 8 minutes, stirring often and adjusting the heat as necessary. Using a slotted spoon, transfer the bacon to a paper towel-lined plate to drain, reserving the bacon fat in the skillet. You should have about 1½ tablespoons of fat. If necessary, pour off enough fat or add enough olive oil to the skillet to measure 1½ tablespoons. Be sure to remove any burnt bacon bits from the skillet.

2 Remove the tough tendon from each scallop (see Note) and pat the scallops dry with paper towels.

3 Heat the bacon fat in the skillet over medium-high heat. Arrange the scallops in the skillet so they are not touching. Cook the scallops without moving them until the bottoms are a rich golden brown, 1 to 3 minutes, depending on the size of the scallops. Using tongs, turn the scallops and cook until the second side is a golden brown, 1 to 3 minutes. When cooked, the scallops should be mostly opaque with a slightly translucent center and firm side. Transfer the scallops to a plate and cover them with aluminum foil to keep warm.

4 Add the edamame, boiling water, and ginger to the skillet, scraping the bottom of the skillet to loosen any brown bits. Cover the skillet, let the water return to a boil over medium-high heat, and let the edamame simmer until tender, 3 to 4 minutes. Drain the edamame and transfer it to a medium-size serving bowl. Add the tomatoes, scallions or red onion, soy sauce, sesame oil, and drained bacon. Toss well to combine. Season the salad with salt and pepper to taste.

5 Spoon the edamame salad onto 3 or 4 serving plates, dividing it equally among them. Place 2 to 3 scallops on each plate alongside the salad and serve.

NOTE: The small tendon or muscle on one side of the scallop that looks a little more tough than the rest of the shellfish is easily removed by pulling it away with your fingers or cutting it away with a small paring knife. If left on the scallop, this muscle tends to toughen up when cooked.

WARM SPINACH SALAD
with Bacon, Shrimp, and Bell Peppers

Serves 4 as a main dish, 6 as an appetizer

S pinach is both delicate in texture and hearty in flavor, which means its taste doesn't get drowned out by bacon. Red bell peppers and shrimp make for a juicy, sweet, nutty combination. Crisp bacon adds flavor and crunch and the pan drippings of bacon fat, the juice of the shrimp, and the bell peppers join for an extraordinarily flavorful salad. Baby arugula or first-of-the year chard or kale also work beautifully in this dish.

7 to 8 packed cups (about 8 ounces) baby spinach, rinsed and patted dry

6 very thin slices red onion

6 slices thick-cut bacon, cut crosswise into ½-inch-wide pieces

3 tablespoons extra-virgin olive oil, or more as necessary

2 medium-size red bell peppers, stemmed, seeded, and cut into ½-inch pieces

1¼ pounds extra-large shrimp (21 to 24 per pound), peeled and deveined

2 to 3 large cloves garlic, finely chopped

3 tablespoons red wine vinegar

½ cup loosely packed, fresh basil leaves, chopped

Grated zest of ½ lemon

Freshly ground black pepper

1 Arrange the spinach leaves on 4 dinner plates (or 6 salad plates if serving the salad as an appetizer). Scatter an equal portion of the red onion slices on top of the spinach.

2 Cook the bacon in a large skillet over medium heat until browned and crisp, 7 to 9 minutes, stirring often and adjusting the heat as necessary. Using a slotted spoon, transfer the bacon to a paper towel-lined plate to drain. Pour all of the bacon fat into a small bowl and wipe the skillet clean with paper towels. Add 3 tablespoons of the bacon fat and the olive oil to the skillet. If necessary, add enough additional

olive oil to the skillet to measure a total of 6 tablespoons. Heat the bacon fat and olive oil over medium-high heat.

3 When the fat mixture starts to shimmer, add the red peppers, reduce the heat to medium, and cook until the peppers start to soften, about 2 minutes, stirring occasionally. Add the shrimp and garlic and cook until the shrimp start to turn pink and firm up, about 2 minutes, stirring occasionally and turning the shrimp so that they cook evenly. Add the wine vinegar and cook, stirring, until the shrimp are cooked through and no longer translucent, about 45 seconds.

Remove the skillet from the heat and stir in the drained bacon, half of the basil, and the lemon zest. Season the shrimp and bacon mixture with black pepper to taste. The bacon contributes a fair amount of salt, so don't add any now; pass salt at the table for those who want it.

4 Divide the shrimp mixture and pan sauce among the dinner plates, spooning them over the onion slices and spinach. Sprinkle the remaining basil evenly over each serving and serve the salad immediately.

BACON AND EGG SALAD
with Fresh Basil and Red Onion

Make about 2 cups, enough for 3 sandwiches

Y ou might ask, "Why a recipe for egg salad?" Because bacon places it on culinary Olympus. The egg salad is wonderful on slices of good-quality multigrain bread, but we have also spread it on white bread, such as Pepperidge Farm sandwich bread, for making those crustless tea sandwiches perfect for a cocktail party, a bridal party, or a Sunday church reception.

3 slices bacon, cut into ¼-inch pieces

6 large hard-cooked eggs
(recipe follows), peeled

⅓ cup mayonnaise

⅓ cup diced red onion

⅓ cup coarsely chopped fresh basil
leaves or flat-leaf parsley

¾ teaspoon curry powder, or according
to taste

Salt and freshly ground black pepper

1 Cook the bacon in a medium-size skillet over medium heat until the bacon is browned and crisp and most of the fat is rendered, 5 to 8 minutes, stirring often and adjusting the heat as necessary. Using a slotted spoon, transfer the bacon to a paper towel-lined plate to drain.

2 Using a paring knife, slice the eggs into a medium-size mixing bowl and then mash them with a fork. Add the mayonnaise, red onion, basil or parsley, curry powder, and the drained bacon and stir well to combine. Season the egg salad with salt and pepper to taste (salt the egg salad lightly, or not at all, as the bacon adds salt).

PERFECT HARD-COOKED EGGS

Makes 6 eggs

There are different methods for cooking hard-cooked eggs, and they call for carefully monitoring the cooking time so the eggs are neither too soft nor too hard when done. We found this method to be the most reliable for producing perfectly hard-cooked eggs without the fragile shells cracking as they cook. Of course, for egg salad, if a shell does break and some of the egg white spills into the cooking water, the egg can still be peeled, mashed, and mixed up with the other ingredients.

6 large eggs (room temperature)

1 Gently arrange the eggs so they fit in a single layer in a medium-size saucepan. Add water to cover the eggs by 1 inch and let come to a boil, uncovered, over high heat, about 9 minutes. (The number of eggs you cook can be increased as long as you use a saucepan or pot that is large enough to hold the eggs in a single layer.)

2 As soon as the water boils, remove the pan from the heat, cover it, and let the eggs sit in the water for 10 minutes. As they sit, fill a large bowl with about 4 cups of water and 2 cups of ice cubes.

3 Using a slotted spoon, transfer the eggs one by one to the ice water and let them sit for exactly 5 minutes.

4 Remove the eggs from the ice water and, starting at the wider end, gently remove the shells. It helps to tap the egg first on a counter surface and roll it back and forth several times before removing the shell.

CHAPTER 5

MEATIER MEATS

Pork Roast Stuffed with
Bacon and Black Mission
Figs, page 112

IN THIS CHAPTER...

If you tried to isolate exactly what it

is that makes cooked meat so attractive and downright irresistible you would probably end up with a list of the qualities that define bacon: crisp, salty, fatty, slightly funky (in a good way), and brimming with umami flavor. Really, for human beings, bacon is like culinary catnip. It can transform a delicious piece of meat into a morsel of divinity. Okay, maybe that's a little bit over the top, but bacon really amps up the pleasure of every cooked critter. In a quickly cooked dish like Argentine grill master Francis Mallmann's beef tournedos, chunks of fillet mignon wrapped in bacon and sage are quickly seared, resulting in the ultimate in savoriness.

At the other end of the spectrum—that is to say, a slowly cooked dish with a long list of ingredients—Bacon Brisket and Beer Chili makes for complexity of flavor and super intensity. Our Pork Roast Stuffed with Bacon and Black Mission Figs includes bacon for a "pig plus pig" pièce de résistance. Osso buco, an Italian family classic, is now something we would never think of making without bacon. Unctuous, smoky, and herbaceous, both the name, *osso buco*, and the finished dish are a mellifluous mouthful. Finally, from the modern métier of blogging the always resourceful and creative Cathy Erway rings some changes on a classic Taiwanese stir-fry.

FILLET FRANCIS

Serves 4

Francis Mallmann is the dean of South America's chefs. Trained in the greatest kitchens of France, his evolution as a chef took him back to the rustic wood-fired cookery of his Patagonian heritage. Here he solves the problem inherent in filet mignon: wonderful texture, not much taste. By wrapping the tournedos (one-inch-thick rounds of beef fillet) in fresh sage and bacon he adds layers of flavor and even more succulence to the meat—an easy and impressive dish.

4 beef tournedos (fillets 1 inch thick and about 5 ounces each)

16 fresh sage leaves

4 slices slab bacon (each about ⅛ inch thick, 1 inch wide, and long enough to wrap around a tournedo), or 4 slices lightly smoked bacon

Salt and freshly ground black pepper

1 Pat the tournedos dry with paper towels. Press 4 sage leaves on the side of each piece of fillet, spacing them evenly. Wrap a slice of bacon around each tournedo so that it holds the sage leaves against the meat. Tie the bacon in place with butcher's string.

2 Heat a large cast-iron skillet over high heat until it starts to smoke and a drop of water sizzles on the surface. Season the tournedos with salt and pepper to taste and place them in the hot skillet on their bacon-wrapped sides.

3 Cook the tournedos without moving them until the bacon is well charred, 1½ to 2 minutes. Rotate the tournedos a quarter turn and cook until that portion of bacon is crisped, then repeat the rotation 2 more times so the bacon is nicely crisped all around.

4 Place the tournedos on a flat side and cook until done to taste, 2 to 3 minutes per side for medium-rare. Transfer the tournedos to a platter and let them rest for 3 minutes. Remove and discard the strings before serving the tournedos.

BRAWNY BACON BEEF BOURGUIGNON

Serves 6

I f you have made more than one beef stew in your life, chances are that sometimes you have ended up with delicious but tough, overcooked meat. It's hard to avoid. We've found that slicing a collagen-rich cut, such as chuck, into large chunks (2 to 3 inches) allows the meat to braise without overcooking as the deep, rich wine sauce permeates the meat. While it's possible to make a beef and wine stew with any red wine, there is something about the pinot noir grape (from which red Burgundies are made) that is almost reminiscent of the heady smell of bacon. Both have many of the same characteristics: a flavor that accents meatiness. Food scientists say that what is happening here is that red wine, bacon, tomato paste, and beef all have a form of umami, the elusive taste that means "yummy" in Japanese.

Quite a few fancier versions of this dish call for wrapping the vegetables, garlic, and herbs in cheesecloth and removing them from the stew at the end of the cooking. We leave them in the stew so that their flavors and textures play off the intense meat flavors. You can make the stew without the pearl onions and mushrooms the day before you plan on serving it. Refrigerate the stew overnight and the next day, about 30 minutes before dinner, reheat it in a 250°F oven until warmed through. Then prepare the onions and mushrooms and add them to the stew.

FOR THE BEEF STEW

5 slices thick-cut bacon, cut into ¼- to ½-inch pieces

4 pounds boneless beef chuck roast or top blade, cut into 2- to 3-inch chunks (see Notes)

Salt and freshly ground black pepper

2 tablespoons olive oil, plus more for browning the beef, if necessary

1 bottle (750 milliliters) pinot noir or red Burgundy

2 large carrots, trimmed, peeled, and coarsely chopped

1 large leek, white and pale green parts only, rinsed well and chopped

1½ cups chopped onion (about 1 large onion)

3 medium-size cloves garlic, minced

2 teaspoons tomato paste

2 bay leaves

½ teaspoon dried thyme

2 tablespoons chopped fresh flat-leaf parsley

1 cup low-sodium beef or chicken stock (see Notes)

3 tablespoons unbleached all-purpose flour

3 tablespoons unsalted butter, at room temperature

FOR THE PEARL ONIONS AND MUSHROOMS

40 frozen pearl onions

½ cup low-sodium beef or chicken stock, or ½ cup water (see Notes)

2 tablespoons (¼ stick) unsalted butter

½ teaspoon sugar

Pinch of salt

12 ounces button or cremini mushrooms (each about 1 inch in diameter), stems trimmed, mushrooms wiped clean

2 to 3 tablespoons brandy

FOR SERVING

Buttered egg noodles

Minced fresh flat-leaf parsley

French bread

1 Make the beef stew: Cook the bacon in a large skillet over medium heat until browned and crisp, 7 to 10 minutes, stirring often and adjusting the heat as necessary. Using a slotted spoon, transfer the bacon to a paper towel-lined plate to drain, leaving all of the bacon fat in the skillet.

2 Preheat the oven to 300°F.

3 Season the beef with salt and pepper to taste. Heat the bacon fat in the skillet over medium-high heat until it is hot but not smoking. Add as many beef chunks as will fit in the skillet in a single layer, leaving some room between each chunk to facilitate browning. Brown the meat, turning the chunks once or twice with tongs, until they are well crusted on all sides, 5 to 6 minutes. Transfer the browned chunks to a large Dutch oven. Repeat with the remaining chunks of beef (if you need more fat for browning, add a little olive oil to the skillet).

4 When all of the beef is browned, pour off any fat remaining in the skillet. Add 1 cup of the wine, let it come to a simmer, and deglaze the skillet by scraping up the brown bits from the bottom with a wooden spoon. Pour the wine mixture over the beef in the Dutch oven and add the drained bacon.

5 Heat the 2 tablespoons of olive oil in the same large skillet over medium-high heat. Add the carrots, leek, and chopped onion and cook, stirring often, until the vegetables are lightly browned, 5 to 7 minutes. Stir in the garlic and cook until fragrant, 1 to 2 minutes. Transfer the vegetables to the Dutch oven. Add the tomato paste, bay leaves, thyme, parsley, 1 cup of beef or chicken stock, the remaining wine, and just enough water to barely cover the meat. Stir to combine. Cover the Dutch oven, set it on the stove over medium-high heat, and let the stew come to a simmer. Then place the Dutch oven in the oven and bake the stew until the meat is nearly tender, about 1 hour and 20 to 30 minutes.

6 Blend the flour and the 3 tablespoons of butter in a small bowl to make a paste to thicken the stew. Remove the stew from the oven and set it on the stove over medium heat. Don't turn off the oven. Stir the flour and butter mixture into the stew 1 teaspoonful at a time and let the stew come to a simmer. Taste for seasoning, adding more salt and pepper as necessary. Return the stew to the oven and bake, uncovered, until the meat is fork-tender but not falling apart, about 30 minutes (avoid overcooking the meat, which will dry it out). Remove and discard the bay leaves. If the stew is still too liquid, using a slotted spoon, transfer the beef to a medium-size bowl. Set the Dutch oven over medium-high heat and let the liquid simmer until it is reduced to the consistency of heavy cream. Return the beef to the Dutch oven and cover the pot. Remove it from the heat and continue with the recipe.

7 Prepare the pearl onions and mushrooms: Combine the pearl onions, 1/2 cup of stock or water, 2 tablespoons of butter, the sugar, and a pinch of salt in a large skillet and let come to a boil over high heat. Cover the skillet, reduce the heat to medium, and cook until the onions are tender, about 5 minutes. Uncover the skillet, increase the heat to high, and let simmer until the liquid is nearly all evaporated, about

NOTES: Buy a boneless chuck roast or top blade roast and cut and trim the meat yourself. A 4-pound roast will yield about 3 1/2 pounds of beef, enough for 6 servings. Pull the meat apart to locate its natural seams. Use a paring knife to trim off the excess fat and silverskin (the opaque connective membrane) and then cut the meat into 2- to 3-inch chunks.

If you don't have time to make your own stock (and few of us do) purchase a good-quality brand such as Kitchen Basics. Bacon lends its own saltiness to the dish, and if you need more salt you can always add it at the end but it's hard to reverse the salt gears. So we recommend buying unsalted or low-sodium stocks for our recipes and always using unsalted butter. For ways to supplement the flavor of store-bought stocks using bacon and vegetables, see Bacon-Flavored Stock on page 54.

3 minutes. Add the mushrooms and cook, stirring occasionally, until the liquid they release evaporates and the mushrooms and onions are lightly browned, 5 to 8 minutes.

8 Stir the mushroom and pearl onion mixture and the brandy into the stew and bring the stew to a simmer over medium-high heat. Cook, partially covered, until just heated through, about 5 minutes. Taste for seasoning, adding more salt and pepper as necessary. Ladle the stew over buttered egg noodles in individual bowls. Sprinkle parsley on top and serve with crusty French bread.

The deep, rich wine sauce permeates the meat as it braises.

BACON BRISKET and Beer Chili

Serves 6

For most of us in the U.S.A. a chile pepper is a chile pepper and we don't make many distinctions. But in Mexico, where the use of this amazing family of ingredients has reached its highest expression, many people can distinguish taste differences in twenty, even thirty, chiles. This recipe takes advantage of some of the pronounced differences that even the most Anglo of us can detect. It starts with ancho chiles (dried poblanos), which are mild chiles with a fruity accent. To that we add a smoky chipotle (a wood-roasted jalapeño), which bears the same relation to a fresh jalapeño as bacon does to fresh pork. Finally, for some more serious heat, we add a fresh jalapeño. The star ingredient is brisket that cooks long and slow until the meat fibers soften and pick up flavor and succulence from the other ingredients. Be advised, this chili takes a while to make—but it's the long cooking that makes it worthwhile. Our advice: Don't watch the pot the whole time. But, then, that's good advice for any slow-cooked dish.

FOR THE CHILI

3 large dried ancho chiles, stems removed

About 1½ cups boiling water

1 flat-cut, also called first-cut, beef brisket (about 3 pounds), trimmed of excess fat and cut into ¾- to 1-inch cubes

Kosher salt and freshly ground black pepper

1 large chipotle pepper, in adobo sauce, seeded and coarsely chopped

2 teaspoons cumin seeds

2 packed teaspoons dark brown sugar

5 slices thick-cut bacon, diced

2 large onions, chopped (about 3 cups)

1 jalapeño pepper, seeded and chopped

Vegetable oil, if necessary

6 large cloves garlic, chopped

2½ teaspoons chili powder

2 teaspoons dried oregano

1 teaspoon ground coriander

2 cans (14½ ounces each) fire-roasted diced tomatoes, with their juices

1 bottle (12 ounces) Mexican beer

1 teaspoon ground cinnamon

1 can (15½ ounces) kidney beans, rinsed and drained

⅓ cup chopped fresh cilantro

FOR SERVING (OPTIONAL)

Sour cream

Grated cheddar, the best you can find

Warm Corn Bread with Bacon Drippings (see page 243), flour tortillas, or boiled white rice

1 Place the ancho chiles in a heatproof medium-size bowl. Pour enough boiling water over the ancho chiles to just cover them and let the chiles soak until they soften, at least 30 minutes.

2 While the ancho chiles soak, pat the brisket cubes with paper towels to remove any excess moisture and facilitate browning. Season the brisket cubes with kosher salt and black pepper to taste and set them aside.

3 Remove the ancho chiles from the soaking liquid and set the soaking liquid aside. Remove and discard any seeds and remaining stem fibers from the chiles. Coarsely chop the ancho chiles and place them in a blender or mini food processor. Strain the chile-soaking liquid, discarding any seeds. Add the chipotle pepper, cumin seeds, brown sugar, and ½ cup of the strained chile soaking liquid to the blender or mini processor with the chiles. Process the chiles until pureed, 30 seconds to 1 minute.

4 Position a rack in the center of the oven and preheat the oven to 350°F.

5 Cook the bacon in a large ovenproof pot, such as a Dutch oven, over medium heat until

lightly browned and most of the fat is rendered, 5 to 8 minutes, stirring often and adjusting the heat as necessary. Using a slotted spoon, transfer the bacon to a paper towel-lined plate to drain, reserving the bacon fat in the pot. Increase the heat to medium-high and, working in batches and being careful not to overcrowd the pot, add the meat cubes to the bacon fat and brown on all sides. Using tongs, transfer the browned meat to a large bowl.

6 Add the onions and jalapeño pepper to the pot and cook over medium-high heat, stirring occasionally, until the vegetables are softened and lightly browned, 6 to 8 minutes. (There should be enough fat in the pan to brown the onions and jalapeño, but if necessary add up to 1 tablespoon of vegetable oil.) Add the garlic, reduce the heat to medium, and cook until the garlic is fragrant, about 1 minute, stirring often.

7 Add the chili powder, oregano, and coriander to the onion mixture and cook until fragrant, about 1 minute, stirring to combine. Add the browned meat cubes, drained bacon, ancho chile mixture, the tomatoes with their juices, beer, and $1/2$ teaspoon of the cinnamon. Stir well to coat the meat evenly with the sauce and spices. Cover the pot and let the chili come to a simmer.

8 Place the pot in the oven and bake the chili until the meat is close to fork-tender, about 2 hours, stirring once. Stir in the kidney beans and the remaining $1/2$ teaspoon of cinnamon. If too much of the liquid has evaporated, add $1/4$ to $1/2$ cup of water, as necessary. Cover the pot and bake the chili until the meat is fork-tender, 10 to 20 minutes longer.

9 Taste for seasoning, adding more kosher salt and black pepper as necessary. Spoon the chili into individual serving bowls and sprinkle some cilantro over each. Serve the chili with your choice of sour cream, grated cheddar cheese, warm corn bread, tortillas, or rice.

OSSO BUCO
with Orange and Lemon Gremolata

Serves 6

T o our way of thinking, veal shank is an overlooked treasure. No meat gets more tender. Our bacon-boosted version uses a long braise to add some pizzazz to the gentle flavor of veal. Bacon *plus* tomatoes pump up the deliciousness. Then there is the bone-sucking treat at the end—the marrow. No matter how full you feel, there's always room for this creamy finishing touch.

The robust and rustic flavors of osso buco want something to focus and brighten their intense meatiness. As in much Italian cookery, this finishing touch is a combination of flavorfully powerful raw ingredients that freshen up and focus each taste. You may be surprised to see a touch of cinnamon in the gremolata here along with the parsley, garlic, and lemon and orange zest. But, when used sparingly, cinnamon flies under the radar, barely registering on your palate, yet it does something magical to tie the dish together. Thanks to Marie's grandma Maria Briccetti, who always insisted on it.

FOR THE OSSO BUCO

6 slices bacon, cut into ¼-inch pieces

About ¼ cup vegetable oil

Unbleached all-purpose flour, for lightly dredging the veal shanks

6 veal shanks (about 1½ inches thick and 10 ounces each)

Salt and freshly ground black pepper

2 cups dry white wine

2 cups finely chopped onions (about 2 medium-size onions)

1 cup diced carrots (about 2 large carrots)

1 cup diced fennel

⅔ cup diced red bell pepper

4 medium-size cloves garlic, finely chopped

4½ teaspoons tomato paste

1 can (14½ ounces) diced tomatoes, with their juices

1½ to 2 cups low-sodium chicken stock

2 bay leaves

1 teaspoon fresh thyme leaves

½ teaspoon chopped fresh rosemary

¼ cup minced fresh flat-leaf parsley

2 medium-size cloves garlic, minced

1 teaspoon finely grated lemon zest

1 teaspoon finely grated orange zest

⅛ teaspoon ground cinnamon

Risotto, buttered noodles, or mashed potatoes, for serving (optional)

1 Prepare the osso buco: Position a rack in the lower third of the oven and preheat the oven to 325°F.

2 Cook the bacon in a large Dutch oven or other heavy-bottomed ovenproof pot over medium heat until lightly browned and most of the fat is rendered, 5 to 8 minutes, stirring often and adjusting the heat as necessary (don't let the bacon brown too darkly). Using a slotted spoon, transfer the bacon to a paper towel-lined plate to drain, reserving 2 tablespoons of the bacon fat in the pot. If necessary, pour off any extra fat or add enough vegetable oil to the Dutch oven to measure 2 tablespoons.

3 Place flour in a shallow bowl. (A pie plate works well for this.) Season 3 of the veal shanks with salt and black pepper to taste. Dredge the seasoned veal shanks in the flour until lightly coated on all sides. Shake off any excess flour. Tie each shank tightly around the middle with butcher's string.

4 Heat the 2 tablespoons of fat in the Dutch oven over medium-high heat until it shimmers, about 1 minute. Add the 3 floured veal shanks in a single layer. Cook the veal shanks until deeply browned, 4 to 5 minutes per side, turning them once with tongs. Transfer the browned veal shanks to a large bowl and set them and the bowl of flour aside.

5 Remove the Dutch oven from the heat and add ½ cup of the white wine, scraping the bottom to loosen any brown bits. Pour the liquid from the Dutch oven over the veal shanks in the bowl.

6 Season the remaining 3 veal shanks with salt and black pepper to taste, dredge them in the flour, and tie them tightly with butcher's string (see page 116). Add 2 tablespoons of oil to the Dutch oven and heat over medium-high heat until the oil shimmers, about 1 minute. Add the veal shanks in a single layer and repeat the browning process. Transfer the shanks to the bowl.

7 After removing the shanks, if you have less than 2 tablespoons of fat in the bottom of the Dutch oven, add more oil to make up the difference. Place the Dutch oven over medium-high heat. Add the onions, carrots, fennel, and red bell pepper and cook, stirring occasionally, until the vegetables soften, 8 to 10 minutes. Add the finely chopped garlic and cook until fragrant, about 1 minute. Add the tomato paste and ½ cup of the white wine and cook until the tomato paste is blended into the mixture, about 1 minute, stirring to mix well.

8 Increase the heat to high, add the drained bacon, tomatoes with their juices, 1½ cups of the chicken stock, the remaining 1 cup of wine, and the bay leaves, thyme, and rosemary to the Dutch oven and stir to mix. Return the veal shanks to the Dutch oven along with all of the juices in the bowl. The liquid should nearly cover the shanks. If necessary, add a little more stock. Cover the Dutch oven and let the liquid come to a full simmer.

9 Adjust the lid of the Dutch oven so that it sits slightly ajar; this allows a little steam to escape as the osso buco braises in the oven. Transfer the Dutch oven to the oven and cook the veal shanks until the meat feels very tender but not falling off the bone when pierced with a fork, 1 hour and 45 minutes to 2 hours.

10 While the osso buco cooks, prepare the gremolata: Combine the parsley, minced garlic, lemon and orange zest, and cinnamon in a small bowl.

11 After the osso buco is cooked, stir half of the gremolata into the Dutch oven. Taste for seasoning, adding salt and black pepper as necessary. Let the osso buco stand for about 5 minutes. Using tongs, transfer the veal shanks to a serving platter. Carefully cut off the butcher's string without separating the meat from the bone. Remove and discard the bay leaves from the Dutch oven. Ladle the sauce over the veal shanks and sprinkle the remaining gremolata over the osso buco. Serve immediately with risotto, buttered noodles, or mashed potatoes, if desired.

PORK ROAST Stuffed with Bacon and Black Mission Figs

Serves 8 to 10

Roast pork can be succulent and delicious but too often it can turn out dry. Brining it is a pretty failsafe method to produce juicy, flavorful pork and it knocks the ball out of the park in this recipe, which has proved to be one of the biggest crowd pleasers in this collection. Honey contributes beautiful floral notes in addition to sweetness. The simple rosemary-garlic rub adds a herbaceous accent. The truly memorable flavor that makes this recipe a standout is the stuffing of bacon and figs: fruity, supremely soft, salty, smoky. We made this for the twenty-ninth birthday of one of our kids and won the highest accolade from a crowd of hip, food-savvy New Yorkers: "Can I have seconds?"

FOR THE PORK ROAST AND BRINE

6 tablespoons honey

⅔ cup Diamond Crystal kosher salt

6 bay leaves

8 medium-size cloves garlic, peeled
and lightly crushed with the flat
side of a chef's knife

1½ teaspoons fennel seeds (optional)

1 tablespoon black peppercorns

1 center-cut boneless pork loin roast
(about 3½ pounds)

FOR THE BACON AND FIG STUFFING (SEE NOTE)

6 slices bacon, diced

1 medium-size onion,
diced (about 1 cup)

1 large shallot, diced

8 ounces dried black Mission figs, stems
removed and discarded, cut into ¼- to
½-inch pieces

3 tablespoons granulated sugar

1 packed tablespoon dark brown sugar

6 tablespoons balsamic vinegar

1 bay leaf

Freshly ground black pepper

1 tablespoon extra-virgin olive oil

⅔ cup coarse-ground homemade bread
crumbs (see page 32)

⅓ cup chopped fresh flat-leaf parsley

1 tablespoon Armagnac or Cognac
(optional)

FOR THE HERB OIL RUB

2 tablespoons extra-virgin olive oil

1 tablespoon chopped fresh rosemary
leaves

1 large clove garlic, finely chopped

¼ teaspoon table salt

⅛ teaspoon black pepper

1 Brine the pork: Combine the honey, ⅔ cup of kosher salt, 6 bay leaves, 8 cloves of garlic, fennel seeds, if using, peppercorns, and 4 cups of water in a large pot. Cover the pot, let come to a boil over high heat, and let boil for about 1 minute, stirring occasionally to dissolve the salt. Remove the brine mixture from the heat and stir in 4 more cups of water. Refrigerate the brine or place it in the freezer to cool to room temperature. Pour the brine into a ceramic or glass bowl or other nonreactive container large enough that the pork roast can be completely submerged. Add the pork, cover the bowl loosely with plastic wrap, and refrigerate the pork for 6 to 8 hours (longer brining may cause the pork to become too salty).

2 Remove the pork from the brine and rinse it under cold water. Pat the pork dry with paper towels and discard the brine.

3 Prepare the bacon and fig stuffing: Cook the bacon in a large heavy-bottomed saucepan over medium heat until the bacon is lightly browned and most of the fat is rendered, 5 to 8 minutes, stirring often and adjusting the heat as necessary. Using a slotted spoon, transfer the bacon to a paper towel-lined plate to drain, reserving the bacon fat in the saucepan. You should have 1 to 2 tablespoons of fat. If there's more, pour off and discard the excess.

4 Heat the bacon fat in the saucepan over low heat. Add the onion and shallot and cook, stirring occasionally, until the onion is very soft and lightly browned at the edges, 8 to 10 minutes.

5 Add the drained bacon, figs, granulated sugar, brown sugar, balsamic vinegar, bay leaf, and 1/2 cup of water to the saucepan and season with pepper to taste. Cover the pan and bring to a boil over high heat. Then, reduce the heat as necessary to maintain an even simmer and cook, uncovered, until most of the liquid has evaporated, 20 to 25 minutes, stirring occasionally. Remove and discard the bay leaf, transfer the fig mixture to a medium-size bowl, and let cool for about 10 minutes.

6 Heat the 1 tablespoon of olive oil in a small skillet. Add the bread crumbs and cook over low heat until evenly browned, 3 to 4 minutes, stirring often. Stir the browned bread crumbs and the parsley and Armagnac or Cognac, if using, into the fig mixture. If desired, season with additional pepper to taste. Set the stuffing aside to cool completely (you will have about 2 1/2 cups stuffing).

7 Make a pocket in the pork roast for the stuffing. Starting at one end and using a long knife (a boning knife works well for this), insert the blade through the center of the roast, making a 1 1/2- to 2-inch-wide horizontal cut that runs from one end of the roast to the other. (If you find it easier, make 2 cuts halfway into the meat, working from each end of the roast toward the center so that the cuts meet in the middle.) Make another 1½- to 2-inch-wide cut through the center of the roast so that it intersects the first cut, forming a cross. Place the pork in a large roasting pan.

8 Using your fingers, pry the cuts open to make a cavity for the stuffing. Stuff the roast, using the handle of a long wooden spoon to push the stuffing deep into the roast. Be sure to force the stuffing well into the middle to fill the center of the roast. It helps to work from both ends of each cut.

9 Preheat the oven to 400°F and tie the roast (see A Simplified Way of Tying a Boned Pork Roast on page 116).

10 Make the herb oil rub: Place the 2 tablespoons of olive oil and the rosemary, chopped garlic, ¼ teaspoon of table salt, and ⅛ teaspoon of pepper in a small bowl or measuring cup and stir to mix. Rub the stuffed pork roast all over with the oil and herb mixture.

11 Roast the pork for 15 minutes, then reduce the oven temperature to 350°F and continue roasting the pork for about 20 minutes longer. Use an instant-read meat thermometer to measure the internal temperature of the roast and gauge how close the pork is to being done, inserting the thermometer into the thickest part of the meat 10 minutes after you have reduced the oven temperature. The roast will be done when the meat thermometer registers 135°F, or 140°F, if you like your pork a little more cooked. The internal temperature will rise rapidly after the roast reaches 125°F; monitor it closely to keep the pork from overcooking.

12 When done, transfer the pork roast to a cutting board. Cover the roast loosely with aluminum foil and let it stand for 15 to 20 minutes before removing and discarding the string. As the roast rests the internal temperature will rise about 5°F. Slice the roast and serve it immediately, drizzling any pan juices over the slices.

NOTE: The bacon and fig stuffing can be prepared and refrigerated, covered, 1 to 2 days ahead of roasting the pork, but let the stuffing come to room temperature before stuffing the roast.

A SIMPLIFIED WAY OF TYING A BONED PORK ROAST

There are more complicated and "official" ways to tie a roast, but we like this simplified method for helping the roast to hold its shape and keeping the stuffing in place.

1 Tie the pork roast using six to seven individual pieces of butcher's string (kitchen twine also works).

2 Evenly space the ties about an inch apart crosswise along the roast from one end to the other.

3 Cut a piece of string 2½ times longer than the roast and weave it lengthwise through the individual pieces of string on both the top and bottom of the roast.

4 Tie the ends of the string together in a knot to secure it and help hold the stuffing in place.

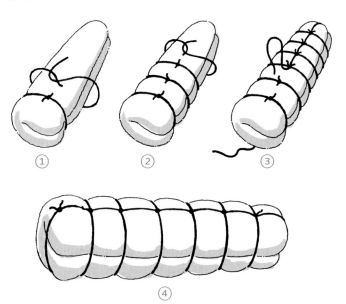

PORK TENDERLOIN
with Bacon, Fennel, and Carrots

Serves 4

To make this recipe, we bought a beautiful pork tenderloin and then used the ingredients we had on hand; as is often the case, kitchen necessity became the nurturing mother of culinary invention. The fat from the bacon flavors the vegetables and moistens the meat. The fruitiness and sweetness of the orange is accented by the fennel. It's a really nice dish to make for company (just double the recipe to serve eight). If you do double it, transfer the pork tenderloins and vegetables from the Dutch oven or skillet to a roasting pan to bake, so that the pork roasts rather than steams and stews, which it would do if you crowd too much in the pan.

3 slices thick-cut bacon, cut into ½-inch pieces

1½ teaspoons fennel seeds

1 pork tenderloin (1 to 1¼ pounds)

Salt and freshly ground black pepper

1 large fennel bulb

3 carrots, trimmed and peeled

¼ cup dry white wine

2 large cloves garlic, finely chopped

½ cup low-sodium chicken stock

1 tablespoon unsalted butter

1½ teaspoons Dijon mustard

Juice and grated zest of half an orange

1 Position a rack in the center of the oven and preheat the oven to 375°F.

2 Cook the bacon in a large ovenproof skillet or a Dutch oven over medium heat until the bacon is lightly browned and most of the fat is rendered, 5 to 8 minutes, stirring often and adjusting the heat as necessary. Using a slotted spoon, transfer the bacon to a paper towel-lined plate to drain, reserving the bacon fat in the skillet.

3 Crush the fennel seeds in a mortar using a pestle or pulse them in a mini food processor until crushed. Rub the pork tenderloin all over with the crushed fennel seeds and season it with salt and pepper to taste.

4 Trim the fennel bulb, setting aside the fennel fronds. Place the trimmed fennel bulb on a cutting board, flat side down, then cut it in half from top to bottom. Cut each half again to make 4 wedges. Then cut each wedge into thin wedges, about ½ inch thick. Slice the carrots in half crosswise and then lengthwise into sticks each about ½ inch thick.

5 Reheat the bacon fat in the skillet over medium-high heat. Add the pork tenderloin and brown it on all sides, about 6 minutes total. Transfer the pork to a plate. Reduce the heat to medium. Add the fennel wedges, carrot sticks, and white wine to the skillet and toss the vegetables to evenly coat. Cover the skillet and cook until the fennel and carrots are tender, about 10 minutes, stirring occasionally. Add the garlic, chicken stock, and butter and let come to a boil over high heat. Then, reduce the heat as necessary and let the fennel and carrot mixture simmer, covered, until the flavors blend, 4 to 5 minutes. Remove the skillet from the heat and add the drained bacon.

6 Place the pork tenderloin on top of the vegetable mixture in the skillet, adding any juices from the plate, and bake until an instant-read meat thermometer inserted into the thickest part of the tenderloin registers 140° to 145°F, 15 to 20 minutes. Transfer the tenderloin to a cutting board, loosely cover it with aluminum foil, and let it rest for about 5 minutes before slicing.

7 As the tenderloin rests, chop enough of the reserved fennel fronds to measure 3 tablespoons. Place the skillet over medium-high heat. Stir in the mustard, orange juice, orange zest, and chopped fennel fronds and let simmer for a few minutes until the liquid is reduced by about half.

8 Slice the pork tenderloin. Using a slotted spoon or tongs, transfer the fennel and carrots to a serving platter and arrange the sliced pork on top, drizzling the sauce from the skillet over all before serving.

SALTIMBACON

Serves 4

I f you have ever seen saltimbocca in a cookbook, no doubt you are familiar with the explanation that, in Italian, *saltimbocca* means jumps in your mouth. Perhaps this refers to how quickly people tend to devour it because it's so delicious. Basically, our version is a "sandwich" of pounded pork cutlets enclosing a layer of bacon and sage that is then dusted with flour and bread crumbs. The fat from the bacon helps to compensate for the lean (often too lean) consistency of much modern pork. If you can find the well-marbled meat from heritage breeds, you will notice the difference in flavor and texture. The completed dish includes a sauce of Marsala wine and mushrooms. In Italy they prefer pancetta to American-style bacon, but given the mix of powerful flavors, we feel the smokiness of the bacon nicely balances the woodsy notes in the Marsala.

4 slices thick-cut bacon

8 thin boneless pork chops (about ½ inch thick and 4 ounces each)

8 fresh sage leaves

Freshly ground black pepper

¼ cup unbleached all-purpose flour, seasoned with salt and pepper

½ cup homemade bread crumbs (see page 32)

2 tablespoons extra-virgin olive oil, or more if necessary

1 large shallot, diced

4 to 6 ounces cremini or baby portobello mushrooms, stems trimmed, mushrooms wiped clean and sliced about ½ inch thick

½ cup Marsala

½ cup low-sodium chicken stock

¼ cup finely chopped fresh flat-leaf parsley

1 Cook the bacon in a large skillet over medium heat until lightly browned, but not crisp, on both sides, 6 to 7 minutes. Turn the slices and adjust the heat, as necessary. Using tongs, transfer the bacon to a paper towel-lined plate to drain, reserving 1 tablespoon of the bacon fat in the skillet. When cool, cut each slice of bacon in half crosswise.

2 Place the pork chops between 2 pieces of plastic wrap or waxed paper and, using a meat mallet or the flat side of a cleaver, pound each several times until it is about ¼ inch thick.

3 Arrange 4 pork chops on a work surface. Arrange 2 sage leaves side by side in the center of each chop, then top each sage leaf with a half slice of the cooked bacon. Season the chops with pepper to taste. Arrange the remaining 4 pork chops on top of the bacon and sage filling to make "sandwiches." Press the edges of the chops together so that they will adhere while cooking.

4 Place the seasoned flour in a shallow bowl; place the bread crumbs in a second shallow bowl (pie plates work well for this). Dredge each of the pork sandwiches lightly on both sides in the seasoned flour and then in the bread crumbs, pressing on the crumbs so they stick to the pork.

5 Add 1 tablespoon of olive oil to the skillet with the bacon fat and heat over medium-high heat until the fats begin to shimmer, about 30 seconds. Place the pork sandwiches in the skillet, reduce the heat to medium, and cook until the bread-crumb crusts are a golden brown on the bottom, 3 to 5 minutes. Carefully turn over each pork sandwich to brown the second side, 3 to 5 minutes. Transfer the pork sandwiches to a platter and set it in a warm place.

6 Add another tablespoon of olive oil to the skillet. Add the shallot and cook until softened, 2 to 3 minutes, stirring and scraping up any brown bits from the bottom of the skillet. Add the mushrooms and Marsala, let come to a boil, and cook until the sauce begins to reduce, 2 to 3 minutes. Add the chicken stock and cook until the sauce has a slightly syrupy consistency, 2 to 3 minutes.

7 Return the pork sandwiches to the skillet. Reduce the heat as necessary so that the

saltimbocca simmer gently until just warmed through, 3 to 4 minutes. Spoon a little of the pan sauce over each serving and sprinkle the chopped parsley on top.

CATHY ERWAY'S TWICE-COOKED BACON with Celery and Leeks

Serves 3 to 4

Cathy Erway is one of the great young food bloggers (her blog is *Not Eating Out in New York*) and food personalities in New York City. Of Taiwanese heritage, she sometimes likes to play around with traditional recipes. We asked her to put her talents to work on bacon and here is the lovely result.

This is a traditional Szechuan dish made with fresh pork belly, which is stewed until tender and then sliced and quickly stir-fried with vegetables. Cathy has used slab bacon in place of the pork belly, and there's enough bacon in the dish to serve as a light lunch or supper with rice. The ingredients make a lovely pan sauce, and it's an interesting use of slab bacon. The flavor of fresh ginger is still making our mouths tingle. We also like that celery plays a prominent role in the dish, and very few recipes, except in Chinese cooking, use celery as a starring vegetable.

Cathy's most recent book is *The Art of Eating In: How I Learned to Stop Spending and Love the Stove.* She hosts the Heritage Radio Network podcast "Let's Eat In."

12 ounces slab bacon, rind removed
(see page 57)

1 tablespoon canola or vegetable oil

1 large leek, white and light green parts
only, cut in half lengthwise, rinsed
well, and sliced ¼ inch thick on the
diagonal

3 ribs celery, preferably Chinese celery,
thinly sliced on the diagonal

1 cup fresh bean sprouts

1 piece (about 1 inch long) fresh ginger,
peeled and cut into julienne strips

½ cup rice wine

1 tablespoon chile and fermented bean
sauce (see Note)

1 teaspoon soy sauce

Salt and freshly ground black pepper

1 teaspoon coarsely crushed Szechuan or
black peppercorns (optional)

Steamed brown or white rice, for serving

1 Bring 2 quarts of water to a boil in a large pot. Add the slab bacon, cover the pot, and let simmer until the bacon softens slightly, 2 to 3 minutes. Using tongs, transfer the slab bacon to a cutting board and let it cool. When cool, slice the bacon into thin, floppy strips about ⅛ to ¼ inch thick, 1 inch wide, and 2 inches long.

2 Set a wok or a large skillet over high heat and when hot add the canola or vegetable oil. Add the bacon slices and cook until just crisped, 2 to 3 minutes per side. Transfer the bacon to a large bowl and set it aside. If after crisping the bacon slices you find that some still have an excessive amount of fat, trim it off before returning the bacon to the wok with the vegetables.

3 Add the leek, celery, bean sprouts, and ginger to the wok or skillet and stir-fry until the vegetables are just softened, 2 to 3 minutes. Return the bacon to the pan and add the rice wine. Let the liquid boil for a few seconds, then add the chile and fermented bean sauce and the soy sauce. Stir and taste for seasoning, adding salt and pepper as necessary. Sprinkle the crushed peppercorns over all, if using. Serve with brown or white rice.

NOTE: Also called hot bean sauce or chile bean sauce, chile and fermented bean sauce is available at Chinese markets, and at Whole Foods and other good-quality supermarkets.

GRILLED MIDNIGHT MOON AND BACON SANDWICH

Makes 2 sandwiches

Make a sandwich with bacon and melted cheese on grilled bread for lunch and everybody's happy. We tried lots of different cheeses and Midnight Moon is our first choice. It's an aged goat's-milk cheese with a firm, dense texture and a taste that is both buttery and nutty. While other cheeses will make a fine grilled cheese, tomato, and bacon sandwich, it's worth hunting for Midnight Moon, as its flavor is distinctive. For best results use a good-quality multigrain bread. If you can't find Midnight Moon in your market or specialty cheese shop, you can substitute a good Swiss, Gouda, or Morbier (which is Daniel Boulud's favorite for his Frenchie Burger).

4 slices thick- or regular-cut bacon

4 slices multigrain bread, each about ½ inch thick

4 to 5 ounces thinly sliced Midnight Moon cheese

2 slices ripe tomato, each about ½ inch thick

Freshly ground black pepper

2 very thin red onion slices

1 Cook the bacon in a large skillet over medium heat until browned and crisp, 6 to 8 minutes, depending on the thickness of the bacon, using tongs to turn the slices and adjusting the heat as necessary. The skillet should be big enough to hold 2 slices of bread side by side. Transfer the bacon to a paper towel-lined plate to drain, reserving the bacon fat in a small cup or bowl. Wipe the skillet clean with paper towels and set it aside.

2 Place 2 of the slices of bread on a work surface. Place a quarter of the cheese on top of each slice of bread. Place a slice of tomato over each stack of cheese. Season the tomato slices with pepper to taste. Place 2 bacon slices on each tomato slice, breaking the bacon into pieces if necessary to fit. Place a red onion slice over the bacon on each sandwich. Divide the remaining slices of cheese evenly between the 2 sandwiches and press the cheese gently onto the onion. Top each sandwich with one of the remaining slices of bread. Gently press down on the top of each sandwich.

3 Heat 2 teaspoons of the reserved bacon fat over medium-low heat in the wiped skillet. Place the sandwiches in the skillet. Brush the top of each sandwich lightly with the remaining bacon fat. Cover the sandwiches with a lid that is slightly smaller than the skillet to weigh the sandwiches down. Cook the sandwiches until both sides are browned, 4 to 5 minutes per side, reducing the heat if the bread browns too quickly. Transfer the sandwiches to individual plates and let stand for 30 seconds to 1 minute to allow the cheese to set slightly before slicing each sandwich in half and serving.

A PERFECT BLAT
(Bacon, Lettuce, Avocado, and Tomato)
Makes 2 sandwiches

Now, everybody knows that a BLT has mayonnaise, but we thought there had to be another way, and then a visit to Ted & Honey, a lovely sandwich shop in Brooklyn's Cobble Hill neighborhood, caused a little lightbulb to shine in the bacon part of our brains: *avocado*. It has the fat and creaminess of mayo and its own nutty and fresh flavor that makes for an even more healthful BLT—or, as we like to think of it, BLAT. To make up for the vinegar in the mayo, a squeeze of lemon juice adds a bright, tart fruitiness. When only mayo will do for your BLT, we suggest going whole hog (!) and slathering your sandwich with Bacon Aioli (recipe follows).

6 slices bacon (thin to medium thickness, depending on your preference)

1 medium-size ripe Hass avocado, peeled and with pit removed

2 teaspoons fresh lemon juice

¼ teaspoon salt, or more to taste

Freshly ground black pepper

2 dashes your choice of hot sauce (optional), or more to taste

2 leaves romaine lettuce, large enough to slightly overlap the edges of the bread

4 slices multigrain bread, toasted

1 medium-size ripe tomato (preferably locally grown), cored and cut into 4 thin slices

1 Cook the bacon in a large skillet (preferably cast-iron) over medium heat until browned and crisp, 6 to 8 minutes, depending on the thickness of the bacon, using tongs to turn the slices and adjusting the heat as necessary. Transfer the bacon to a paper towel-lined plate to drain.

2 Combine the avocado, lemon juice, salt, pepper, and hot sauce, if using, in a small bowl and mash the avocado with a fork until smooth. Taste for seasoning, adding more salt and/or hot sauce as necessary. Set the avocado spread aside. Rinse the romaine lettuce leaves and pat them dry with paper towels.

3 Place 2 of the slices of bread on a work surface. Spread each slice with half of the avocado spread. Layer the lettuce, tomato, and bacon over the spread, dividing the ingredients evenly between each sandwich. (If the bacon slices overlap the bread, simply cut or fold them in half to fit within the bread's edges.) Top each sandwich with the remaining slice of bread, then cut the sandwiches in half and serve immediately.

BACON AIOLI
Makes about 1 cup

First a confession: We are not huge fans of straight old-fashioned mayonnaise. But aioli is a horse of a different color. Garlic gives aioli a completely different aspect and bacon steps right in and lets garlic know there is more than one powerful flavor in this game. The apple cider vinegar lends a bit of subtle sweetness. Try the aioli as a sandwich spread, a dip for raw vegetables, a sauce for grilled fish, or a filling for hard-cooked eggs; or toss enough of it to coat a salad mixture of romaine leaves and croutons. And don't forget to try the aioli on a BLT. You may never eat another one without it.

3 slices bacon, diced

1 whole large head garlic

⅔ cup mayonnaise

1⅓ teaspoons apple cider vinegar

Salt and freshly ground black pepper

1 Position a rack in the center of the oven and preheat the oven to 400°F.

2 Cook the bacon in a medium-size skillet over medium heat until the bacon is lightly browned and most of the fat is rendered, 5 to 8 minutes, stirring often and adjusting the heat as necessary. Using a slotted spoon, transfer the bacon to a paper towel-lined plate to drain, reserving the bacon fat in the skillet.

3 Cut off and discard the top of the head of garlic to expose the cloves, then generously brush the exposed cloves with some of the bacon fat. Wrap the head of garlic in aluminum foil and bake the garlic until the cloves are tender, about 35 minutes. Let the garlic cool until slightly warm, 5 to 10 minutes.

4 Squeeze the garlic cloves from their skins into a medium-size mixing bowl and mash them well with a fork. Add the mayonnaise, cider vinegar, and drained bacon and stir to blend well. Season the aioli with salt and pepper to taste. Cover the aioli and refrigerate it for a few hours to let the flavors bloom before using. The aioli can be refrigerated, covered, for up to 1 week.

THE BLT—DECONSTRUCTED AND RECONSTRUCTED

A BLT is simple to make but, like anything truly delicious, demands the best ingredients. The bread must be toasted and its thickness carefully considered. If it's too thick, you'll miss that sublime experience of biting into the sandwich and tasting all its delicious layers at once. Some people insist on using white packaged sandwich bread, the kind that has a soft, tight crumb to absorb some of the tomato's wonderful juices. We like a multigrain bread for its firmness and flavor, but even a thinly sliced brioche can work.

Buy the best bacon you can find. If you prefer it to have a little chewiness, choose a thick-sliced bacon. If you like a crisp and crunchy contrast to the tomato slices, choose one that's thinly sliced. Since bacon is the main feature in this production, here's your chance to audition different artisanal bacons. Try a whiskey barrel-smoked or a black pepper–rubbed bacon.

The canonical BLT calls for using iceberg lettuce, but this recipe, like so many others, is always being fiddled with and improved upon by inventive cooks. Follow your muse here. Use whatever greens you fancy: Red leaf lettuce is lovely. Boston lettuce offers a creamy contrast to the toasted bread. Romaine, which we favor, adds crunch. Arugula or watercress are wonderful for the way that their sharpness counterbalances the broad flavors of bacon.

Find the very best summer tomatoes for your BLT. We recommend using ripe, firm, locally grown tomatoes for their unique floral scent. Never refrigerate a quality ripe tomato; that diminishes its flavor. Store tomatoes away from the sun and use them within a couple of days of purchase.

BRAWNIER
BIRDS

Chicken Tagine with Bacon,
Butternut Squash, and Prunes,
page 136

IN THIS CHAPTER...

Of all the political promises ever

made, "a chicken in every pot" is perhaps the most practical and friendliest. Anyone who puts a chicken in your pot and fills the house with the seductive scent of a flavorful hen and aromatic vegetables is our kind of candidate (provided he or she comes through on that promise). Throw bacon into that pot and you amp up the flavor, unctuousness, and succulence of your bird immeasurably. A free-range organic chicken has a nutty, buttery flavor that plays well off of the taste and texture of bacon. Come to think of it, even a so-so chicken is kind of fun when you add bacon to the mix, whether it's the crispier, tastier coq au vin that our friend, the great chef Robert Wiedmaier, achieves with his Belgian version or the brawnier Chicken Cacciatore we have reinterpreted here.

From the Moroccan part of the world we have taken the liberty to add bacon to a softly sweet and fruity tagine in the hope that our departure from the no-bacon strictures of North African cuisine will be forgiven because it's so darn good. Basically every culture has a dish with chicken as a base and deeply flavored fruits, veggies, and spices. Season it with bacon and you are just adding to the pleasure.

A SUNDAY CHICKEN

Serves 4

A wonderful dish to anticipate as the house fills with the aroma of chicken, bacon, and herbs, this is a recipe that smells like Sunday—a lazy, peaceful Sunday afternoon. Lots of recipes call for tucking gobs of butter under the chicken's skin before roasting it. Conventional cooking wisdom holds that the butter bastes the breast meat and keeps it from drying out. What really happens is the butter quickly melts and rather than moistening the meat, it pools at the bottom of the roasting pan. Instead of using butter, we tuck raw bacon, herbs, garlic, fresh ginger, and salt and pepper under the chicken skin. As it cooks, the bacon provides "time-release" fat and seasoning that is absorbed in the breast meat.

The medley of brussels sprouts and potatoes in the pan caramelizes and puts the pan drippings to delicious use. Also, we butterfly the raw chicken by removing the bird's backbone before roasting. This allows the chicken's thighs to lie flat over the roasting pan for even cooking. Butterflying also makes it easier to carve the roasted chicken.

4 slices bacon, diced

4 medium-size cloves garlic, minced

2 teaspoons fresh thyme leaves

2 teaspoons minced fresh rosemary leaves

2 to 3 teaspoons minced peeled fresh ginger

Salt and freshly ground black pepper

1 whole organic chicken (4 to 4¼ pounds)

Vegetable oil cooking spray or olive oil, for oiling the broiler pan

12 small (about golf ball-size) red-skinned potatoes, scrubbed and cut in half lengthwise

12 to 14 brussels sprouts, trimmed and cut in half lengthwise if wider than 1 inch

1 small yellow onion, cut in quarters

1 tablespoon plus 2 teaspoons extra-virgin olive oil

1 Combine the bacon, garlic, thyme, rosemary, ginger, ⅛ teaspoon of salt, and pepper to taste in a small mixing bowl and set the bacon and herb seasoning mixture aside.

2 Rinse the chicken under cold running water and pat it dry with paper towels. Butterfly the chicken by placing it, breast side down, on a large cutting board and, using a pair of poultry shears, cutting through the bones on both sides of the backbone. Remove and discard the backbone. Trim any excess fat off the chicken. Turn the chicken over and use your hand to press the breastbone down and flatten the bird.

3 Slip your fingers between the skin and breast meat to loosen the skin. You might find it easier to slip a sharp boning knife under the skin to separate it from the meat. Spoon half of the bacon and herb seasoning mixture under the skin on each side of the breast, working it down toward the legs. (Set the remaining bacon and herb mixture aside.) Using your fingers and working on the outside of the chicken, press down on the skin to distribute the seasonings evenly over the breast and into the thigh areas. If you have the time, at this point refrigerate the chicken, uncovered, for 8 to 24 hours (see Note); refrigerate the remaining bacon and herb mixture separately, covered. Let the chicken come to room temperature before proceeding with the recipe.

4 Position a rack in the lower third of the oven and preheat the oven to 450°F. Line the bottom of a deep broiler pan with aluminum foil and spray it with vegetable oil cooking spray or brush it with olive oil.

5 Place the potatoes, brussels sprouts, and onion in the aluminum foil-lined broiler pan. Drizzle 1 tablespoon of the olive oil over the vegetables, tossing them to coat. Arrange the vegetables cut side down in the pan. Sprinkle the reserved bacon and herb mixture evenly over the top of the vegetables and season them lightly with salt and pepper.

6 Place the broiling rack in the pan over the vegetables and place the chicken on the rack skin side up. Rub the chicken breast, wings, and legs with the remaining 2 teaspoons of olive oil.

7 Bake the chicken until lightly browned, about 20 minutes, then rotate the broiler pan 180 degrees so the back of the pan faces the front of the oven. Continue baking the chicken until the skin is golden brown and an instant-read meat thermometer inserted into the thickest part of a thigh, but not touching a bone, registers 165°F, 15 to 20 minutes longer.

8 Transfer the chicken to a cutting board. Using a flat metal spatula, transfer the potatoes and brussels sprouts to a serving platter. Cut the chicken into pieces and serve with the vegetables and any juices.

NOTE: We recommend air-drying the raw chicken in the refrigerator, uncovered, for 8 hours or overnight after you have inserted the bacon and herb mixture under its skin. This allows the surface moisture to evaporate so that when the chicken roasts the skin becomes quite crisp and browned, and it also allows the bacon and herbs to infuse the bird with more flavor. Before putting it in the oven, remove the chicken from the refrigerator about 1 hour ahead to let it come to room temperature.

ROBERT WIEDMAIER'S COQ AU VIN A LA BRUXELLES

Serves 5

F or most of us, coq au vin is a braised chicken dish that we first ordered in an old-fashioned French restaurant—not a fancy one but, instead, a place that served the kind of food that French grandmas made. Or, for millions of aspiring American home cooks, Julia Child's coq au vin may be the most popular recipe in her classic *Mastering the Art of French Cooking.*

Julia's is a great recipe, but this version by Robert Wiedmaier, a Belgian American who is one of the greatest chefs in Washington, D.C., blew us away when we tried it at his restaurant Brasserie Beck. Rather than thickening his wine sauce with a roux, Robert reduces it to achieve intensity of flavor. The combination of bacon and thyme is truly thrilling.

1 organic chicken (4½ pounds), cut into 10 pieces (see the facing page)

4¼ cups cabernet sauvignon

2 tablespoons Ghent or Dijon mustard

8 ounces slab bacon, rind removed (see page 57)

1 tablespoon unsalted butter

2 tablespoons extra-virgin olive oil

½ pound white pearl onions, peeled

1 pound white button mushrooms, stems trimmed, mushrooms wiped clean

Unbleached all-purpose flour, for dredging the chicken

Salt and freshly ground black pepper

1 cup low-sodium chicken stock, or more if necessary

2 teaspoons fresh thyme leaves

¼ cup finely chopped fresh flat-leaf parsley

1 Trim any excess fat off the chicken pieces. Rinse the chicken pieces under cold running water and pat them dry with paper towels. Place the chicken in a large deep bowl. Place ¼ cup of the cabernet sauvignon and the mustard in a small bowl or measuring cup and stir to mix. Pour this mixture over the chicken and add the remaining 4 cups of cabernet. Cover the bowl with plastic wrap and refrigerate the chicken for 24 hours.

2 Remove the chicken from the marinade, setting aside the marinade. Pat the pieces of chicken dry with paper towels. Set the chicken aside.

CHICKEN PARTS

When a recipe calls for a chicken cut in ten pieces, you can have your butcher cut the chicken or you can cut up a whole chicken yourself. To do this, separate each chicken leg and thigh. Remove the backbone from the chicken and cut each breast half crosswise into two pieces. Use a boning knife to cut through the joint that attaches each wing to the breast. If you wish, you can cut off the tip of each wing. You will have two drumsticks, two thighs, four breast pieces, and two wing pieces. When Robert Wiedmaier makes his coq au vin, he also "French cuts" the thigh bones by removing the tendons and pulling the meat back off the bone until the bone is exposed; but he says it's an optional technique for a home cook.

A cut-up chicken purchased at the supermarket typically has eight pieces in the package. We recommend slicing each breast piece in half crosswise. The skin will brown better, and you'll have two more pieces of breast for those who like white meat.

3 Make the lardons: Cut the slab of bacon crosswise into slices about ½ inch thick. Stack 2 slices and cut them lengthwise into ½-inch-thick strips. Finally, cut the slices crosswise into lardons about 1 inch long.

4 Place the butter and olive oil in a large Dutch oven and set it over medium-high heat. When the butter has melted, add the lardons and onions and cook until they are lightly browned, 7 to 8 minutes, stirring occasionally. (A pair of tongs is useful for turning the lardons and onions to facilitate even browning.) Add the mushrooms and cook until the lardons and onions are cooked through and the mushrooms are lightly browned, 7 to 8 minutes, stirring occasionally. Reduce the heat to medium if at any time the lardon mixture browns too quickly. Using a slotted spoon, transfer the lardons, onions, and mushrooms to a medium-size mixing bowl and set them aside. Reserve the fat in the Dutch oven.

5 Position a rack in the center of the oven and preheat the oven to 325°F.

6 Place the flour in a shallow bowl (a pie plate works well for this). Season the pieces of chicken lightly with salt and pepper. The lardons will add a good amount of salt, so feel free to omit salt in this step. You can always taste at the end and add salt. Dredge each piece of chicken lightly in the flour, shaking off the excess.

7 Heat the fat in the Dutch oven over medium-high heat until it shimmers, about 1 minute, then add 3 or 4 floured chicken pieces to the Dutch oven, being careful not to overcrowd it. Cook the chicken until it is seared and golden brown, 3 to 5 minutes per side. Transfer the browned chicken pieces to a large plate and repeat with the remaining pieces of chicken.

8 Add half of the reserved marinade (about 2 cups) and 1 cup of chicken stock to the Dutch oven. Discard any remaining marinade. Add the browned chicken pieces, pushing them down into the liquid. Cover the Dutch oven and adjust the heat as necessary to bring the mixture to a simmer. Place the Dutch oven in the oven and bake the chicken until an instant-read meat thermometer inserted into the thickest part of a thigh, but not touching a bone, registers 165°F, 25 to 30 minutes.

9 Transfer the chicken from the Dutch oven to a large bowl. Skim the fat off the top of the sauce. Set the Dutch oven over medium-high heat and let simmer until the sauce is reduced by half, continuing to skim the fat and foam off the surface. The sauce should be of medium thickness: As Chef Wiedmaier says, "not quite thick enough to coat the back of a spoon." If the sauce is too thick, add a little more chicken broth. If it is too thin, let it reduce further. Strain the sauce through a strainer into a medium-size bowl.

10 To assemble the coq au vin, wipe the Dutch oven clean with paper towels. Place the chicken, lardons, onions, and mushrooms back in the Dutch oven. Pour the sauce over all and sprinkle the thyme and parsley on top. Place the Dutch oven over medium heat, partially cover it, and let the chicken, sauce, and vegetables simmer gently until they are just heated through before serving.

CHICKEN CANZANESE

Serves 4

Even if you don't speak Italian, you might look at the title of this recipe and think that it's chicken done in the style of the city of Canzano in Abruzzo, but the wonderful food writer Amanda Hesser has reported that, after extensive research, she couldn't find confirmation of this in any of the great Italian cookbooks. However, Craig Claiborne, who more than anyone else began the *New York Times* tradition of well-researched and delicious recipes, wrote in 1969 that it was done this way in Canzano and that has been how it has been thought of ever since. Two trustworthy writers: You decide.

Whatever its origins, versions of this dish can be found all over Italy. It's a simple one-pot meal that is lighter than coq au vin or chicken cacciatore (perhaps because of the white wine). Smoky bacon instead of prosciutto adds another layer of flavor. We felt that the bracing freshness of ginger would balance the bacon nicely, which makes our version even less likely to be found in Canzano.

3 tablespoons kosher salt

2 tablespoons sugar

1 organic chicken (3½ to 3¾ pounds),
   cut into 8 pieces

3 carrots, trimmed, peeled, and cut into
   2- to 3-inch pieces

2 medium-size boiling potatoes
   (about 10 ounces total), cut in
   quarters

1 small onion, cut in quarters

3 slices thick-cut bacon, cut into
   ½-inch pieces

6 fresh sage leaves

2 bay leaves

1 piece (about ½ inch long) fresh ginger,
   peeled and chopped

3 whole cloves

1 large clove garlic, slivered lengthwise

1 fresh rosemary sprig (3 to
   4 inches long)

¼ teaspoon crushed red pepper flakes

¾ cup dry white wine

1 loaf French or Italian bread

1 Combine the kosher salt, sugar, and 1 cup of warm water in a large bowl and stir until the salt and sugar dissolve. Trim the excess fat off the chicken pieces. Rinse the chicken pieces under cold running water. Place the chicken in the bowl and add enough cold water to cover. Cover the bowl with plastic wrap and refrigerate the chicken for about 1 hour. Then, drain the chicken well and discard the brine.

2 Arrange the chicken in a single layer in a large deep pot, fitted with a lid. Scatter the carrots, potatoes, onion, and bacon over the chicken. Add the sage, bay leaves, ginger, cloves, garlic, rosemary, and red pepper flakes. Add the white wine and ¾ cup of water. Cover the pot and let the liquid come to a boil over high heat. Then, reduce the heat as necessary and let the chicken simmer until it is just cooked through, 30 to 35 minutes. (An instant-read meat thermometer inserted into the thickest part of a thigh, but not touching a bone, should register 165°F. Avoid overcooking the chicken or it will be dry.)

3 Transfer the chicken and vegetables to a large shallow serving bowl. Let the sauce in the pot come to a boil, then reduce the heat and let simmer until the liquid reduces and becomes slightly syrupy, about 5 minutes. Remove and discard the bay leaves, whole cloves, and rosemary sprig. Pour the sauce over the chicken and vegetables in the serving bowl. Serve with slices of French or Italian bread for sopping up the plentiful sauce.

CHICKEN TAGINE with Bacon, Butternut Squash, and Prunes

Serves 4

Tagines are named for the North African crockery in which these slow braises are prepared. A tagine has a high clay dome that allows the vapor given off by the ingredients to condense and fall back on the gently bubbling stew, slowly building flavor. We have found that a good Dutch oven also does the trick. Although many tagines are made with savory ingredients only, we love the combination of fruits with meat and poultry that typify many Moroccan and Algerian tagines. Of course they also include the aromatic spices used in much Middle Eastern cuisine. The marriage of meat, fruits, and spices was also widespread in medieval European cookery (for those with the money to afford such luxuries). We think that the strong flavors really work well with bacon, but of course, in North Africa, where religious practices forbid pork, there are no bacon-based tagines.

Browning the chicken is the most time-consuming part of the preparation. If you want to speed up the process, use two skillets at once. You should have enough bacon fat for two skillets, but if not, simply add 1 to 2 tablespoons of olive oil. The onion is not browned in a tagine but slowly cooked until very soft to concentrate its flavor. Onion gives the tagine a delicious foundation to which half a dozen intensely individual seasoning ingredients—orange zest, cinnamon, garlic, saffron, star anise, and honey—are added to make a complex and satisfying sauce that imparts a distinct flavor to the chicken.

6 slices thick-cut bacon, coarsely chopped

1 large onion, cut in half lengthwise and thinly sliced crosswise

1¼ cups low-sodium chicken stock

1 organic chicken (about 4 pounds), cut into 10 pieces (see page 133)

Salt and freshly ground black pepper

Olive oil, if necessary

3 medium-size cloves garlic, minced

1 strip (3 by 1 inch) orange zest, finely chopped (see Notes)

2 large pinches saffron threads

¼ teaspoon ground cinnamon

¼ teaspoon ground ginger

⅛ teaspoon cayenne pepper

1 star anise point (see Notes)

About 3 tablespoons fresh orange juice (from ½ navel orange)

2 tablespoons honey

1 bay leaf

12 pitted prunes

1 pound butternut squash, peeled and cut into 2-inch pieces

Couscous or quinoa (optional), for serving

1 Cook the bacon in a large Dutch oven over medium heat until browned and most of the fat is rendered, 7 to 10 minutes, stirring often and adjusting the heat as necessary. Using a slotted spoon, transfer the bacon to a paper towel-lined plate to drain. Pour all but about 1½ tablespoons of the bacon fat into a small bowl and set it aside.

2 Heat the bacon fat in the Dutch oven over medium heat. Add the onion and stir to coat it with the bacon fat. Add 1 tablespoon of the chicken stock, cover the Dutch oven, reduce the heat to low, and cook the onion until it is very soft but not browned, about 25 minutes, stirring occasionally.

3 As the onion cooks, trim any excess fat off the chicken pieces. Rinse the chicken pieces under cold running water and pat them dry with paper towels. Season the chicken lightly with salt (the bacon will also impart salt) and black pepper to taste. Heat 2 tablespoons of the reserved bacon fat in a large skillet over medium heat until it shimmers, about 1 minute. If necessary, add enough olive oil to the skillet to measure a total of 2 tablespoons. Working in batches so as not to crowd the pieces in the skillet, brown the chicken until golden, 6 to 8 minutes per side. Transfer the browned chicken to a plate.

4 When the onion has cooked, add the garlic and orange zest to the Dutch oven and

cook over medium heat until fragrant, about 1 minute. Stir in the saffron, crushing it first between your fingers, and the cinnamon, ginger, cayenne pepper, and star anise point. Cook

until fragrant, about 30 seconds. Stir in the orange juice, honey, bay leaf, and the remaining 1 cup and 3 tablespoons of chicken stock, scraping up any brown bits from the bottom of the Dutch oven.

5 Scatter the prunes and drained bacon over the onion mixture. Add the browned chicken and any juices on the plate. Cover the Dutch oven, let the mixture come to a boil, then reduce the heat and let the chicken simmer for about 20 minutes. Add the butternut squash and let simmer until the squash is tender and the chicken is cooked through, about 20 minutes. The chicken is cooked when an instant-read meat thermometer inserted into the thickest part of a thigh, but not touching a bone, registers 165°F.

6 Using a slotted spoon, transfer the chicken, prunes, and squash to a serving bowl and cover the bowl with aluminum foil to keep warm. Using a large spoon, skim the fat off the surface of the pan juices. If the pan juices are more than about 1 cup, let them boil for a few minutes to concentrate them. Remove and discard the bay leaf and anise point and pour the pan juices over the chicken before serving it with couscous or quinoa, if desired.

NOTES: To remove the zest from the orange, run a vegetable peeler or a paring knife from the stem to the blossom end, removing as little as possible of the bitter white pith under the orange-colored peel. Then, finely chop the zest.

To remove a point from a star anise, using your fingers simply snap it off of the whole anise star.

CHICKEN MARSALA
with Bacon and Sage

Serves 4

Browning chicken breasts in a skillet and then pan-roasting them at a low temperature produces succulent white meat—a state of juiciness for the chicken breasts that is often (and dispiritingly) otherwise hard to achieve. Don't worry if during the initial browning the chicken sticks a little to the pan and tears away when you turn it. Adam Perry Lang, who is a truly gastronomic griller, calls this "scruffing" and says that it creates more little nooks and crannies in the surface of the food, which means more area to crisp up and turn golden brown. The combination of bacon, sage, Marsala, and butter has massive mouth-filling flavor. Marsala wine is a sweet match for such mild-tasting meat as veal or chicken breasts. In the unlikely event that you have some leftover sauce, it's wonderful with pan-seared scallops.

4 skinless, boneless organic chicken breasts (6 to 8 ounces each), trimmed of fat

Salt and freshly ground black pepper

About ½ cup unbleached all-purpose flour, for dredging the chicken

6 slices bacon, diced

Olive oil, if necessary

10 ounces cremini mushrooms, stems trimmed, mushrooms wiped clean and sliced about ¼ inch thick

½ cup low-sodium chicken stock

1 ripe plum tomato, seeded and chopped

2 medium-size cloves garlic, thinly sliced

2½ teaspoons minced fresh sage

1⅓ cups Marsala

2 tablespoons (¼ stick) unsalted butter

Grated zest of half a lemon

1 Position a rack in the lower third of the oven and preheat the oven to 225°F. Place a large shallow baking dish on the oven rack.

2 Pat the chicken breasts dry with paper towels and season the chicken lightly with salt and pepper. Place the flour in a shallow dish (a pie plate works well for this). Dredge both sides of the chicken breasts in the flour, lifting and shaking them to remove any excess flour. Set the chicken aside.

3 Cook the bacon in a large heavy skillet over medium heat until lightly browned and most of the fat is rendered, 5 to 8 minutes, stirring often and adjusting the heat as necessary. Using a slotted spoon, transfer the bacon to a paper towel-lined plate to drain, reserving about 2 tablespoons of bacon fat in the skillet. If necessary, add enough olive oil to the skillet to measure 2 tablespoons.

4 Place the skillet over medium-high heat and heat the bacon fat until it shimmers, about 1 minute. Arrange the chicken breasts in a single layer in the skillet and brown them on both sides, 3 to 4 minutes per side, turning them once with tongs. Transfer the browned chicken breasts to the baking dish in the oven. They will continue to cook slowly as you prepare the Marsala and sage sauce.

5 Place the skillet over medium heat. Add the mushrooms and ¼ cup of the chicken stock and, using a wooden spoon or flat metal spatula, scrape up any brown bits from the bottom of the skillet. Increase the heat to medium-high and cook the mushrooms until most of the liquid in the skillet evaporates and the mushrooms start to brown, about 5 minutes. Add the tomato, garlic, 1½ teaspoons of the sage, and the drained bacon and cook, stirring, until the garlic is fragrant, about 1 minute.

6 Add the Marsala and the remaining ¼ cup of chicken stock. Increase the heat to high and let the sauce come to a boil. Then, reduce the heat as necessary and let simmer vigorously, scraping up any brown bits from the bottom of the skillet. Let the sauce simmer until it is reduced and slightly thickened, 5 to 7 minutes. Remove the skillet from the heat and whisk in the butter. Stir in the remaining 1 teaspoon of sage and taste for seasoning, adding pepper, if necessary.

7 The chicken breasts should be fully cooked at this point but use an instant-read meat thermometer to check that they have reached an internal temperature of 165°F. Or, using a paring knife, cut into the thickest part of each breast to check for doneness; the chicken meat should appear white and opaque, without a trace of pink. If necessary, place the breasts in the skillet and let them simmer in the sauce until they are completely done, 1 to 2 minutes. Transfer the chicken breasts to serving plates. Pour the sauce over the chicken breasts, sprinkle them with the lemon zest, and serve.

VELVETY CHICKEN with Rosemary-Bacon Biscuit Topping

Serves 4 to 6

Our favorite part of this recipe? The biscuit topping. The combination of bacon and rosemary makes the biscuits more than something to soak up sauce. They are a full savory partner to the rich pie filling. The first time we tested this recipe it was a cold and rainy Sunday afternoon so we poured ourselves a glass of sherry. A lightbulb went off: Why not add a touch of earthy sweetness to the sauce? So in went the sherry.

2¼ to 2½ pounds skin-on, bone-in
  organic chicken breasts

3 cups low-sodium chicken stock

5 whole peppercorns

4 slices bacon, cut crosswise into
  ½-inch-wide strips

Olive oil, if necessary

1 medium-size onion,
  diced (about 1¼ cups)

3 medium-size carrots, trimmed, peeled, and sliced into ¼-inch-thick rounds

1 rib celery, cut crosswise into ¼-inch-thick pieces

2 medium-size cloves garlic, thinly sliced

Salt and freshly ground black pepper

⅔ cup fresh green peas, or ⅔ cup thawed frozen peas if fresh are not available

4 tablespoons (½ stick) unsalted butter

4 tablespoons unbleached all-purpose flour

⅓ cup half-and-half

2 tablespoons dry sherry

½ teaspoon freshly ground nutmeg

Rosemary-Bacon Biscuit Topping (recipe follows)

1 Combine the chicken breasts, chicken stock, and peppercorns in a 4- or 5-quart saucepan. Add enough water to just cover the chicken. Cover the pan and let the liquid come to a boil over high heat. Then, reduce the heat as necessary and let the chicken simmer, partially covered, until it is just cooked through, 8 to 10 minutes. To check for doneness, using a paring knife, cut into the thickest part of one of the breasts; the chicken meat should appear white and opaque, without a trace of pink. Transfer the chicken to a large bowl to cool; strain the broth into a medium-size bowl and set it aside.

2 While the chicken poaches, cook the bacon in a large skillet over medium heat until the bacon is browned and crisp and most of the fat is rendered, 5 to 8 minutes, stirring often and adjusting the heat as necessary. Using a slotted spoon, transfer the bacon to a paper towel-lined plate to drain, reserving the bacon fat in the skillet. If necessary, add enough olive oil to the skillet to measure a total of 1½ tablespoons. Heat the skillet over medium-high heat. Add the onion, carrots, and celery and cook until just crisp-tender, about 5 minutes, stirring occasionally. Add the garlic and cook until fragrant, about 1 minute, stirring often.

Season the vegetables with a pinch of salt and pepper to taste and set them aside.

3 Transfer the poached chicken to a large bowl to cool. Strain the broth into a medium-size bowl and set it aside. When cool enough to handle, remove the meat from the chicken, discarding the skin and bones. Cut the chicken meat into bite-size pieces. Scatter the chicken, the cooked vegetables, drained bacon, and the peas evenly in a 13- by 9-inch baking dish and set the dish aside.

4 Pour 2 cups of the reserved chicken broth into a small saucepan and let come to a simmer. (Set aside any remaining broth for another use.)

5 Melt the butter over medium heat in the skillet used to cook the vegetables. Add the flour and cook, whisking constantly, until the flour lightly colors, about 1 minute. Gradually stir in the 2 cups of hot broth and cook, whisking often, until the sauce comes to a boil and thickens, 3 to 4 minutes. Stir in the half-and-half and let the sauce simmer until it is about as thick as cream, about 3 minutes. Remove the skillet from the heat and stir in the sherry and nutmeg. Taste for seasoning, adding more salt and pepper as necessary.

6 Pour the sauce over the chicken mixture. Cover the baking dish with aluminum foil and set it aside in a warm place while you make the Rosemary-Bacon Biscuit Topping. Or, you can prepare the chicken filling up to a day before. Refrigerate the baking dish, covered, then rewarm the filling for about 15 to 20 minutes in an oven preheated to 300°F before topping it with the biscuits.

7 Preheat the oven to 400°F.

8 Arrange the biscuit rounds in an even layer on top of the chicken filling and bake in the middle of the oven until the biscuits are browned and the filling is bubbling, about 25 minutes. If after 20 minutes the biscuits appear to be browning too quickly, tent the baking dish with aluminum foil and continue to bake until the filling is warmed through. Serve the chicken and biscuits warm.

ROSEMARY-BACON BISCUIT TOPPING

Makes 8 to 9 biscuits

B acon and fresh rosemary add just the right accent notes to these buttery biscuits.

3 slices bacon, diced

2 tablespoons (¼ stick) cold unsalted butter, cut into ¼-inch pieces, plus melted butter, if necessary, for adding to the bacon fat

1⅔ cups packaged dry biscuit mix, such as Bisquick

1 teaspoon fresh minced rosemary leaves

Freshly ground black pepper

½ cup milk

Unbleached all-purpose flour, for rolling out the biscuits

1 Cook the bacon in a medium-size skillet over medium heat until browned and crisp and most of the fat is rendered, 5 to 8 minutes, stirring often and adjusting the heat as necessary. Using a slotted spoon, transfer the bacon to a paper towel-lined plate to drain, setting aside 1 tablespoon of the bacon fat in a large mixing bowl. If necessary, add enough melted butter to measure 1 tablespoon.

2 Add the biscuit mix, cold butter, rosemary, a few grindings of black pepper, and the drained bacon to the mixing bowl with the bacon fat. Using a fork or your fingers, blend the butter into the biscuit mix until the mixture resembles coarse crumbs. Stir in the milk and blend until a soft dough forms (it will be very soft).

3 Generously sprinkle a work surface with flour. Transfer the dough to the work surface and sprinkle it with a little flour to firm it up. Generously dust your hands and the rolling pin with flour. Roll out the dough into a round that is ¼ to ½ inch thick.

4 Using a small inverted glass or a cookie cutter with about a 2½-inch diameter, cut the biscuit dough into 8 or 9 rounds. (Dip the edge of the glass or cookie cutter into flour each time you use it to help release the biscuit from the glass or cookie cutter.) Continue with Step 7 of the Velvety Chicken with Rosemary-Bacon Biscuit Topping recipe.

VARIATION: You can bake these tasty biscuits separately from the velvety chicken casserole and serve them alongside other dishes or as a treat with your morning eggs and coffee. Just roll and cut out the biscuits as directed above. Preheat the oven to 400°F. Arrange the biscuits on a parchment paper-lined rimmed baking sheet and bake them until the tops are evenly browned, 13 to 14 minutes. If desired, brush the tops of the biscuits lightly with melted butter when they come out of the oven. Serve immediately.

CHICKEN CACCIATORE

Serves 4

There are food facts most of us learn early in life that we never think to question. For example, the word *cacciatore,* we were told, means hunter's style. Fair enough, yet the only way most of us heard that word was in connection with chicken. But who hunts chickens? We never asked. In fact, what the word *cacciatore* probably refers to is the strongly flavored ingredients, on the theory that with such bold flavors even the scrawniest game would taste full-flavored and delicious. It occurred to us that bacon with its inherent smokiness adds the aroma of the autumn woods and a crackling fire, which is exactly what a hunter wants after a long day in the field. Because this is a recipe that stews, we find that dark meat keeps its succulence much better than white meat so our *cacciatore* is made with chicken thighs.

6 slices thick-cut bacon, cut crosswise into ½-inch-wide pieces

8 skin-on, bone-in organic chicken thighs, trimmed of excess skin and fat

1 cup chopped onion

1 large red or yellow bell pepper, stemmed, seeded, and cut into thin 2-inch-long strips

1 carrot, trimmed, peeled, and cut into thin disks

½ cup diced fennel or celery

3 medium-size cloves garlic, minced

4½ teaspoons unbleached all-purpose flour

1⅓ cups dry white wine

1 cup low-sodium chicken stock

1 can (14½ ounces) diced tomatoes, with their juices

2 teaspoons fresh thyme leaves

⅛ teaspoon crushed red pepper flakes

2 teaspoons chopped fresh oregano leaves

Salt and freshly ground black pepper

2 tablespoons chopped fresh flat-leaf parsley (optional)

1 Cook the bacon over medium heat in a large heavy saucepan or Dutch oven until the bacon is lightly browned and most of the fat is rendered, 7 to 10 minutes, stirring often and adjusting the heat as necessary. Using a slotted spoon, transfer the bacon to a paper towel-lined plate to drain, reserving 1 tablespoon of bacon fat in the saucepan.

2 Heat the bacon fat over medium-high heat until it shimmers, about 1 minute. Add 4 of the chicken thighs, skin side down, and cook until the skin is well browned, about 5 minutes. Using tongs, turn the chicken thighs over and brown the second side, 4 to 5 minutes. Transfer the browned chicken thighs to a plate and brown the remaining 4 thighs. When the chicken is cool enough to handle, remove and discard the skin. Drain off and discard all but 1½ tablespoons of fat from the pan.

3 Add the onion, bell pepper, carrot, and fennel or celery to the pan. Cook over medium-high heat, stirring occasionally, until the vegetables begin to brown, 6 to 7 minutes. Add the garlic and cook until fragrant, about 1 minute, stirring often. Stir in the flour and cook, stirring constantly, to blend well, about 1 minute. Add the white wine and let simmer for about 1 minute, scraping up any brown bits from the bottom of the pan with a wooden spoon. Stir in the chicken stock, tomatoes with their juices, thyme, red pepper flakes, oregano, and half of the drained bacon. Add the browned chicken thighs and any juices that have accumulated on the plate.

4 Cover the pan, let the stew come to a simmer, adjusting the heat as necessary, and let simmer until the chicken is cooked through, about 30 minutes. Add the remaining bacon and let simmer, uncovered, until the thighs are very tender when pricked with a fork, about 5 minutes. Season the stew with salt and black pepper to taste, and garnish it with the parsley, if using.

PAELLA WITH CHICKEN AND BACON

Serves 6

Paella is one of those dishes, like pizza, that everyone seems to like. Go ahead and mention paella to a friend; we're willing to bet you will raise an affectionate smile. There is something about the almost magical way that the juices in all the ingredients swell into the rice to produce a creamy, savory, elegant, and complex flavor that is just short of divine. The *soccarat*—or rice crust—that forms where the rice comes in contact with the cooking vessel is as delicious as the crust on a thick, charbroiled steak. (Please note, if you don't get a crusty *soccarat,* which happens to the best of us, the paella will still be delicious.) Some people shy away from using saffron because it is an expensive ingredient but, in this dish, the experience is truly worth it. And using bacon in place of the traditional Spanish chorizo, a peppery sausage, provides smoky, savory drippings for sautéing the chicken and shrimp, giving them more flavor!

5 slices thick-cut bacon, cut crosswise into ½-inch-wide pieces

Extra-virgin olive oil, if necessary

5 to 6 cups low-sodium chicken stock, or more as necessary

½ cup dry white wine

12 colossal shrimp (1¼ to 1½ pounds), peeled and deveined, shells reserved for the stock

2 large pinches saffron threads, crumbled

Kosher salt and freshly ground black pepper

3 skinless, boneless organic chicken thighs (about 1¼ pounds total)

½ large onion, grated on the largest holes of a box grater

2 medium-size ripe tomatoes, cut in half and grated on the largest holes of a box grater (skin discarded)

6 medium-size garlic cloves, diced

1 tablespoon seeded and diced jalapeño pepper

½ teaspoon pimentón de la Vera (Spanish paprika)

1⅔ cups Arborio rice

18 mussels, scrubbed and debearded (see page 171)

1 whole roasted red bell pepper, cut into long 1-inch-wide strips

1 cup frozen peas

⅓ cup chopped fresh flat-leaf parsley or cilantro

1 Cook the bacon in a large skillet over medium heat until the bacon is browned and most of the fat is rendered, 7 to 10 minutes, stirring often and adjusting the heat as necessary. Using a slotted spoon, transfer the bacon to a paper towel-lined plate to drain. Pour all of the bacon fat into a small bowl. Add enough olive oil to the bacon fat to measure ¼ cup and set it aside.

2 Place 4¼ cups of the chicken stock in a medium-size saucepan. Cover the pan and let the stock come to a boil over high heat. Add the white wine and shrimp shells and let come to a boil. Then, reduce the heat as necessary and let simmer, partially covered, until the shrimp shells impart their flavor, about 10 minutes. Strain the stock and return it to the saucepan. Add the saffron, season with salt and black pepper to taste, and set the shrimp stock aside.

3 Trim any excess fat off the chicken thighs. Cut any large pieces in half crosswise. Season the chicken with salt and black pepper to taste. Pour the reserved ¼ cup of fat into a 13- to 14-inch paella pan and heat over medium-high heat. Add the chicken thighs and cook until lightly browned on both sides, 2 to 4 minutes per side. Transfer the browned chicken thighs to a platter and set aside. Add the shrimp to the paella pan and cook until just lightly browned on both sides, 1 to 2 minutes per side. Shrimp get rubbery if overcooked, so watch them closely. They will fully cook later in the recipe. Transfer the shrimp to a plate and set aside.

4 Set the paella pan over medium heat. If the pan is too dry, add 1 or 2 tablespoons more of olive oil. Add the onion and cook until soft-

ened, about 5 minutes. Add the tomatoes, garlic, jalapeño, and *pimentón* and cook, stirring occasionally, until the mixture—the sofrito—turns a very deep red and has the consistency of a thick fruit sauce, 15 to 20 minutes. (If the sofrito sticks to the pan or starts to burn, lower the heat and add a little water.) The paella can be prepared up to this point several hours or even a day ahead. Cover the bacon, shrimp stock, chicken thighs, shrimp, and sofrito and refrigerate them separately.

5 About 1 hour before you are ready to serve the paella, bring the shrimp-flavored stock back to a simmer in the saucepan over medium-high heat. Place the paella pan with the sofrito over the largest burner of your stove (if necessary, you can place the paella pan over two burners). Heat the sofrito over medium-high heat, add the rice, and cook, stirring and coating the rice with the sofrito, 1 to 2 minutes.

6 Spread the rice in the paella pan in an even layer. Add the reserved bacon and pour in the simmering shrimp-flavored stock. Shake the pan a little to evenly distribute the rice. Do not stir the rice after this point. Adjust the heat to bring the broth to a vigorous simmer and turn the pan occasionally to distribute the heat so that the rice cooks evenly. When the rice and the stock are at about the same level, after 8 to 10 minutes, reduce the heat to medium-low.

7 Heat the remaining chicken stock in a small saucepan over medium heat. Add ½ to 1 cup of stock and cook the rice for about 5 minutes longer, rotating the pan to distribute the heat evenly. Taste a grain of rice that's nestled just below the top layer. It should be al dente, with a little firm bite. If the rice is not cooked, and all the liquid is absorbed, add another ½ cup (more or less as needed) of stock to the pan and cook the rice for 5 minutes longer. Repeat this process until the rice is done but still firm to the bite.

8 Add the chicken and mussels, hinged side down, burying them in the rice as much as possible. Cook until the mussels just begin to open, about 5 minutes, depending on their size. Add the shrimp, pushing them into the rice, the roasted pepper strips, and the peas. If necessary add just enough stock to keep the rice moistened. Cover the pan (use aluminum foil if you don't have a large lid) and cook the paella until the chicken and shrimp are cooked and the mussels have fully opened. Discard any mussels that have not opened.

9 To make the *soccarat,* increase the heat to medium-high and rotate the paella pan as you cook the paella for about 2 minutes longer to brown and caramelize the bottom layer of rice. You will hear the rice crackle as the *soccarat* (the crust) forms. If it starts to burn, remove the paella pan immediately from the heat.

10 Sprinkle the paella with the parsley or cilantro, set the paella pan in the center of the table, and invite your guests to help themselves.

A BIT OF BACON FOR FLAVOR

There are many simple ways to add a little bacon flavor and/or to use bacon to add moisture to your own favorite roast chicken recipe. Simply cut two slices of bacon in half crosswise and, about 20 minutes before beginning to cook the chicken, arrange the slices of bacon side by side so they cover the whole chicken breast. Or, simmer some chopped cooked bacon in the roasting pan juices, adding a little wine or chicken broth, to make a smoky, bacon-enhanced pan sauce.

ROAST CORNISH GAME HENS
with Mushroom and Bacon Brandy Stuffing

Serves 2 to 4, depending on the size of the hens and appetite of the diners

Cornish game hens are kind of like the food version of the Holy Roman Empire. Voltaire said of this crazy quilt of mini countries and languages that it was neither holy, nor Roman, nor an empire. So far as we can tell these delicious birds aren't from Cornwall. They are domesticated animals so they aren't really game. They are young chickens bred for juicy white meat. Their great virtue is that you can cook a whole hen to serve one, maybe two, people. Not to be deterred by the fact that they aren't really game at all, we prepared ours with a robust bacon brandy stuffing as if they were full-flavored game birds. Surely no wild Scottish grouse or Georgia quail ever made a bolder flavor statement.

2 Cornish game hens (about 1½ pounds each, see Notes)

Olive oil, as necessary

5 slices thick-cut bacon

¾ cup finely chopped shallots (about 2 medium-size shallots)

¼ pound fresh button, cremini, chanterelle, or baby portobello mushrooms, stems trimmed, mushrooms wiped clean and coarsely chopped (about 1½ cups)

2 medium-size cloves garlic, minced

1 cup dry medium-ground homemade bread crumbs (see page 32)

¼ cup chopped fresh flat-leaf parsley

2 tablespoons brandy or sherry

Salt and freshly ground black pepper

1 tablespoon butter, if necessary

Store-bought chutney, such as Major Grey's mango chutney, for serving (see Notes)

1 Remove the livers, if any, from the hens, coarsely chop them, and set them aside. Remove and discard the gizzards and hearts, if any. Rinse the hens under cold running water and pat them dry with paper towels. Trim off any excess fat around the cavities of the hens.

2 Position a rack in the center of the oven and preheat the oven to 425°F. Grease the bottom of a roasting pan lightly with olive oil.

3 Chop 4 of the slices of bacon into ¼- to ½-inch pieces and cook them in a medium-size skillet over medium heat until lightly

browned and most of the fat is rendered, 5 to 8 minutes, stirring often and adjusting the heat as necessary. Using a slotted spoon, transfer the browned bacon to a paper towel-lined plate to drain. You should have about 2 tablespoons of bacon fat in the skillet. If necessary add enough olive oil to the skillet to measure 2 tablespoons. Reserve $1\frac{1}{2}$ tablespoons of the bacon fat in the skillet, and pour the remaining $1\frac{1}{2}$ teaspoons into a small bowl, and set it aside.

4 Add the shallots to the skillet and cook over medium-high heat until softened, 2 to 3 minutes, stirring occasionally. Stir in the mushrooms and cook until slightly softened, about 1 minute, stirring often. Remove the skillet from the heat, let cool about 1 minute, and using a rubber spatula, scrape the mushroom mixture into a medium-size mixing bowl.

5 Set the skillet over medium heat and add the reserved $1\frac{1}{2}$ teaspoons of bacon fat. Add the chopped livers, if using, and the garlic and cook, stirring occasionally, until the livers are lightly browned and the garlic is fragrant, 30 seconds to 1 minute. Scrape the liver mixture into the bowl with the mushrooms. Add the bread crumbs, parsley, and drained bacon to the bowl. Sprinkle the brandy or sherry over the stuffing and toss to moisten. Season the stuffing with salt and pepper to taste.

6 Place the hens in the prepared roasting pan. Loosely fill the main and neck cavities of each hen with about $\frac{3}{4}$ cup of stuffing. Place any additional stuffing in a small ovenproof ramekin baking dish. Dot the top of the stuffing with the butter and cover the baking dish with aluminum foil. Tuck the wings under the hens and tie their legs together with butcher's string. Season the hens lightly with salt and pepper and arrange them in the roasting pan without touching, breast side up. Cut the remaining slice of bacon in half crosswise and place one half across the breast of each hen.

7 Bake the hens for 20 minutes, then rotate the roasting pan 180 degrees so the back of the pan faces the front of the oven. Reduce the heat to 375°F and bake the hens until an instant-read meat thermometer inserted into the thickest part of a thigh, but not touching a bone, registers 165°F, 20 to 25 minutes longer. The exact roasting time will depend on the size of the hens. Remove the baking dish of stuffing from

VARIATION: If you like, add 6 chopped dried apricots, or $\frac{1}{3}$ cup of dried cranberries, or $\frac{1}{2}$ cup of chopped lightly toasted pecans to the stuffing for the game hens. Also, if you wish, you can brush the breasts and wings of the hens with some of the chutney about 5 minutes before removing them from the oven to create a lovely warm glaze.

the oven once the stuffing is warmed through and lightly crisped on top, about 25 minutes.

8 Remove the hens from the oven, cover them loosely with aluminum foil, and let them rest for about 5 minutes. Remove and discard the string from around the legs of the hens. You can serve the hens whole or use a sharp chef's knife or poultry shears to cut the hens in half from front to back along the breast and backbones. Set the whole or halved hens on a platter and serve with the additional stuffing and the chutney.

NOTES: In testing this recipe, we discovered that there are a couple of differences between brands of Cornish game hens. Perdue's hens tend to be slightly larger than Bell & Evans hens. Perdue hens range from 1½ to 1¾ pounds, while the Bell & Evans hens averaged slightly less than 1½ pounds. Both were quite sweet and succulent and make lovely presentations at the table when served whole or cut in half. But the Perdue hen is probably a better choice if you are planning on serving two diners per hen.

Additionally, in our testing we found a package of the liver, heart, neck, and gizzard in the Perdue hens but didn't find the same package in the Bell & Evans hens. The livers do add a nice gaminess to the stuffing and work well with the bacon; however, the stuffing is good without them, so if you unwrap the hen and there isn't a liver packed inside its cavity (or if you don't like chicken livers), simply proceed with the recipe omitting the livers in the stuffing.

You can also use the chutney to glaze the hens. Five minutes before the hens have finished cooking, heat ¼ cup chutney with 1 to 2 tablespoons water in the microwave for about 30 seconds. Brush the warmed chutney over the hens and continue roasting for 5 minutes more.

SMOKIER
SEAFOOD

Halibut Poached in Bacon Broth
with Baby Spinach and Creamer
Potatoes, page 163

IN THIS CHAPTER...

History does not record who first

paired bacon with seafood. Probably it was the first person who raised a pig near a body of water, because the two are really made for each other. With such mild-fleshed fish as cod or halibut, bacon adds some oomph to the flavor as in Flakey Cod Fillets with Bacon and Wine-Braised Fennel or Halibut Poached in Bacon Broth with Baby Spinach and Creamer Potatoes. With such strongly flavored fish as salmon and tuna, bacon has the brawn to turn an assertive recipe into a powerhouse, as in Crusted Salmon with Avocado and Red Onion Green Salad. As for shellfish, we've never met one that didn't go swimmingly— hmm, can shellfish swim?—with bacon. From the intensity of Mussels with Saffron, Bacon, and Tomato to the delicate nuances of Sea Scallops Bronzed in Clarified Butter with Oven-Braised Bacon to our neoclassic, slightly Asian-inflected Lake House Clambake with Bacon Ginger Herb Broth, our feeling is if it comes in a shell or had a fin, and once had a curly tail and went *oink,* it's worth combining in a recipe. "Surf 'n' snout" is our motto.

FLAKY COD FILLETS with Bacon and Wine-Braised Fennel

Serves 4

One day, while walking down a narrow and beautiful old street in Rome, we happened to pass by a local lunch spot when the chef—by the looks of her, the best-fed customer at her own restaurant—lifted the lid from a pan of artichokes and was enveloped by a great billow of wine-scented steam. The idea for rapid wine steaming came from that moment. Adding white wine in small amounts to a pan of thin fennel slices, tossing them with bacon toward the end of the cooking time, and then laying a fillet of fish on top and letting it steam for a few minutes makes for a simple one-pot meal, or in this case, a one-skillet meal. Moist flaky cod is perfection, but we have tried it with more delicate fish such as freshly caught flounder or, as a way to welcome spring, by using the first shad fillets of the year.

We have been making this recipe for many years. Recently, inspired by the delicious old-time sauerkraut recipe of Virginia McIlwain of Rockford, Illinois, we have started to add ½ teaspoon of caraway seeds. Yum.

4 slices bacon, diced

2 medium-size fennel bulbs

2 tablespoons (¼ stick) unsalted butter

2 cups dry white wine, such as pinot grigio or sauvignon blanc

4 cod fillets (each about 1½ inches thick and 6 ounces)

Extra-virgin olive oil

Salt and freshly ground black pepper

1 Cook the bacon in a large skillet (the skillet should be large enough to hold all 4 cod fillets in a single layer) over medium heat until the bacon is lightly browned and most of the fat is rendered, 5 to 8 minutes, stirring often and adjusting the heat as necessary. Using a slotted spoon, transfer the bacon to a paper towel-lined plate to drain. Wipe out the skillet with a paper towel, leaving a thin film of bacon fat.

2 Cut the fennel bulbs in quarters lengthwise. Using a mandoline or chef's knife, cut the fennel into thin slices.

3 Add the butter to the skillet and cook over medium heat until the butter melts and foams. Add the fennel and cook, stirring, about 2 minutes. Add a splash of wine. It should turn to steam immediately; if it doesn't, increase the heat. Add 2 or 3 more tablespoons of wine and cover the skillet but not super tightly; you want steam to escape. Keep adding a splash of wine every 2 minutes or so, as the liquid evaporates, replacing the lid so that the fennel continues to steam rapidly in the wine. After approximately 10 minutes, the fennel should still be slightly crunchy with a pleasant, tart taste from the wine. Add the drained bacon to the fennel and stir to combine.

4 Reduce the heat to low. Arrange the cod fillets on the bed of fennel, cover the skillet,

and let the cod steam until cooked through, about 8 minutes.

5 Transfer a cod fillet to a serving plate by sliding a metal spatula under the fennel and bacon mixture so that you lift it and the cod fillet out of the skillet in one movement. Repeat with the remaining cod fillets. Drizzle some olive oil over the cod fillets and season them with salt and pepper to taste.

LENTIL SALAD with Seared Yellowfin Tuna and Bacon-Scallion Garnish

Serves 4

This is actually two recipes in one. For a very simple main course or side salad, you can prepare the delicious lentil salad on its own. Or, as we do here, use the lentils as a bed for seared slices of tuna. Bacon and lentils are natural partners: Bacon's saltiness and umami wake up the subtle flavor of lentils.

There are so many ways to vary this lentil dish. You can substitute shallots for the scallions or add sautéed mushrooms or spinach. Try curry powder rather than cumin, or perk the salad up with a little hot sauce or crushed red pepper flakes. French lentils, also called green lentils, are easy to find in specialty food markets and, more and more, in regular supermarkets. If you can't find them, you can use the more commonly found brown lentils, but we strongly recommend the little green guys: They're more tender and cook more quickly.

FOR THE LENTIL SALAD

- 1¼ cups French green lentils (lentilles du Puy), rinsed and picked over
- 1 small onion, peeled and cut in half
- 2 whole cloves
- 1 medium-size carrot, trimmed, peeled, and cut into quarters
- 1 large clove garlic, peeled and lightly crushed with the flat side of a chef's knife

- 1 bay leaf
- 3½ cups low-sodium chicken stock or water
- Salt and freshly ground black pepper
- 2 tablespoons red wine or sherry vinegar
- 1 teaspoon Dijon mustard
- 1 teaspoon ground cumin
- ⅓ cup extra-virgin olive oil

FOR THE BACON-SCALLION GARNISH AND TUNA

- 5 slices thick-cut bacon, sliced crosswise into ½-inch-wide pieces
- 4 scallions, both white and green parts, trimmed and thinly sliced
- 2 tablespoons chicken stock or water

- 4 yellowfin tuna steaks, each about 1 inch thick and 6 ounces
- Salt and freshly ground black pepper
- 2 to 3 tablespoons vegetable oil
- 4 thin lemon or lime wedges

1 Prepare the lentil salad: Place the lentils in a medium-size saucepan. Stud each onion half with a clove and add them and the carrot, garlic, and bay leaf to the saucepan. Add the 3½ cups of stock or water, season with salt and pepper to taste, and bring to a boil over high heat. Then, reduce the heat as necessary and let simmer, partially covered, until the lentils are almost tender, 20 to 25 minutes. (Taste the lentils after about 15 minutes and every 4 to 5 minutes thereafter; be careful not to overcook the lentils or they will become mushy.) As the lentils cook, using a large spoon, skim off any foam or solids that rise to the top. When the lentils are done cooking, drain them, setting aside 1 tablespoon of the cooking liquid in a medium-size mixing bowl. Discard the onion halves, carrot, garlic, and bay leaf. Transfer the lentils to the bowl with the cooking liquid.

2 Place the vinegar, mustard, and cumin in a small mixing bowl and stir to mix. Whisk in the olive oil until the dressing is well blended. Pour the dressing over the lentils and toss well to combine. Cover the lentil salad with aluminum foil to keep it warm and set it aside.

3 Prepare the bacon-scallion garnish and tuna: Cook the bacon in a large skillet over medium heat until the bacon is lightly browned and most of the fat is rendered, 5 to 8 minutes, stirring often and adjusting the heat as necessary. Add the scallions and cook, stirring often, until the scallions are softened and the bacon is crisp, 3 to 4 minutes. Using a slotted spoon, transfer the bacon and scallions to a paper towel-lined plate, blot them with paper towels to absorb the excess fat, and set the garnish aside.

4 Place the large skillet over medium heat, add the 2 tablespoons of chicken stock or water, and deglaze the pan, scraping up any brown bits from the bottom of the skillet. Stir the pan liquid into the lentil salad.

5 Season the tuna steaks with salt and pepper to taste. Add the vegetable oil to the skillet and heat over medium-high heat until the oil starts to shimmer, about 1 minute. Place the tuna steaks in the skillet and cook them until nicely browned on the bottom, 2 to 4 minutes. Turn the tuna steaks, reduce the heat to

medium, and cook until browned on the second side but still dark pink in the center, 3 to 5 minutes. To test for doneness, make a small incision with a paring knife in the center of a tuna steak and check the color. Transfer the tuna to a cutting board and cut each steak in half.

6 To serve, divide the lentil salad and the tuna among 4 dinner plates. Sprinkle the bacon-scallion garnish over each serving and garnish each plate with a lemon or lime wedge.

CRUSTED SALMON with Avocado and Red Onion Green Salad

Serves 4

For this dish we owe a debt to the great chef Daniel Boulud, who is both a friend and a cooking mentor. His simple recipe for pancetta-wrapped tuna loin is supremely flavorful and combines a cracklingly crisp texture on the outside with smooth tuna, cooked rare, on the inside. We once assisted Boulud when he made it for President Clinton at a dinner in East Hampton, New York. We prepared a few extra portions for his Secret Service detail and their looks of delight meant as much as the rave reviews from the commander in chief.

For our version we have gone with a similarly fatty fish—salmon. The result is so good our hope is that we, too, can make it for a president some day. Use thin or medium-thick sliced bacon, as thicker-cut bacons will overwhelm the salmon. Make sure to cook the bacon-wrapped salmon on the stove until the bacon is browned and crisp before putting it in the oven. The salmon does not bake long enough to brown the bacon much more once it leaves the stovetop.

Since salmon is a fish many people like to eat rare, and even raw, how long you cook the fish depends on how done you like it. Rare salmon has a deep orange color and looks slightly translucent; medium salmon leans more to pink in color with opaque flesh. An instant-read meat thermometer will help you gauge doneness, but with salmon it is best to make a small incision into the thickest part of the fish and take a look.

FOR THE SALMON

7 to 8 slices thin-cut or regular-cut bacon

1 to 1¼ pounds skinless salmon fillet, center cut like a roast (9 to 10 inches long, 1½ inches thick at thickest point, and 3 inches wide), pin bones removed

Salt and freshly ground black pepper

¼ teaspoon ground ginger

2 teaspoons extra-virgin olive oil

FOR THE SALAD

3 tablespoons extra-virgin olive oil

Juice of 1 lime (about 1 tablespoon)

¼ teaspoon Dijon mustard

Salt and freshly ground black pepper

4 packed cups baby spinach, rinsed and patted dry

2 loosely packed cups arugula, rinsed and patted dry

1 ripe avocado

Half a small red onion, very thinly sliced

1 Prepare the salmon: Place a 10- to 12-inch-long piece of plastic wrap on a work surface. Arrange the bacon slices side by side on the plastic wrap so that one end of each slice is positioned at the edge of the plastic wrap nearest you and the slices overlap just a little. Season the salmon very lightly with salt (remember the bacon will add salt) and pepper to taste, and the ginger. Place the salmon across the overlapped slices of bacon, positioning it at one end of the slices. Tuck the thinner end of the salmon under toward the center, so the salmon fillet is roughly even in thickness and 7 to 8 inches long from end to end. Holding 2 corners of the plastic wrap at one end, roll the bacon around the outside of the salmon fillet, keeping the rows of slices as even as possible. Secure the bacon to the salmon by tying it with butcher's string or unwaxed dental floss at 1-inch intervals, as you would tie a meat roast (see page 116). Wrap the salmon in the plastic wrap and set it aside.

2 Position a rack in the center of the oven and preheat the oven to 350°F.

3 Heat the 2 teaspoons of olive oil in a large

ovenproof pan over medium heat (a cast-iron skillet works well for this) for about 30 seconds. When the oil is hot, remove and discard the plastic wrap from the bacon-wrapped salmon and add the salmon to the pan. Sear the salmon until the bacon is browned and the fat is rendered, about 2 minutes on each of the 4 sides.

4 Transfer the pan to the oven and bake the salmon for 4 to 5 minutes, then use an instant-read meat thermometer to test for doneness, inserting it into the thickest part of the salmon. When the salmon is done to rare, it will register 120° to 125°F. For medium salmon, cook the fish a few minutes longer until the instant-read meat thermometer registers 130° to 135°F. Once you remove the salmon from the oven, tent it lightly with aluminum foil. The internal temperature will rise another 5 degrees as it sits.

5 Prepare the salad: Place the 3 tablespoons of olive oil and the lime juice and mustard in a small mixing bowl and whisk to mix. Season with salt and pepper to taste. Or put all of the ingredients for the lime and mustard dressing in a small jar, cover it, and shake vigorously just before serving.

6 Place the spinach and arugula on a serving platter. Slice the avocado and scatter it and the red onion on top of the greens.

7 To serve, transfer the salmon to a cutting board. Remove and discard the string. Cut the salmon into slices about 1 inch thick and arrange them on top of the salad. Whisk or shake the lime and mustard dressing to fully recombine it and drizzle it over the salmon and salad. Serve immediately.

HALIBUT POACHED IN BACON BROTH with Baby Spinach and Creamer Potatoes

Serves 4

P oaching is one of the most surefire ways to cook fish without compromising its delicate texture. The magical thing about this particular recipe is that the depth of flavor in the bacon broth ties the main ingredients together and adds power yet doesn't overwhelm. This works best with a firm-fleshed fish such as halibut. You can also use salmon or striped bass or a combination of these fish.

If you want to get a little more creative, throw in some scallops, clams, and mussels and you have a wonderful seafood stew that can hold its own against any bouillabaisse or cioppino. Cooking times will of course vary, depending on the thickness and type of fish or shellfish you use.

2½ cups low-sodium fish or chicken stock

8 ounces slab bacon, rind removed (see page 57), cut into 8 pieces, or 8 ounces thick-cut bacon

1 medium-size onion, peeled and cut into quarters

1 large carrot, trimmed, peeled, and cut in half crosswise

2 large cloves garlic, peeled

2 sprigs fresh dill or thyme

5 black peppercorns

8 Yukon Gold (creamer) or red-skinned potatoes, scrubbed

Pinch of salt

4 halibut fillets (each about 1 inch thick and 6 ounces)

1 package (9 ounces) baby spinach, rinsed

1 Combine the stock, bacon, onion, carrot, garlic, dill or thyme, and peppercorns in a medium-size saucepan. Cover the pan and let come to a boil over high heat. Then, reduce the heat as necessary and let simmer gently, partially covered, until the flavors blend, about 40 minutes. Strain the bacon broth and discard the solids (or save the bacon to panfry with your morning eggs). Refrigerate the broth until chilled, about 1 hour. Using a slotted spoon, skim off and discard the solidified fat from the top of the bacon broth. You should have about 1½ cups of broth.

2 About 30 minutes before you plan to serve, place the potatoes in a medium-size saucepan and add water to barely cover. Add the salt, cover the pan, and let come to a boil over high heat. Then, reduce the heat as necessary and let the potatoes simmer until just tender, 10 to 15 minutes. Drain the potatoes, return them to the pan, and cover to keep warm.

3 Bring the skimmed bacon broth to a boil in a large saucepan or skillet over high heat. Add the halibut fillets, cover the pan, and reduce the heat as necessary to let the halibut fillets simmer until partially cooked, about 3 minutes. Using tongs or a metal spatula, turn the fillets and let them simmer for 3 minutes longer. After 6 minutes, check for doneness by inserting the tip of a thin-bladed knife into the center of a halibut fillet. When it's cooked, the flesh should be opaque, not translucent, and the knife should enter the fish easily, without resistance. To avoid overcooking, continue checking for doneness after every minute. Transfer the cooked halibut to a platter and cover it with aluminum foil to keep warm.

4 Add the spinach to the saucepan with the bacon broth, increase the heat to high, cover the pan, and cook the spinach until just wilted, about 1 minute.

5 Place 1 halibut fillet in each of 4 soup bowls. Divide the spinach and potatoes evenly among the bowls, spoon some of the bacon broth over each fillet, and serve.

BACON AND SHRIMP RISOTTO
with Spinach

Serves 2 to 3

A s long as you have good risotto-making rice (it should be short grain, such as Arborio) and a few ingredients on the shelves and in the fridge, you can always whip up a pleasing meal. Short-grain rice adds creaminess and highlights the flavor of the dish. Because the bacon is not fully crisped before being added to the rice, the bacon fat continues to slowly release into the rice, imparting moisture and flavor. The final dish is plenty creamy without classic additions of butter or cheese. As a rule, Italians don't like to combine fish and cheese in one dish, so there's no Parmesan in this risotto, and it's not missed. What a lovely use of bacon!

Lemon zest, unlike lemon juice (which is acidic), contributes a fragrant floral oil without adding acidity. It adds another flavor dimension that we think complements the bacon, spinach, rice, and shrimp.

To make this or any other risotto successfully, be sure to have all your ingredients ready before cooking. You don't want to be waiting for the broth to heat up at the moment the sautéing rice requires you to add the hot cooking liquid.

You can vary this risotto in many ways, substituting lightly sautéed asparagus for the spinach, for example, or using sea scallops instead of shrimp.

2½ cups low-sodium chicken stock

3 slices thick-cut bacon, coarsely chopped into ½-inch pieces

1 small onion, finely chopped (about ⅔ cup)

1 cup Arborio or other short-grain Italian rice

½ cup dry white wine

Scant ¼ teaspoon freshly grated nutmeg

¾ pound extra-large shrimp (21 to 24 per pound), peeled and deveined

4 packed cups (4 ounces) fresh spinach, well-rinsed, coarse stems removed and leaves coarsely chopped

Salt and freshly ground black pepper

Freshly grated zest of half a lemon (optional)

1 Combine the chicken stock and 1 cup of water in a medium-size saucepan over high heat. Cover and bring to a simmer, about 5 minutes. Reduce the heat as low as possible and move the pan to the back burner. You want to keep the broth warm without allowing it to evaporate.

2 Cook the bacon over medium heat in a large heavy saucepan or skillet (see Note), stirring occasionally, until very lightly browned and some fat is rendered, 2 to 3 minutes. Add the onion and cook, stirring often, until the onion is softened and lightly browned, about 5 minutes. Stir in the rice, reduce the heat to medium-low, and cook, stirring with a wooden spoon, until all the rice kernels are coated in the bacon fat, 1 to 2 minutes. Stir in the wine and cook until it has been completely absorbed by the rice, about 2 minutes.

3 Stir in 1½ cups of the hot stock mixture into the rice and raise the heat as necessary to bring the risotto to a simmer. Let simmer until the liquid is absorbed and the bottom of the pan is nearly dry, 10 to 12 minutes. Stir well every 3 to 4 minutes and adjust the heat as necessary to maintain a simmer.

4 Stir in ½ cup more of the hot stock mixture and cook until the liquid has nearly evaporated, 3 to 5 minutes. (You don't want the bottom of the pan to become dry.) Stir often and adjust the heat to maintain the simmer. Stir in another ½ cup of the stock mixture and cook until the liquid has nearly evaporated (but before the bottom of the pan becomes dry), 3 to 5 minutes, again stirring often and maintaining a simmer. After 8 to 10 minutes, the risotto should be nearly cooked through but still firm to the bite and appears slightly

wet and creamy. (Different brands of rice will use different amounts of broth, so we call for a little more liquid than you will probably need to cook the risotto. On the other hand, if all the broth is used up before the rice is cooked, add hot water to the risotto, ¼ to ½ cup at a time, and continue to cook until the rice is nearly firm to the bite and slightly creamy.)

5 Add the nutmeg, another ¼ cup of the stock mixture (or hot water if no stock remains), and the shrimp. Cover the skillet; reduce the heat to medium-low and cook until the shrimp is nearly cooked through, 2 to 3 minutes.

6 Remove the cover and gently fold the spinach into the risotto, cover and cook just until the spinach has wilted but is still bright green and the shrimp are cooked, 1 minute more. Season with a little salt and pepper, if desired.

7 Spoon the risotto onto individual serving plates and garnish with freshly grated lemon zest, if using. Serve immediately.

NOTE: Choose a wide heavy-bottomed, 2- to 3-quart skillet or saucepan. A wide pot will distribute the heat evenly and allow the rice to sit on the bottom of the pan in a thin, even layer so the broth is evenly absorbed.

LAKE HOUSE CLAMBAKE
with Bacon Ginger Herb Broth

Serves 8

A clambake conjures delicious memories of summer by the sea: Picture digging a pit in the sand and steaming shellfish and sausages between layers of corn, potatoes, and seaweed while the kids run in and out of the surf, the grown-ups sip ice-cold beer, and the sky is a happy unbroken blue. If you don't live by the shore, you're not out of luck in the clambake department. In fact, we made this on a July Fourth weekend at an upstate lake house in a four-gallon pot with a tight-fitting lid. Instead of seaweed (we were a hundred and fifty miles from the nearest ocean) we used a bunch each of parsley and cilantro, which lent a fresh and grassy flavor to the corn and potatoes. A half-pound piece of slab bacon added to the steaming liquid of wine and water along with garlic, ginger, and a little salt makes for a rich, satiny finish to the broth. Buy the biggest shrimp you can find (in some markets they are called colossal or jumbo) and allow them to steam with the mussels and clams just until they are pink and no longer translucent, four to five minutes.

14 to 16 hard-shell clams
(each about 2 inches in diameter)

8 ounces slab bacon
(see page 173)

1 cup dry white wine

4 large cloves garlic, peeled and
lightly crushed with the flat side of
a chef's knife

3 to 4 quarter-size pieces fresh ginger

½ teaspoon sea salt

8 medium-size red potatoes (each about
4 inches around), scrubbed

Large bunch fresh parsley

Large bunch fresh cilantro

1 to 1¼ pounds chorizo or andouille
sausage, cut into 1-inch pieces

1½ pounds mussels, scrubbed and
debearded (see page 171)

4 large ears corn, cut in half crosswise

1 to 1½ pounds colossal shrimp
(10 to 15 per pound), unpeeled

3 tablespoons unsalted butter, melted

1 loaf French bread, sliced

1 Place the clams in a large bowl, cover them with cold water, and let them soak for about 20 minutes so they can release their sand and grit. After soaking and draining the clams, use a firm brush to scrub off any additional sand or barnacles that may cling to the shells.

2 Place the slab bacon in the bottom of a 4-gallon (16-quart) pot. Add the white wine, garlic, ginger, sea salt, and enough water to bring the liquid in the pot to a depth of about 1½ inches. Place a steamer rack on top of the slab bacon, cover the pot, and bring the liquid to a boil over high heat.

3 When the liquid boils, place the potatoes on the steamer rack. Top them with half of the parsley and cilantro. Cover the pot and cook until the potatoes have softened slightly, about 10 minutes.

4 Remove the cover and layer the clams, then the sausage, the mussels, and the corn in the pot. Place the remaining parsley and cilantro on top of the corn, cover the pot tightly, and let steam over high heat for 10 minutes. Add the shrimp, cover the pot, and cook until the clams and mussels have opened and the shrimp are pink and no longer translucent, about 5 minutes. If the shrimp are done before the clams and mussels open, use tongs to remove them from the pot to keep them from becoming over-done and rubbery. Discard any clams or mussels that have not opened after steaming.

5 To serve, using tongs, transfer the shrimp, corn, mussels, sausage, clams, and potatoes to 8 large soup bowls, dividing them evenly. Remove and discard the slab bacon (see Note). Strain 4 to 5 cups of the broth from the pot through a fine-mesh sieve set over a medium-size bowl. Discard the garlic, ginger, parsley, and cilantro. Add the melted butter to the strained broth.

6 Spoon ⅓ to ½ cup of the broth and butter mixture over each serving of the clambake and serve immediately with the sliced French bread.

NOTE: If you wish, you can slice the bacon slab into large pieces, place the pieces in a bowl, and serve them alongside the clambake for those who want bacon. Or, wrap and refrigerate the bacon slab and fry it up the next day to crumble it on salad.

MUSSELS WITH SAFFRON, BACON, AND TOMATO

Serves 2 as a main dish, 4 as an appetizer

A bacon trifecta: We sauté the shallots in bacon drippings, add bacon to the pot to infuse the poaching liquid, and garnish the mussels with a mix of cooked bacon and cilantro. Saffron is a powerful ingredient so, even though it's not cheap, a little goes a long way—bacon has the oomph to balance it perfectly. You'll notice that we eliminated the heavy cream called for in many recipes for steamed mussels. Just about a tablespoon per serving of the lighter half-and-half marries the flavors of saffron, clam juice, tomatoes, and white wine in a soft velvety broth.

3 slices thick-cut bacon, cut into ½-inch pieces

1 tablespoon unsalted butter

1 large shallot, diced

2 medium-size cloves garlic, minced

⅓ cup dry white wine

⅓ cup clam juice

1 large ripe tomato, seeded and diced

Scant ¼ teaspoon saffron threads

⅛ teaspoon crushed red pepper flakes

⅓ cup half-and-half

Salt and freshly ground black pepper

3 tablespoons chopped fresh cilantro or flat-leaf parsley

1 baguette, sliced and toasted

Extra-virgin olive oil

2 pounds mussels, scrubbed and debearded (see page 171)

1 Cook the bacon in a large deep saucepan over medium heat until browned and some of the fat is rendered, 5 to 8 minutes, stirring often and adjusting the heat as necessary. Using a slotted spoon, transfer the bacon to a paper towel-lined plate to drain, reserving about 1½ teaspoons of bacon fat in the pan.

2 Add the butter and shallot and cook over medium heat until the shallot has softened, 3 to 4 minutes, stirring occasionally. Add the garlic and cook until fragrant, 1 to 2 minutes. Add the white wine, clam juice, tomato, saffron threads (crushing them first between your fingers), red pepper flakes, and half of the drained bacon and stir to combine. Let come to a boil with the pan partially covered. Then, reduce the heat as necessary and let the broth simmer gently until the flavors blend, 3 to 4 minutes. Remove the saucepan from the heat

and stir in the half-and-half. Season with salt and black pepper to taste.

3 Combine the remaining drained bacon and the cilantro or parsley in a small bowl, then set the bacon and cilantro garnish aside. Toast the slices of baguette and drizzle olive oil over them.

4 Place the saucepan over medium-high heat and add the mussels to the poaching broth. Cover the pan and let the mussels simmer until they open, 4 to 8 minutes, depending on the size of the mussels. Remove and discard any mussels that do not open after 8 minutes. Divide the mussels and the broth equally among individual serving bowls and sprinkle the bacon and cilantro garnish evenly over each serving. Serve with the toasted bread slices to sop up the sauce.

CLEANING AND DEBEARDING MUSSELS

Most of the mussels sold today in markets are farm raised or "cultivated" and contain little sand or grit and very little of the "beard" you'll find on "wild" mussels. To remove the small web of vegetative matter (the beard) on a mussel, simply grip it and give it a good pull toward the hinged end of the mussel shell. If it's a little stubborn, try using a small paring knife or kitchen shears to remove it. Wait to debeard the mussels until you are just ready to cook them; debearding causes the mussels to die.

If the mussels are especially dirty, you can soak them for twenty to thirty minutes in fresh cool water before cooking, allowing them to expel their sand and grit. But again, most of the farmed mussels will only require you to rinse them under cold running water while brushing each to remove any dirt on the shell's surface. It's best to use shellfish the day they are purchased, but if you must, you can store clams and mussels in a bowl in the refrigerator (never under water or wrapped in plastic, which causes them to die) for a day.

SEA SCALLOPS BRONZED IN CLARIFIED BUTTER
with Oven-Braised Bacon

Serves 4

Many recipes feature bacon-wrapped sea scallops that are sautéed or baked until the bacon is crisp. Our recipe takes a different approach, serving braised bacon alongside caramelized sea scallops. It achieves maximum deliciousness when you prepare the braised bacon ahead of time, allowing it to sit in the strained braising liquid in the refrigerator for a day or two. Just before serving, you sauté the scallops very quickly in clarified butter and then arrange them on a serving platter with the chunks of bacon. You can complete this meal with a simple salad, a serving of grilled asparagus, or sautéed baby spinach with a squeeze of lemon.

Oven-Braised Slab Bacon (recipe follows)

5 tablespoons unsalted butter, cut into 1-inch-thick pieces

12 large sea scallops (1 to 1¼ pounds)

Salt and freshly ground black pepper

2 tablespoons brandy

1 Remove the slab of bacon from the braising liquid (save the liquid for flavoring soups, stews, or sauces). Cut the slab into ½-inch-thick slices.

2 Add 1 tablespoon of butter to a skillet and heat over medium-high heat. Place the braised bacon slices in the skillet and cook until lightly browned on both sides, 4 to 5 minutes per side, turning once. Cover the skillet to keep the bacon warm and set it aside.

3 Remove the tough tendon from each scallop (see Note, page 95). Pat the scallops dry with paper towels and sprinkle them lightly with salt and pepper to taste.

4 Melt the remaining 4 tablespoons of the butter in a small saucepan over very low heat without stirring. Using a large spoon, skim off and discard the foamy layer that rises to the top. Carefully pour off the clear yellow liquid into a large stainless steel skillet. The liquid is the clarified butter; there should be at least 2 tablespoons. Set the skillet over medium-high heat and heat until the clarified butter just begins to smoke.

5 Add the scallops to the clarified butter in the skillet without any of them touching. (If necessary, cook the scallops in 2 batches.) Cook the scallops without moving them until the bottoms are a rich golden brown, 2 to 3 minutes. Turn the scallops and cook them until the second side is golden brown, 1 to 3 minutes, depending on the size of the scallops. When cooked the scallops will be mostly opaque with a slightly translucent center and firm sides. Transfer the scallops and the bacon to a serving platter and cover them with aluminum foil to keep warm.

6 To deglaze the skillet that cooked the scallops, pour in the brandy and scrape up any brown bits from the bottom. Pour the liquid from the pan over the scallops and bacon and serve.

OVEN-BRAISED SLAB BACON

Makes one 12-ounce slab

One of the most popular comfort dishes to appear on restaurant menus in the last decade is pork belly. Restaurant owners like it because it's an inexpensive cut of meat. Guess what? Bacon is nothing more than cured and smoked pork belly. By braising the belly until it is pull-apart fork-tender, it becomes supremely unctuous and much less salty, and much

of the fat is rendered. Depending on what you use as a braising medium, you can create any number of complex, satisfying, soul-warming flavors. We've tried it with apple cider, spiked the cider with bourbon, and braised the bacon with beer and parsnips for a sweet-bitter combo. Cloves give an aromatic touch; rosemary, lemon zest, and garlic will add a Mediterranean feel that is a light counterpoint to the punch of the bacon.

12 ounces slab bacon, rind removed (see page 57)

1 medium-size carrot, trimmed, peeled, and coarsely chopped

1 rib celery, coarsely chopped

1 small yellow onion, thickly sliced

1 bay leaf

½-inch-thick piece peeled fresh ginger (optional), chopped

1 whole clove

1 large clove garlic, peeled and lightly crushed with the flat side of a chef's knife

3 black peppercorns, crushed

½ cup dry white wine

¼ cup brandy or dry white vermouth

Low-sodium chicken stock

1 Position a rack in the center of the oven and preheat the oven to 300°F.

2 Place the bacon slab, fat side up, in a small Dutch oven or other stovetop-to-oven dish just large enough to hold the bacon and vegetables in a single layer, cutting the bacon into 2 pieces if necessary. Add the carrot, celery, onion, bay leaf, ginger, if using, whole clove, garlic, peppercorns, white wine, and brandy or vermouth to the Dutch oven. Add enough chicken stock to fill the Dutch oven to a depth of about 1 inch. Place the Dutch oven over medium heat and let the liquid come to a boil.

3 Cover the Dutch oven with a lid or aluminum foil and bake until the bacon is very tender, 2 to 2½ hours. Uncover the Dutch oven, turn on the broiler, and broil the bacon just until the top layer of fat is browned and golden, 3 to 4 minutes. Or transfer the bacon to a cast-iron skillet, arranging it fat side down, and cook it over medium heat until the fat is browned, 5 to 7 minutes.

4 Transfer the browned slab of bacon to a bowl and strain the braising liquid through a wire-mesh strainer into a saucepan, discarding the vegetables. Pour the strained liquid over the bacon, cover the bowl with plastic wrap, and refrigerate the braised bacon for at least 2 hours or until ready to use.

A FEW SUGGESTIONS FOR USING OVEN-BRAISED SLAB BACON

〰 *Toss cubes of oven-braised bacon into a macaroni and cheese casserole.*

〰 *Add cubes to hearty bean, onion, or split pea soups.*

〰 *Pump up the flavor of brown gravy for chicken or turkey by adding cubes of the bacon.*

〰 *Toss cubes into a salad of yellow and red cherry tomatoes, basil, and homemade croutons.*

〰 *Add oven-braised sliced bacon to vegetable stir-fries.*

〰 *Panfry slices of the braised bacon and serve them with scrambled or fried eggs, in omelets, or with French toast, pancakes, or grits.*

〰 *Add panfried cubes of bacon to rice dishes, sautéed spinach, Swiss chard, or mustard greens.*

〰 *Panfry cubes and toss them into mixed green salads with hard-cooked eggs and grilled asparagus spears.*

MEDITERRANEAN SEAFOOD STEW with Bacon

Serves 4

A full-on fish stew: Using bacon fat to sweat the leeks, carrots, and bell pepper ("aromatics" in chef speak) allows the vegetables to become tender, sweetly caramelized, and beautifully smoky. This infuses the whole stew with a depth of flavor that pairs beautifully with the bright acidity and almost smoky sweetness of ripe tomatoes. If any recipe ever cried out for mopping every last drop of juice up with a piece of crusty bread, this is the one. If you double the recipe, it becomes a simple and quick dish to make for a good-size dinner party.

8 small, hard-shell clams
(no larger than 2 inches in diameter)

¾ pound sea scallops

4 slices bacon, cut into ½-inch pieces

Olive oil, as necessary

2 large leeks, white parts only,
rinsed and chopped

2 carrots, trimmed, cut in half
lengthwise, and thinly sliced
crosswise

1 small red bell pepper, stemmed,
seeded, and diced

3 ripe plum tomatoes
(about ¾ pound total), cored and
diced

1 cup dry white wine

1 bottle (8 ounces) clam juice

2 large cloves garlic, minced

1 teaspoon ground cumin

1 bay leaf

¼ teaspoon crushed red pepper flakes

¾ pound extra-large shrimp
(20 to 24 per pound), shelled and
deveined

2 tablespoons coarsely chopped fresh
cilantro or flat-leaf parsley

1 loaf French or Italian bread, sliced and
toasted

1 Place the clams in a large bowl, cover them with cold water, and let them soak for about 20 minutes so they can release their sand and grit. After soaking and draining the clams, use a firm brush to scrub off any additional sand or barnacles that may cling to the shells. Remove the tough tendon from each scallop (see Note, page 95). Cut the scallops in half.

2 Cook the bacon in a heavy 3-quart saucepan over medium heat until lightly browned and most of the fat is rendered, 5 to

8 minutes, stirring often and adjusting the heat as necessary. Using a slotted spoon, transfer the bacon to a paper towel-lined plate to drain, reserving 2 tablespoons of bacon fat in the pan. If there are less than 2 tablespoons of bacon fat, add enough olive oil to make up the difference.

3 Place the pan over medium heat. Add the leeks and carrots and cook until the leeks soften, about 4 minutes, stirring occasionally and scraping up any brown bits from the bottom of the pan. Add the red bell pepper and cook, stirring occasionally, until the pepper softens, about 2 minutes. Add the tomatoes, white wine, clam juice, garlic, cumin, bay leaf, red pepper flakes, and ¾ cup of water. Cover the pan and let come to a boil. Then, reduce the heat as necessary and let the stew simmer, partially covered, until the flavors blend, 10 to 12 minutes.

4 Add the shrimp, clams, scallops, and drained bacon. Cover the pan, increase the heat to high, and let the stew come to a boil. Then, reduce the heat as necessary and let the stew simmer, partially covered, until the shrimp is evenly pink, the scallops are opaque, and the clams have opened, 4 to 5 minutes. If after 5 minutes some of the clams have not opened, using tongs transfer the shrimp and scallops to a plate and cover them loosely with aluminum foil to keep warm. Cook the clams 2 to 3 minutes longer, then discard any that don't open (the length of time the clams will take to cook depends upon the size of the clams and the pan). Remove and discard the bay leaf. Divide equal portions of the seafood stew into 4 individual soup bowls and sprinkle each serving with the cilantro or parsley. Serve the stew with thick slices of toasted French or Italian bread.

PASTA
AND
BACON

Linguine with Cauliflower
and Bacon Bread Crumbs,
page 188

IN THIS CHAPTER...

If you like pasta, bacon, and fresh

vegetables, you'll love these healthy dishes where all these ingredients shine. These recipes allow you to have your cake—at least your spaghetti—and eat it, too.

When you've tested dozens of recipes with bacon, you begin to have favorite combinations, and one of ours turned out to be bacon and cauliflower. It was not a stretch to combine these two winning partners with pasta in Linguine with Cauliflower and Bacon Bread Crumbs. The bacon bread crumbs added to the steaming pasta-cauliflower sauce provide a garnish of delicious crunch and saltiness. Yes, sir! What a pleasure to make and eat!

Three Variations on a Theme

Roman home cooks always have some cured pork around, which probably explains why the go-to pasta sauces of Rome all feature cured pork. In the Eternal City pancetta or *guanciale* (cured pork jowls) are the cured meat of choice, but American bacon adds smokiness to these simple sauces, all of which are robust enough to gain extra power from smoke.

PASTA ALLA GRICIA

Serves 3 as a main dish, 6 as a first course

We start with *pasta alla gricia*, perhaps the simplest sauce of all—just a blending of bacon and grated sharp cheese. It's quick to prepare, so is perfect any time of the week. A little crusty bread on the side and call it a night.

2 tablespoons extra-virgin olive oil, plus more olive oil if necessary

5 slices bacon, diced

Salt

12 ounces linguine or other long, thin pasta

½ cup freshly grated pecorino romano cheese, plus additional cheese for serving

Freshly ground black pepper

1 Bring 4 to 5 quarts of water to a rolling boil in a large pasta or soup pot.

2 While waiting for the water to boil, heat the olive oil in a medium-size skillet over medium heat. Add the bacon and cook until browned and most of the fat is rendered, 5 to 8 minutes, stirring often and adjusting the heat as necessary. Turn off the heat and set the skillet aside.

3 Salt the boiling water. Add the linguine, stir to separate the strands, and cook until al dente, following the package instructions. Set aside about 1 cup of the pasta cooking water, then drain the linguine and return it to the cooking pot.

4 Add the bacon with its fat to the drained linguine and stir in the pecorino romano cheese. If the pasta mixture seems too dry, add a little of the pasta cooking water or a little more olive oil. Season the linguine with plenty of pepper and serve it with more pecorino romano on the side for those who want it.

CARBONARA with a Hint of Lemon

Serves 4 as a main dish, 6 as a first course

T iming is the most important element in carbonara. The secret to doing this recipe justice is to make sure the sauce has finished cooking just before it's tossed with the pasta. Don't let the cooked pasta sit waiting while you're finishing the sauce. So, do your prep and be sure the cheeses are grated, the garlic is peeled, and the wine is uncorked and measured before you turn on the heat. One other thing: Since you've worked so hard to time the preparation steps, call your dinner guests to the table and have them seated and waiting for you to serve. Pour them some wine and they'll be happy.

We find that some lemon and white wine—although not part of the old-fashioned recipe—sharpen and lighten the traditional recipe. But, of course, you can eliminate the lemon altogether, if you prefer a more classic carbonara.

Half a small lemon

3 tablespoons extra-virgin olive oil

4 medium-size cloves garlic, peeled and lightly crushed with the flat side of a chef's knife

6 slices thick-cut bacon, cut into ¼- to ½-inch pieces

⅓ cup dry white wine

Salt

1 pound spaghetti or linguine

3 large eggs

⅔ cup freshly grated Parmigiano Reggiano cheese, plus additional cheese for serving

¼ cup freshly grated pecorino romano cheese

Freshly ground black pepper

1 Using a vegetable peeler remove the zest from the lemon half, being careful to remove only the yellow part and not the bitter white layer (the pith) beneath it. Chop or slice the zest into very thin slivers ½ to 1 inch long.

2 Bring 4 to 5 quarts of water to a rolling boil in a large pasta or soup pot.

3 While waiting for the water to boil, place the olive oil and garlic in a large skillet over medium heat and cook until the garlic turns

golden, 30 seconds to 1 minute. Remove and discard the garlic. Increase the heat to medium-high, add the bacon, and cook until it is browned and most of the fat is rendered, 7 to 10 minutes, stirring often and adjusting the heat as necessary. Add the white wine and cook until the wine reduces slightly, 1 to 2 minutes. Add the lemon zest. Remove the sauce from the heat and cover the skillet to keep the sauce warm.

4 Salt the boiling water. Add the spaghetti, stir to separate the strands, and cook until al dente, following the package instructions.

5 While the spaghetti cooks, break the eggs into a serving bowl large enough to hold the cooked spaghetti and the carbonara sauce. Beat the eggs with a fork. Add the Parmigiano Reggiano and pecorino romano cheese and a few generous gratings of pepper and stir to combine.

6 When the pasta is done, set aside ½ cup of the pasta cooking water, then drain the spaghetti. Add the spaghetti to the serving bowl with the eggs and cheese and toss to coat the strands well. Add the bacon and lemon mixture to the spaghetti and toss to mix. If the spaghetti mixture seems too dry, add a little of the reserved pasta cooking water. Serve the spaghetti at once with more pepper and Parmigiano Reggiano cheese on the side for those who want it.

BUCATINI ALL'AMATRICIANA

Serves 4

B acon, tomatoes, and Parmigiano Reggiano: A food scientist will tell you that this comprises a trinity of umami savoriness. A food lover will simply say "Bring it!" It is a larder meal par excellence, made from ingredients that are always on hand. In the dead of winter canned or frozen oven-roasted tomatoes do the trick, but come early summertime, sweet cherry tomatoes make this rib-sticking stalwart into a lighter meal, well suited to the season. Our method of superheating the tomatoes in a very hot pan produces a pleasing char yet preserves juiciness.

You can serve this sauce with just about any shape pasta, but there is something special about bucatini, which is nothing more than hollow spaghetti. You get all the fun of slurping a forkful of spaghetti and then, as you draw air through the empty center of the bucatini, you draw in a jet of *amatriciana*-flavored vapor.

6 slices bacon, coarsely diced

1 medium-size onion, diced

Salt

1 pound bucatini

1 pound cherry tomatoes, stems removed

About ¼ cup extra-virgin olive oil

½ cup chopped fresh flat-leaf parsley

½ cup (2 ounces) best-quality freshly grated Parmigiano Reggiano cheese

½ teaspoon crushed red pepper flakes

1 Bring 4 to 5 quarts of water to a rolling boil in a large pasta or soup pot.

2 While waiting for the water to boil, cook the bacon in a large skillet over medium heat until browned and crisp and the fat is rendered, about 5 to 8 minutes, stirring often and adjusting the heat as necessary. Using a slotted spoon, transfer the bacon to a paper towel-lined plate to drain, reserving 1 to 2 tablespoons of bacon fat in the skillet.

3 Add the onion to the bacon fat and cook over medium heat until soft and golden, 5 to

6 minutes, stirring occasionally. Transfer the onion to a small bowl and set it aside. Wipe the skillet clean with a paper towel.

4 Salt the boiling water. Add the bucatini, stir to separate the strands, and cook until al dente, following the package instructions.

5 While the bucatini cooks, place the skillet over high heat. Place the tomatoes and 2 tablespoons of the olive oil in a bowl and toss to mix. When the skillet is hot, add the tomatoes, shaking the skillet vigorously. If you get a flare-up from the tomatoes, it's okay; it will char them nicely. Cook the tomatoes until charred, about 2 minutes. Reduce the heat to medium. Prick the tomatoes with a fork to release their juices. Add the onion and drained bacon to the skillet and continue cooking.

6 When the pasta is done, drain the bucatini and add it to the skillet. Add the parsley, Parmigiano Reggiano cheese, and crushed red pepper flakes and toss to combine. If the bucatini mixture seems too dry, toss it with the remaining 2 tablespoons of olive oil. Serve immediately.

BROCCOLI with Bacon, Orecchiette, and Fresh Lemon

Serves 3 to 4

We personally like the earthy "cabbagey" flavors of broccoli but we know there is a world of broccoli bashers (and cauliflower complainers) out there who are immune to the healthy-vegetable arguments advanced by moms everywhere. Fair enough. Here we hope to win some hearts by teaming up broccoli with garlic, fragrant lemon, and of course, bacon. Instead of cooking the broccoli to the point of soggy surrender, we sauté it lightly in bacon fat before finishing it in just a little water and lemon juice. The florets come out crisp-tender and appealingly green. All the ingredients retain their individual flavors and textures.

4 slices thick-cut bacon, cut into
¼- to ½-inch pieces

1 tablespoon extra-virgin olive oil,
plus more olive oil if necessary

Salt

8 ounces orecchiette
(little ear-shaped pasta)

1 pound broccoli crowns, cut into
1- to 2-inch florets (about 5½ cups,
from 1¼ pounds untrimmed broccoli)

1 tablespoon minced garlic

2 teaspoons fresh lemon juice

1 tablespoon grated lemon zest

3 tablespoons freshly grated pecorino
romano cheese

Freshly ground black pepper (optional)

1 Bring 4 to 5 quarts of water to a rolling boil in a large pasta or soup pot.

2 While waiting for the water to boil, cook the bacon in a large skillet over medium heat until lightly browned and most of the fat is rendered, 5 to 8 minutes, stirring often and adjusting the heat as necessary. Using a slotted spoon, transfer the bacon to a paper towel-lined plate to drain, reserving 3 tablespoons of bacon fat in the skillet. If necessary, add enough olive oil to the skillet to measure 3 tablespoons.

3 Salt the boiling water. Add the orecchiette, stir to separate the pasta, and cook until al dente, following the package instructions.

4 While the orecchiette cooks, cook the broccoli (you want the broccoli to be ready to toss into the pasta as soon as it is drained). Heat the bacon fat in the skillet over medium heat until it begins to shimmer, about 30 seconds. Add the broccoli and garlic and cook until the garlic is fragrant, about 1 minute, stirring to coat the broccoli with the bacon fat. Increase the heat to high. Carefully remove about ¾ cup of boiling water from the pasta pot and add ½ cup of the water and the lemon juice to the skillet. Cover the skillet and cook the broccoli until it begins to turn bright green,

about 2 minutes. Uncover the skillet and cook, stirring occasionally, until the liquid has evaporated and the broccoli is crisp-tender and bright green, 3 to 5 minutes longer. If all of the water has evaporated before the broccoli is cooked, add 1 to 2 tablespoons more pasta cooking water to the skillet.

5 When the pasta is cooked, drain it and return it to the cooking pot. Add the broccoli, the drained bacon, 1 tablespoon olive oil, the lemon zest, and pecorino romano cheese to the steaming pasta. Taste for seasoning, adding salt and pepper, if desired. Toss the pasta well to combine and serve immediately.

These florets come out crisp-tender and appealingly green.

FETTUCCINE with Bacon and Kale

Serves 3 as a main dish, 4 as first course

Years ago nobody ate kale, at least nobody we knew, but with the growth of locally sourced food and farmers' markets we've discovered just how great this readily available late-season green is. Kale stands up to the salty smokiness of bacon and the nutmeg adds a nutty, floral, spicy note, like the finish you get from a glass of red wine.

You really should prepare the sauce as the pasta cooks so that at precisely the moment when the pasta is done, the sauce is ready and the flavors are at their peak. Feel free to use other kinds of pasta, but choose a pasta that's not too thin, one with some heft or thickness. Fettuccine coils nicely around the bacon and the greens. Perciatelli, pappardelle, or even linguine would all work.

We cook the kale first in a pot of boiling water and then boil the pasta in the same kale-enriched water. Finally we use a little of the very same flavorful cooking water to make the kale and bacon sauce for the pasta. (We like adding a little pasta water to finish the sauce. The starchy cooking water leaves a tad of pleasant creaminess and helps the sauce adhere to the pasta.)

5 slices bacon, cut into ½-inch pieces

Salt

8 ounces kale, tough stems and ribs removed and discarded, leaves coarsely chopped and rinsed

8 ounces fettuccine

Extra-virgin olive oil, as necessary

3 medium-size cloves garlic, thinly sliced

¼ teaspoon crushed red pepper flakes, or more to taste

½ cup low-sodium chicken stock

½ cup (2 ounces) finely, freshly grated pecorino romano cheese, plus additional cheese for serving

Freshly grated nutmeg (see Note)

1 Bring 4 to 5 quarts of water to a rolling boil in a large pasta or soup pot.

2 While waiting for the water to boil, place the bacon in a large skillet over medium heat and cook until lightly browned and most of the fat is rendered, 5 to 8 minutes, stirring often and adjusting the heat as necessary. Using a slotted spoon, transfer the bacon to a paper towel-lined plate to drain, reserving the bacon fat in the skillet.

3 Salt the boiling water. Add the kale and blanch it, uncovered, for about 5 minutes.

Using a slotted spoon or tongs, transfer the kale to a sieve or colander to drain.

4 Let the cooking water return to a boil. Add the fettuccine, stir to separate the strands, and cook until al dente, following the package instructions.

5 While the fettuccine cooks, add enough olive oil to the bacon fat in the skillet to measure 2 to 3 tablespoons. Heat over medium heat until the fats begin to shimmer, 30 seconds to 1 minute. Add the garlic and cook until fragrant, about 30 seconds. Add the blanched kale and crushed red pepper flakes and, using tongs, toss the kale in the oil until it is thoroughly coated, 2 to 3 minutes. Add the chicken stock and the drained bacon and let simmer until warmed through, 1 to 2 minutes.

6 When the pasta is done, set aside ½ cup of the pasta cooking water. Drain the fettuccine and return it to the pot over low heat. Add the kale and bacon mixture to the drained pasta and toss to combine. Add the pecorino romano cheese and about ¼ cup of the reserved pasta cooking water to thin the sauce as desired.

7 Divide the pasta among serving bowls, grating a little nutmeg over each portion. Serve the pasta immediately with more pecorino romano on the side for those who want it.

NOTE: The best tool for grating nutmeg, cheese, or citrus peel is a rasp (Microplane) or stainless steel zester. With either of these tools, you can easily grate very fine pieces of cheese or citrus peel right into the finished dish.

LINGUINE with Cauliflower and Bacon Bread Crumbs

Serves 4

For this wintry pasta, we wanted a crusty finish so we created a topping of crisply cooked bacon and browned bread crumbs. Once you've made this recipe you'll see that bread crumbs with bacon can raise the appeal of many everyday dishes: Toss a handful into a salad of mixed greens; sprinkle them over sliced ripe summer tomatoes, sautéed zucchini, or green beans; or stir them into hearty winter soups.

6 slices bacon, diced

½ cup coarsely ground homemade bread crumbs (see page 32)

¼ cup extra-virgin olive oil

1 head cauliflower (about 2½ pounds), cored and cut into 1- to 2-inch florets (about 8 cups)

Salt and freshly ground black pepper

5 large cloves garlic, finely chopped

1 large shallot, diced

¼ to ½ teaspoon crushed red pepper flakes

½ cup dry white wine

¼ cup low-sodium chicken stock or water

¾ pound linguine

½ cup loosely packed chopped fresh flat-leaf parsley

½ cup (2 ounces) finely, freshly grated Parmigiano Reggiano cheese, plus additional cheese for serving

1 Cook the bacon in a large skillet over medium heat until lightly browned and most of the fat is rendered, 5 to 8 minutes, stirring often and adjusting the heat as necessary. Using a slotted spoon, transfer the bacon to a paper towel-lined plate to drain, reserving 1 tablespoon of the bacon fat in the skillet and pouring any remaining bacon fat into a small bowl.

2 Heat the bacon fat in the skillet over medium heat. Add the bread crumbs and cook, stirring often, until crisp and golden, 2 to 3 minutes. Using a rubber spatula, scrape the bread crumbs into a small bowl. Add half of the drained bacon to the bread crumbs and toss to combine. Set the bread crumb mixture aside.

3 Wipe the skillet clean with a paper towel. Add the remaining bacon fat and the olive oil to the skillet and heat over medium heat until the fats begin to shimmer, about 1 minute. Add the cauliflower to the skillet and stir to coat the florets with the oil. Season the cauliflower with salt and black pepper to taste. Cook the cauliflower, stirring occasionally,

until it is lightly browned but still firm, about 10 minutes.

4 While the cauliflower cooks, bring 4 to 5 quarts of water to a rolling boil in a large pasta or soup pot.

5 While the water is coming to a boil, stir the garlic, shallot, and crushed red pepper flakes into the browned cauliflower. Cook until the garlic is fragrant, about 1 minute, stirring often. Add the remaining drained bacon and the white wine and chicken stock or water. Partially cover the skillet, reduce the heat to medium-low, and cook until the cauliflower is tender and the sauce is slightly reduced, about 5 minutes.

6 While the sauce finishes cooking, salt the boiling water. Add the linguine, stir to separate the strands, and cook until al dente, following the package instructions. Set aside about ½ cup of the pasta cooking water, then drain the linguine and return it to the cooking pot.

7 Immediately add the cauliflower mixture, parsley, and Parmigiano Reggiano cheese to the drained linguine and toss to mix over very low heat for about 1 minute. Add enough of the reserved pasta cooking water, ½ cup at a time, to thinly coat and moisten the linguine. Toss to mix and cook over low heat until well combined and heated through, about 1 minute longer.

8 Remove the linguine from the heat, sprinkle half of the bread crumb mixture over it, and toss to combine. Divide the linguine among 4 shallow bowls and sprinkle an equal amount of the remaining bread crumb mixture over each serving. Serve immediately with more Parmigiano Reggiano on the side.

WHEN TIMING IS EVERYTHING

In many of these pasta dishes, we keep emphasizing the importance of timing. You need to plan on having the sauce cooked and ready to mix into the steaming, just-drained pasta. Otherwise, the undressed pasta sits around, getting cold and gummy. To avoid this dilemma, we recommend you first start boiling the pasta water, then start making the sauce. About 5 to 6 minutes before the sauce is done, add the pasta to the boiling water to cook it to al dente. However, if you find that the pasta is done a few minutes before the sauce, don't continue to cook it. Simply drain the pasta and toss it with a little extra-virgin olive oil, which will help prevent the strands from sticking together until the pasta can be sauced.

BACON BOLOGNESE with Saffron

Serves 4 as a main dish, 6 as a first course

This is our new favorite quick and delicious red sauce, putting the lie to the notion that the two most important ingredients in a classic Italian sauce are time (like four hours) and a grandmother who stirs the sauce all through those four hours, pausing now and again to taste from her well-worn wooden stirring spoon, raising her eyes to heaven as she signals her approval. About a half hour is all you need here to get a wonderful sauce. We like it with orecchiette, cavatelli, or, if you can find it, authentic Sardinian *malloreddus:* The key is a smallish pasta shape with a curve or cup to catch the chunks of hearty sauce. The classic *malloreddus* is made with saffron incorporated in the flour. It gives the pasta a sharp floral fragrance that balances the rich sauce. If there's no *malloreddus* around, adding saffron to the pasta cooking water yields the same flavor and an eye-pleasing yellow color.

- 4 to 5 slices bacon, finely chopped
- 1 medium-size onion, finely chopped
- 1 pound ground pork
- ⅓ cup chopped fresh flat-leaf parsley
- 2 medium-size cloves garlic, finely chopped
- 1 can (28 ounces) crushed tomatoes with added puree
- 2 bay leaves

- 2 teaspoons chopped fresh oregano leaves, or 1 teaspoon dried oregano
- Salt and freshly ground black pepper
- 12 to 14 ounces orecchiette (little ear-shaped pasta) or medium-size macaroni
- 2 generous pinches saffron threads crumbled
- ¼ cup freshly grated pecorino romano cheese, plus additional cheese for serving

1 Cook the bacon in a large deep pot or saucepan over medium heat until it begins to brown and some of the fat is rendered, 2 to 3 minutes. Add the onion and cook until the onion softens, about 5 minutes, stirring occasionally. Add the ground pork, parsley, and garlic and cook until the pork is lightly browned, about 8 minutes, breaking up any large chunks of meat with a wooden spoon,

adjusting the heat as necessary if the pork browns too quickly, and stirring occasionally.

2 Stir in the crushed tomatoes with their puree and the bay leaves, oregano, and ⅓ cup of water. Cover the pan and let come to a boil. Then, reduce the heat as necessary and let the sauce simmer, partially covered, stirring occasionally, until the sauce thickens and the flavors blend, about 25 minutes. Remove and discard the bay leaves. Season the sauce with salt and pepper to taste.

3 Bring 4 to 5 quarts of water to a boil in a large pasta or soup pot 10 to 15 minutes before the sauce is done. Salt the boiling water. Add the orecchiette and crumbled saffron threads and cook until the orecchiette is al dente, following the package instructions. Set aside

¼ cup of the pasta cooking water, then drain the orecchiette.

4 Return the orecchiette and the reserved pasta cooking water to the cooking pot. Immediately add the sauce and the pecorino romano cheese and toss to mix well. Serve the orecchiette with more pecorino romano on the side.

LINGUINE WITH FRESH CLAMS, BACON, AND BASIL
(and a Touch of Cream)

Serves 4

The brininess of the clam broth (a combination of clam juice and the liquid released by the clams as their shells steam open) matches well with the saltiness of bacon. The tanginess of white wine tames the overall salty taste and some cream added at the end smoothes everything out. Finally, a generous amount of basil adds a fresh herbal accent to the dish.

24 littleneck clams

5 slices thick-cut bacon, cut into ¼- to ½-inch pieces

Extra-virgin olive oil, if necessary

Salt

12 ounces linguine

2 to 3 large cloves garlic, finely chopped

2 teaspoons fresh thyme leaves, or 2 teaspoons chopped fresh oregano

½ cup bottled clam juice

⅓ cup dry white wine

¼ to ½ teaspoon crushed red pepper flakes

¾ cup light cream, or more if necessary

1 cup loosely packed fresh basil leaves, coarsely chopped

2 tablespoons freshly grated Parmigiano Reggiano cheese, plus additional cheese for serving

Freshly ground black pepper

1 Place the clams in a large bowl, cover them with cold water, and let them soak for about 20 minutes so they can release their sand and grit. After soaking and draining the clams, use a firm brush to scrub off any additional sand or barnacles that may cling to the shells.

2 Cook the bacon in a large skillet or wide saucepan over medium heat until browned and most of the fat is rendered, 6 to 9 minutes,

stirring often and adjusting the heat as necessary. Using a slotted spoon, transfer two thirds of the bacon to a paper towel-lined plate to drain. Reserve 2 tablespoons of the bacon fat and the remainder of the browned bacon in the skillet. If necessary, add enough olive oil to the skillet to measure 2 tablespoons.

3 Bring 4 to 5 quarts of water to a rolling boil in a large pasta or soup pot. Salt the boiling water lightly or not at all. (Remember, the bacon and the clams will add salt to the dish.) Add the linguine, stir to separate the strands, and cook until al dente, following the package instructions.

4 You want to toss the linguine with the clam sauce just after the pasta is drained. So, while waiting for the pasta water to boil, start making the clam sauce. Add the clams, garlic, thyme or oregano, clam juice, white wine, and crushed red pepper flakes to the skillet, cover the skillet, and let come to a boil over high heat. Then reduce the heat as necessary and let the mixture simmer until the clams start to open, 4 to 6 minutes depending upon the size of the clams. Uncover the skillet and, using tongs, transfer any clams that have opened to a bowl. Cover the skillet again and continue cooking, checking frequently for opened clams and transferring them to the bowl. Discard any clams that do not open after 8 minutes. Increase the heat to high and cook the sauce until it is reduced by about half. Reduce the

heat to low, add the ¾ cup cream, and let the sauce simmer gently, stirring often, until it thickens slightly, 4 to 5 minutes. Remove the skillet from the heat.

5 Return the opened clams to the skillet with any juices in the bowl and add the basil and the drained bacon. Cover the sauce, set it aside, and keep it warm.

6 When the linguine is done, drain it and return it to the pot. Set aside 8 of the clams. Add the remaining clams and skillet sauce, the Parmigiano Reggiano, and a couple of grindings of black pepper to the linguine and toss to mix well. If the sauce is too thick or a little dry, add a little more light cream to moisten it as desired. Cook over low heat until warmed through, about 1 minute. Divide the pasta and clam sauce among 4 individual serving bowls, garnishing each serving with the reserved clams. Serve immediately with more Parmigiano Reggiano on the side for those who want it.

VEGGIES AND SIDES

Grilled Tomatoes Stuffed
with Bacon, Basil,
and Blue Cheese, page 222

IN THIS CHAPTER...

There are very few rules for using

bacon to liven up a recipe other than: If you like something, you might like it even more with a little bacon. Mario Batali once said that in Italy, "pancetta [Italian bacon] is considered a vegetable." His was a comment made half in jest, but the other half is true. In other words, when bacon is used to heighten the flavor of really good vegetables harvested at their peak, you are not masking second-rate ingredients with the pleasing taste of bacon. That's a big culinary no-no.

You will find that cooking vegetables with bacon allows you to be a more improvisational cook, a real advantage when you come home from work, are pressed for time, and need to put something wonderful on the table. So, when you next go vegetable shopping literally "bring home the bacon!" You'll soon see how indispensible bacon will become to your pantry and everyday cooking. It will even help you be a more improvisational cook, an important skill to cultivate when you need something good, fast.

If you're like us veggie enthusiasts and often make vegetables the star attraction and meat the supporting actor in a dish, you might consider serving some of these sides for the main course.

SLOW-COOKER PULLED BACON
and Bourbon Beans

Serves 4

This slow-cooker baked bean recipe transforms slab bacon into a mouthwatering, shredded-pork tenderness. Bourbon picks up a sweet smokiness from the charred-oak barrels in which, by law, it is aged, so you might say bourbon was made to be paired with bacon. The beans and bacon are first parboiled to soften them somewhat, and then all the ingredients are dumped into the slow cooker and allowed to steam in a subtle and sweet bourbon-molasses sauce. While you can bake the beans in a very low oven, the combination of the slow cooker and beans, like bourbon and bacon, is a match made in food heaven.

2 whole cloves

1 small onion, cut in half

8 to 10 ounces slab bacon, rind removed (see page 57)

1½ cups dried cannellini beans, rinsed, drained, and picked over

⅓ cup packed dark brown sugar

⅛ teaspoon cayenne pepper

Pinch of salt

Freshly ground black pepper

1 medium-size onion, diced

1¼ cups Jim Beam bourbon or your bourbon of choice

2 teaspoons molasses

1 Stud the side of each onion half with 1 whole clove. Place the onion halves and the bacon and beans in a large saucepan. Add water to cover the beans by about 2 inches. Cover the pan and let come to a boil over medium-high heat. Then, reduce the heat as necessary and let the beans simmer, partially covered, until the bacon renders some of its fat, about 5 minutes. Transfer the slab of bacon to a plate. Let the beans continue to simmer, partially covered, until they are just barely tender, 40 to 45 minutes.

2 As the beans cook, use a sharp knife to score the fat side of the bacon slab in a cross-hatch or diamond pattern. Combine the brown sugar, cayenne pepper, salt, and a couple of grinds of black pepper on a plate. Generously coat the bacon slab on all sides in the brown sugar and pepper mixture and set it aside.

3 Drain the beans, discarding the cooking liquid, onion, and cloves (or you can save the cooking liquid for making soup or seasoning stews). Place the drained beans, the bacon, fat side up, and any remaining rub from the plate in a slow cooker. Add the diced onion, bourbon, and molasses. Cover the slow cooker and cook the beans until the bacon is very tender, 7 to 8 hours on low heat, 5 hours on high heat. When ready to serve, shred or cube the bacon, removing and discarding its layer of fat, if desired. (Some people like finding cubes of bacon fat in the bean pot, while others want the fat removed. It's your choice.) Stir the bacon into the beans before serving.

TUSCAN WHITE BEANS with Slab Bacon and Sage

Serves 4

While Americans love their baked beans with molasses and brown sugar, Italians prefer dried beans dressed up with such savory ingredients as sage, white wine, garlic, and onions or shallots. Cooking beans doesn't require a lot of culinary skill, but somehow, they often come out tough-skinned and ropy tasting, like old starch. Blame the beans, not the cook. It makes all the difference in the world if you buy beans that were picked and dried recently. Farmers' markets and premium brands in the supermarket are your best bets. Only beans that have been recently dried cook to a creamy finish. You can cook old, hard beans until the next millenium and they'll never be soft and smooth textured.

These beans make a lovely side dish for roasted chicken or pan-roasted fish.

1¼ cups (8 ounces) dried cannellini beans, rinsed and picked over

½ medium-size onion, peeled

1 large carrot, trimmed, peeled, and cut in half

15 fresh sage leaves

4 ounces slab bacon, rind removed (see page 57)

4½ teaspoons extra-virgin olive oil

1 large shallot, minced

2 teaspoons chopped garlic

¼ cup low-sodium chicken stock

¼ cup dry white wine

Salt and freshly ground black pepper

1 Place the beans in a medium-size pot or saucepan. Add the onion, carrot, and enough water to cover the vegetables. Let come to a boil over medium-high heat. Add 12 of the sage leaves, then reduce the heat as necessary and let the beans simmer gently, partially covered, until tender but not falling apart, 50 to 55 minutes.

2 While the beans cook, heat a medium-size saucepan over high heat until very hot. Add the slab bacon, fat side down. Lower the heat to medium-low and cook the bacon until it is browned on all sides and cooked through, about 4 minutes per side, 12 to 16 minutes total. Using a metal spatula, press down on each side of the slab of bacon a couple of times as it cooks to help render the fat.

3 Transfer the slab of bacon to a cutting board, reserving the bacon fat in the pan. When the slab of bacon is cool enough to handle, chop it coarsely.

4 Add the olive oil to the pan with the bacon fat and heat over medium heat. Add the shallot and garlic and cook until fragrant, without browning the garlic, 1 to 2 minutes.

5 Drain the beans, discarding the onion and carrot. Add the drained beans, chopped bacon, chicken stock, and white wine to the pan with the shallot and garlic and stir gently to combine. Adjust the heat to bring the bean mixture to a simmer and cook until heated through, 2 to 3 minutes. Season the beans with salt and pepper to taste. Chop the 3 remaining sage leaves and sprinkle them over the beans before serving.

BROCCOLI RABE with Bacon and Garlic

Serves 4

The always commonsensical Mark Bittman wrote in *The New York Times,* "Why broccoli rabe was not a part of the American vegetable culture until relatively recently is completely beyond me. What can you not cook it with?"

He's right. Done simply with olive oil or garlic it's just the thing to serve with white-fleshed fish or to toss into a soup or pasta. The more mature the broccoli rabe, the stronger the flavor, and the stronger the flavor, the better suited the broccoli rabe is to being prepared with bacon. Garlicky olive oil and rosemary round out the flavor profile—a lot of flavor bang for a relatively few bucks. Prepared this way broccoli rabe is quite lovely with roasted chicken or pork.

1 bunch (about 1 pound) broccoli rabe

4 slices bacon, cut crosswise into ½-inch strips

2 to 3 tablespoons olive oil, as necessary

3 large cloves garlic, coarsely chopped

1 teaspoon chopped fresh rosemary leaves, or ½ teaspoon dried rosemary

Grated zest of half a lemon

Salt and freshly ground black pepper

1 Cut off and discard the bottom 2 inches of the broccoli rabe stems. Cut the remaining broccoli rabe into 3-inch-long pieces. Bring 2 quarts of water to a boil in a large saucepan. Add the broccoli rabe, cover the pan, and cook the broccoli rabe until wilted and barely tender, but still a dark green, 3 to 4 minutes. Drain the broccoli rabe in a colander and set it aside.

2 Using paper towels, wipe the saucepan dry. Add the bacon to the saucepan and cook over medium heat until lightly browned and some fat is rendered, 4 to 5 minutes, stirring often and adjusting the heat as necessary. Add

2 tablespoons of the olive oil and the garlic and cook until the garlic is fragrant, about 1 minute, stirring often. Add the drained broccoli rabe and the rosemary. Using tongs, toss the broccoli rabe to coat it in the oil, then cook, partially covered, just until tender, about 2 minutes. If the broccoli rabe seems a little dry, drizzle the remaining 1 tablespoon of olive oil over it.

3 Sprinkle the lemon zest over the broccoli rabe. Taste for seasoning, adding salt and pepper as necessary, and serve.

APPLE AND BACON BRUSSELS SPROUT HASH

Serves 4

When brussels sprouts are crisped to a golden brown on one side and tossed with crumbled bacon and sautéed apples, you get one of those holiday dishes that never winds up in a Tupperware container the day after. The funkiness of the brussels sprouts, the crunchy, smoky saltiness of the bacon, and the tart, smooth sweetness of the apple are a trio that makes for a beautiful food melody.

4 slices bacon, cut into ¼-inch pieces

Kosher salt

1 pound brussels sprouts, trimmed and cut in half

2 tablespoons (¼ stick) unsalted butter

1 Granny Smith apple, peeled, cored, and cut into about ¼-inch dice

1 teaspoon white wine vinegar

Pinch of sugar

Freshly ground white pepper

1 Cook the bacon in a medium-size skillet over medium heat until lightly browned and most of the fat is rendered, 5 to 8 minutes, stirring often and adjusting the heat as necessary. Using a slotted spoon, transfer the bacon to a paper towel-lined plate to drain.

2 Bring a medium-size pot of water to a boil over high heat. Add the salt and brussels sprouts and blanch them by boiling them for about 2 minutes. Drain the brussels sprouts, then shock them by placing them in cold water to stop the cooking process. Drain the brussels sprouts again.

3 Melt 1½ tablespoons of the butter in a large skillet over medium-high heat. Add the

brussels sprouts, cut side down, and cook them without moving until the bottoms turn a tempting brownish gold, about 2 minutes. Stir the sprouts and continue cooking them until crisp-tender, 3 to 4 minutes longer. Transfer the brussels sprouts to a bowl and set them aside.

4 Add the remaining 1½ teaspoons of butter and the apple to the skillet and cook over medium-high heat until the apple softens and lightly browns, about 2 minutes, stirring occasionally. Transfer the apple to a bowl and set it aside.

5 Place the skillet over medium heat and add the brussels sprouts, drained bacon, wine

vinegar, and sugar. Season with white pepper to taste. Cook until the vinegar steams off, which should happen rapidly. Return the apple to the skillet and mix gently until all of the ingredients are heated through, about 2 minutes.

Remember this dish next November. It's a great variation on a Thanksgiving standby.

THREE "Bs"—BUTTERNUT SQUASH, BACON, BRUSSELS SPROUTS

Serves 4

Add ginger and bacon to butternut squash and brussels sprouts and two fall vegetables become the basis of a sweet, creamy yet crunchy and fresh autumn medley. Don't feel constrained about adding other ingredients such as chopped shallots, diced green apple, currants, or dried cranberries.

Because the brussels sprouts are shredded before they are added to the skillet, they need no blanching to retain their color, flavor, and crunch. Use a sharp chef's knife to slice the sprouts first in half and then into shreds. Or use a food processor fitted with a slicing blade; it does the job in a few seconds. Serve as a side dish with pork, chicken, or fish.

6 slices bacon, cut into ½-inch pieces

Extra-virgin olive oil, if necessary

1 pound butternut squash, peeled and cut into ½-inch pieces (about 3 cups)

8 brussels sprouts, trimmed and thinly sliced or shredded

4 teaspoons coarsely shredded, peeled fresh ginger

2 medium-size cloves garlic, diced

1 tablespoon olive oil

Salt and freshly ground black pepper

1 Cook the bacon in a large skillet over medium heat until lightly browned and most of the fat is rendered, 5 to 8 minutes, stirring often and adjusting the heat as necessary. Using a slotted spoon, transfer the bacon to a paper towel-lined plate to drain, reserving 3 tablespoons of bacon fat in the skillet. If necessary, add enough olive oil to the skillet to measure 3 tablespoons.

2 Add the squash to the skillet and cook over medium-high heat, stirring occasionally, until lightly browned at the edges and just tender, 6 to 8 minutes. Add the drained bacon and the brussels sprouts, ginger, garlic, and olive oil and stir to combine. Reduce the heat to medium and cook, partially covered, until the flavors blend, 2 to 3 minutes, stirring occasionally. Uncover the skillet and cook until the sprouts are just wilted, 3 to 5 minutes longer, stirring occasionally.

BACON-ROASTED CAULIFLOWER

Serves 4

A terrific way to cook cauliflower is to roast it until it's lightly browned and slightly caramelized. Roasting in a dry heat with a little fat and no water releases Mr. Cauliflower's pleasing nuttiness. In some ways this recipe is in fact a "recipe-free" dish because the basic method gives you a direction, but you can alter the amounts of bacon, ginger, or curry powder as you wish, or even add a couple of cloves of garlic to the mix . . . or pine nuts . . . or dried cranberries . . . or Swiss chard . . . or, or, or . . .

2 tablespoons olive oil, plus more for oiling the baking dish or broiler pan

1 medium-size head cauliflower (about 2 pounds), cored and cut into 2-inch florets

2 to 3 slices thick-cut bacon, coarsely chopped

1 piece (about 1 inch long) fresh ginger, peeled and chopped

1 teaspoon curry powder, or more to taste

Salt and freshly ground black pepper

1 Position a rack in the center of the oven and preheat the oven to 375°F. Lightly coat a shallow baking dish or broiler pan with olive oil.

2 Place the cauliflower in the prepared baking dish or broiler pan. Drizzle the olive oil over the cauliflower and toss to coat. Scatter the bacon and ginger over the cauliflower.

Sprinkle the curry powder over the cauliflower and season it with salt and pepper to taste.

3 Bake the cauliflower until it is tender but still firm, 25 to 30 minutes, stirring it once after about 15 minutes. Serve immediately.

IMPROVISE!

Maybe you'll want to take our simple Bacon-Roasted Cauliflower recipe (see page 205) to another level—that's the fun part. Remove and discard the core from half of a large head of cauliflower. Cut the cored half into 1- to 2-inch florets. Scatter the florets in a large, shallow baking dish or broiler pan. Cut a large red or yellow bell pepper in half, remove its stem and seeds, and cut the pepper into 2-inch pieces. Scatter the pieces of bell pepper over the cauliflower florets. Add some large cherry tomatoes, if you want and you have them on hand. Dice a small onion or two large shallots and a couple of large garlic cloves and scatter them over the vegetables. If you have some fresh ginger, peel a 1-inch piece and cut it into thin slivers. Scatter the ginger over the vegetables. Cut four slices of thick-cut bacon crosswise into ½-inch strips and scatter the strips over the vegetables. Drizzle a tablespoon or two of olive oil over the vegetable mixture and season it all with salt and pepper. If you like, add some herbs or spices, such as crushed fresh rosemary or thyme or some curry powder. Place the baking dish in an oven preheated to 375°F and bake the vegetables until the cauliflower is lightly browned and tender but still firm, 25 to 30 minutes, stirring the vegetables once after about 15 minutes.

Other vegetables, such as thick asparagus cut into 2- to 3-inch pieces; 2-inch cubes of eggplant; brussels sprouts or mushrooms cut in half; or small peeled pieces of potato, beets, sweet potato, and butternut squash, can also be cooked using this easy roasting method. So, go ahead and improvise; just don't leave out the bacon. The cooking times will vary, of course, depending on the vegetables you use.

CAULIFLOWER
with Bacon, Olives, and Thyme

Serves 4

Cauliflower can turn out bland and mushy, but it's not the vegetable's fault that most cooks boil the flavor out of it. The best way to cook cauliflower is to sauté or roast it, using little or no cooking liquid and allowing cauliflower's natural sugars to caramelize to a nutty brown. This recipe was created as a side to accompany a grilled or broiled piece of chicken or fish, but it works equally well tossed into a bowl of steaming fusilli with a generous lashing of olive oil.

3 slices thick-cut bacon, cut into ½-inch pieces

½ large head cauliflower, cored and cut into 1- to 2-inch florets (about 4 cups)

⅓ cup dry white wine

15 cherry tomatoes, cut in half

⅓ cup pitted oil-packed kalamata olives

1 large clove garlic, finely chopped

1 teaspoon fresh thyme leaves

Freshly ground black pepper

1 Cook the bacon in a large skillet over medium heat until lightly browned but not yet crisp and some of the fat is rendered, 5 to 6 minutes, stirring often and adjusting the heat as necessary. Add the cauliflower florets, cover the skillet, and cook the cauliflower until it is lightly browned, 5 to 6 minutes, stirring occasionally.

2 Add the white wine, tomatoes, olives, garlic, and thyme. Increase the heat to medium-high, cover the skillet, and let the cauliflower simmer until it is tender but still firm and the wine has evaporated, about 5 minutes. Season the cauliflower with pepper to taste and serve.

CAULIFLOWER BACON GRATIN

Serves 6 to 8

This gratin recipe started as a lighter alternative to mac and cheese—same cheesy, gooey deliciousness, fewer calories. We've also added a little curry, some nutmeg, and some hot sauce, and topped it with a scallion-bread crumb mix for a layer of crunch. We prefer thicker-cut bacon when cooking casseroles since the bacon cooks twice: First it's sautéed and then it's baked with the cauliflower. You can substitute Gruyère cheese for the cheddar and add a little Parmesan to the sauce. Curry is traditionally paired with cauliflower in Indian cuisine and the nutmeg is used by Europeans to add aromatic spiciness. We first served this dish at our Labor Day picnic with grilled steak and chicken and when we asked our guests how to improve the sauce or seasoning, they gratefully replied, "Don't change a thing!"

First rule of cooking for a crowd: Never argue with a good review.

2 tablespoons (¼ stick) unsalted butter, plus butter for greasing the baking dish

5 slices thick-cut bacon, cut crosswise into ½-inch pieces

Extra-virgin olive oil, if necessary

2 large shallots, diced

1¼ cups low-sodium chicken stock

1 large head cauliflower (2½ to 2¾ pounds), cored and cut into 2-inch florets

2 tablespoons unbleached all-purpose flour

½ cup half-and-half or light cream
1 cup whole-milk ricotta

6 ounces good-quality sharp yellow cheddar, coarsely grated (about 1¾ cups)

½ teaspoon curry powder

¼ teaspoon grated nutmeg, preferably freshly grated

4 generous dashes of your choice of hot sauce, or more to taste

Salt and freshly ground black pepper

1 cup coarsely ground, homemade whole-wheat bread crumbs (see page 32)

½ cup finely chopped scallions, green parts only

1 Position a rack in the center of the oven and preheat the oven to 400°F. Butter a shallow 3-quart baking dish (a 13- by 9-inch Pyrex casserole dish works well).

2 Cook the bacon in a large heavy saucepan over medium heat until browned but not crisp and most of the fat is rendered, 6 to 8 minutes, stirring often and adjusting the heat as necessary. Using a slotted spoon, transfer the bacon to a paper towel-lined plate to drain, setting aside 1 tablespoon of the bacon fat in a small bowl and reserving 2 tablespoons of the bacon fat in the pan. If necessary, add enough olive oil to the pan to measure 2 tablespoons.

3 Add the shallots to the pan and cook over medium heat until they just begin to soften, about 2 minutes. Add the chicken stock, using a wooden spoon to scrape up the brown bits at the bottom of the pan. Add the cauliflower, cover the pan, and let come to a boil. Reduce the heat and cook until the cauliflower is barely tender, about 6 minutes. (Don't overcook the cauliflower as it will continue to cook when the gratin bakes.) Using a slotted spoon, transfer the cauliflower to the prepared baking dish, reserving the liquid and shallots in the pan.

4 Increase the heat to medium-high and let the liquid simmer until it is slightly reduced, about 2 minutes. Add the butter and whisk it over medium heat until melted. Whisking constantly, add the flour and cook until the flour is well blended into the butter mixture, 1 to 2 minutes. Slowly add the half-and-half or light cream, whisking until smoothly blended, 2 to 3 minutes. Reduce the heat to medium-low and add the ricotta and half of the cheddar cheese. Let the sauce simmer, whisking often, until smooth and thickened, 2 to 3 minutes. Remove the pan from the heat and stir in the curry powder, nutmeg, and hot sauce. Taste for seasoning, adding salt and pepper and more hot sauce as desired.

5 Pour the cheese sauce over the cauliflower and stir gently to combine. Scatter the drained bacon and the remaining cheddar cheese evenly over the cauliflower. Cover the baking dish loosely with aluminum foil and bake the gratin until warmed through, 15 to 20 minutes.

6 While the gratin bakes, place the remaining 1 tablespoon of bacon fat in a medium-size skillet set over medium heat. Add the bread crumbs and the scallions and toss well to coat the crumbs in the fat.

7 Remove the gratin from the oven and increase the oven temperature to 450°F. Sprinkle the bread crumb and scallion mixture evenly over the top. Return the gratin to the oven and bake, uncovered, until the cheese is bubbly and the bread crumbs are a golden brown, 5 to 10 minutes. Serve the gratin immediately.

UTICA GREENS

Serves 4

One of the great legacies of the wave of Italian immigration in the early twentieth century is that different Italian American communities have come up with their own unique homages to the tradition of the homeland. For example, one rarely thinks of Utica, New York, a small upstate city, as very Italian, but many Italian Americans settled there, and one of the things they invented was the dish known as Utica greens, which we first tasted at Dominique's Chesterfield Restaurant in Utica. While some interpretations call for adding potatoes and most recipes call for prosciutto, we like this pared-down version for its emphasis on the greens and the smokiness of the bacon. Escarole is the traditional green of choice, but kale and Swiss chard (or even a combination of these two) work well. And, you can also add a handful of toasted pignoli (pine) nuts. Utica greens are delicious served with a simple roasted chicken, roasted lamb, or thick pork chops.

P.S. Our thanks to Nicholas Reiter (son of Marie) for suggesting the visit to Dominique's while Nicholas was clerking for a federal judge in Utica.

Butter, for greasing the baking dish

4 slices thick-cut bacon, cut into ¼- to ½-inch pieces

3 tablespoons extra-virgin olive oil, plus more if necessary

⅓ cup fine plain dry bread crumbs, homemade (page 32) or store-bought

¼ cup (1 ounce) finely freshly grated Parmigiano Reggiano cheese

1 medium-size onion, chopped (about ¾ cup)

2 large cloves garlic, chopped

8 to 10 ounces escarole, cored and coarsely chopped

½ cup low-sodium chicken stock

4 pickled hot or sweet cherry peppers, or a combination of the two, drained and thinly sliced

Salt and freshly ground black pepper

1 Position a rack in the center of the oven and preheat the oven to 400°F. Butter a shallow 2-quart baking dish.

2 Cook the bacon in a large deep saucepan over medium heat until the bacon is browned and most of the fat is rendered, 6 to 8 minutes,

stirring often and adjusting the heat as necessary. Using a slotted spoon, transfer the bacon to a paper towel-lined plate to drain. Pour 2 tablespoons of the bacon fat into a medium-size bowl. If necessary, add enough olive oil to the bowl to measure 2 tablespoons. Stir the bread crumbs and the Parmigiano Reggiano cheese into the bacon fat and set the bowl aside.

3 Add the 3 tablespoons of olive oil to the saucepan and heat over medium heat. Add the onion and cook until softened, about 3 minutes, stirring occasionally. Add the garlic and cook until fragrant, about 1 minute. Add the escarole and the chicken stock, cover the pan, and cook until the escarole is wilted,

about 8 minutes. Stir the pickled peppers and the drained bacon into the escarole and season with salt and black pepper to taste.

4 Spoon the escarole mixture into the prepared baking dish. Evenly sprinkle the bacon and bread crumb mixture over the top of the escarole. Bake until the bread crumbs are golden brown, 12 to 15 minutes. Serve immediately.

GARLICKY ROSEMARY BACON AND KALE

Serves 4 to 5

The advent of farmers' markets and the catechism of "Eat seasonal, eat local" has awakened many of us to the pleasures of winter greens—hearty late-season foods. Unsurprisingly, we believe bacon is the secret ingredient that complements the strong flavors of these greens in a way that matches rather than overpowers them (something that can happen when you combine bacon with the more easily overwhelmed greens of summer). Lacinato (aka Tuscan) kale is a little more tender and doesn't have as much fibrous stem as other greens, but we've also used mustard greens, escarole, and even beet tops instead of kale. For another variation, garnish the kale with toasted, butter-flavored bread crumbs.

1 to 1¼ pounds Tuscan kale, tough stems and ribs removed and discarded, leaves rinsed

6 slices bacon, cut into ½-inch pieces

Extra-virgin olive oil, if necessary

4 large cloves garlic, cut in half and lightly crushed

2 to 3 sprigs fresh rosemary

Juice of half a lemon

Salt and freshly ground black pepper

1 Pile a few of the trimmed and rinsed kale leaves on top of each other and slice them crosswise into 2 inch-wide pieces. Repeat with the remaining kale leaves.

2 Cook the bacon in a 4- to 5-quart pot over medium heat until lightly browned and most of the fat is rendered, 5 to 8 minutes, stirring often and adjusting the heat as necessary. Using a slotted spoon, transfer the bacon to a paper towel-lined plate to drain. Pour off and discard all but 3 tablespoons of the bacon fat from the pot. If necessary, add enough olive oil to measure 3 tablespoons.

3 Add the garlic to the pot and cook over very low heat until the garlic is a pale golden color, about 5 minutes, stirring occasionally. Add the rosemary sprigs and cook until fragrant, about 1 minute, turning the sprigs a few times. Remove any burnt or overly browned garlic. Add the kale and, using tongs, turn the kale to coat it in the fat.

4 Add the lemon juice and 1 cup of water. Increase the heat to medium and let simmer, partially covered, until the kale is just tender, 8 to 10 minutes. Remove and discard the rosemary sprigs. Add the drained bacon and toss to combine. Season the kale with salt and pepper to taste before serving.

BACON MUSHROOM STEW
with Glazed Potatoes and Olives

Serves 8

We know what you're thinking: "Olives and bacon together. Won't that be too salty?" You might think so but it isn't, especially if you boil the olives to tame them. What's so nice is the way the saltiness showcases the personality of two wonderful ingredients—the chewy and meaty bacon and the smooth and floral olives. Similarly, the long-cooked potatoes that soak up all the juices and the satiny porcini mushrooms are two different ways of adding a smooth texture. As for the onions and garlic, they turn this mostly vegetable side dish into a stew. Serve it as a main course along with a green salad and a sweetish, fruity wine such as riesling or a buttery California chardonnay. Thanks to "The Master," Michel Richard, with whom we worked on this dish in his wonderful book *Happy in the Kitchen*.

1 cup pitted flavorful oil-cured black olives

5 ounces slab bacon (about ¾ inch thick), rind removed and cut into 8 pieces (see page 57)

⅓ cup extra-virgin olive oil

10 porcini mushrooms, stems trimmed, mushrooms wiped clean and sliced in half lengthwise

Salt

1 cup peeled pearl onions

2 teaspoons sugar

6 Yukon Gold potatoes, peeled and cut into quarters

12 large cloves garlic, peeled

6 sprigs fresh thyme

½ cup low-sodium chicken stock

Freshly ground black pepper

1 Position a rack in the center of the oven and preheat the oven to 325°F.

2 Place the olives in a small saucepan, add water just to cover, and bring to a boil. Strain the olives, return them to the saucepan, and refill it with cold water to cover. Bring to a boil, strain the olives, and set them aside.

3 Place a skillet large enough to hold the mushrooms in a single layer over high heat. Add the pieces of slab bacon and 1 tablespoon of the olive oil. Cook the bacon, stirring, for 1 minute, then turn the pieces over. Cook the bacon until some of the fat begins to render, 1 minute longer. Remove the skillet from the heat, transfer the bacon pieces to a paper towel-lined plate to drain, and set aside.

4 Add the mushrooms to the skillet, cut side down, and season them lightly with salt. Place the skillet over high heat and cook the mushrooms until nicely browned, 3 to 4 minutes. Transfer the mushrooms to the plate with the bacon as they brown.

5 Wipe the skillet clean with paper towels and return it to the heat. Add another tablespoon of olive oil to the skillet, then add the pearl onions. Cook the onions, swirling the pan occasionally, until the onions are lightly golden, about 3 minutes. Sprinkle the sugar over the onions and cook them until browned, 3 to 4 minutes, swirling the pan.

6 Place the drained bacon, the browned mushrooms, the sugared onions, and the potatoes, garlic, thyme sprigs, and chicken stock in an enameled cast-iron casserole large enough to hold all of the ingredients in a single layer. Pour the remaining olive oil over the top.

7 Cover the casserole and bake the mushroom stew until the potatoes are glazed and tender, about 1 hour, stirring once to coat all of the ingredients with the juices. Season the mushroom stew with pepper to taste before serving.

NON-SUFFERING SUCCOTASH

Serves 4

L ike many Americans, we were introduced to the word *succotash* by Sylvester the cat. "Sufferin' succotash" was his favorite exclamation. It wasn't until some years later that we came to know that it is also the name of a traditional Native American vegetarian stew. As they do with many starchy protein-rich plants, bacon and ginger enliven a sometimes lackluster taste. When the corn is fresh and the lima beans are just picked, succotash is a full-flavored seasonal treat. In fact, that's the only time we make it.

2 tablespoons extra-virgin olive oil

3 slices bacon, cut into ½-inch pieces

2 large shallots, chopped (about ¾ cup)

2 teaspoons diced, peeled fresh ginger

2 small yellow squash (about 8 ounces total), trimmed and cut into ½-inch rounds

2 cups corn kernels (cut from 2 freshly shucked ears)

1 cup fresh lima beans, or 1 cup thawed frozen lima beans, if fresh are unavailable

3 tablespoons heavy cream

Salt and freshly ground black pepper

1 Heat the olive oil in a large skillet over medium-high heat. Add the bacon and cook until some of the fat begins to render, about 2 minutes, stirring occasionally. Add the shallots and ginger and cook until the shallots are translucent, about 2 minutes. Add the yellow squash, stir to coat well, and cook until the squash begins to soften, about 2 minutes, stirring occasionally. Add the corn and lima beans, cover the skillet, and reduce the heat to medium.

2 Cook until the squash is just tender but still firm, about 5 minutes. Stir in the heavy cream and cook until just heated through, 30 seconds to 1 minute. Season with salt and pepper to taste before serving.

ROASTED SWEET POTATO STICKS
with Bacon-Bourbon Sauce

Serves 4 to 6

Bourbon, bacon, shallots, ginger, sweet potatoes . . . what's not to like! Although we have nothing against french fries, if you would like a change of pace, try this with anything that goes with fries: fried fish, steak, burgers. Likewise, for a change of pace from mushy Thanksgiving sweet potatoes, serve sweet potato sticks with roasted turkey, or pair them with Christmas ham. We tested the recipe two ways—with and without peeling the sweet potatoes. It worked in both cases, but we prefer not having to peel the potatoes (and the skin is loaded with nutrients). Word of caution: Just like french fries or potato chips, once you start eating sweet potato sticks it's hard to stop, as we found when we took our first test batch from the oven.

3 medium-size sweet potatoes (2¼ to 2½ pounds total), trimmed and well scrubbed

5 slices bacon, cut into ½-inch pieces

Unsalted butter

¾ cup diced shallots (about 2 large)

2 teaspoons chopped, peeled fresh ginger

⅓ cup bourbon or dark rum

4½ teaspoons packed dark brown sugar

Salt and freshly ground black pepper

1 Position a rack in the center of the oven and preheat the oven to 425°F.

2 Cut the sweet potatoes in half lengthwise. Cut each sweet potato half lengthwise into 3 wedges. Place the sweet potato wedges in a single layer in a large roasting pan or shallow baking dish (they should fit snugly) and set them aside.

3 Cook the bacon in a large skillet over medium heat until lightly browned but not crisp, 5 to 7 minutes, stirring often and adjusting the heat as necessary. Transfer the bacon to a paper towel-lined plate to drain, reserving the bacon fat in the skillet. You should have about 2 tablespoons of fat. If necessary, pour off enough fat or add enough butter to the skillet to measure 2 tablespoons.

4 Place the skillet over medium-high heat, add the shallots and ginger and, using a wooden spoon, stir and scrape up any brown bits from the bottom of the skillet. Cook the shallot mixture until the shallots have softened, about 2 minutes, stirring occasionally. Stir in

1½ teaspoons of butter, the bourbon or rum, and the brown sugar and cook just until the butter melts and the sugar dissolves, about 1 minute.

5 Drizzle the bourbon sauce over the sweet potatoes. Sprinkle the drained bacon evenly over the potatoes and season them with salt and pepper to taste.

6 Cover the roasting pan with aluminum foil and bake the sweet potatoes for about 20 minutes. Then, uncover the pan and gently turn the sweet potatoes over. Continue baking the sweet potatoes until they are just tender, about 10 minutes longer. Spoon some of the browned bits of bacon and shallots from the bottom of the pan over the potatoes before serving.

TOMATOES AND CORN
("The Fire Song")
Serves 4 to 6

From Peter: This is the first recipe I ever invented. It is the final recipe in my book *Culinary Intelligence: The Art of Eating Healthy (and Really Well)*. My friend the late Johnny Herald was a great guitar picker and singer. He was also a great mushroom picker. One day he left some tomatoes and corn on the stove while he went mushrooming. He was gone a little too long and somehow a fire started, burning his house to the ground. He wrote "The Fire Song" about tomatoes and corn and I liked the sound of it, so I did some composing of my own, the culinary kind. It's a high-summer treat when corn is at its sweetest and fresh Jersey beefsteak tomatoes are plump, juicy, and almost smoky.

6 slices bacon, diced

2 tablespoons (¼ stick) unsalted butter

4 to 6 cups sweet corn kernels, cut from 4 to 6 freshly shucked ears

2 large ripe beefsteak tomatoes, coarsely chopped

Freshly ground black pepper

½ cup coarsely chopped basil

1 Cook the bacon in a large skillet over medium heat until the bacon is browned and crisp and the fat is rendered, 6 to 9 minutes, stirring often and adjusting the heat as necessary. Using a slotted spoon, transfer the bacon to a paper towel-lined plate to drain. Discard the bacon fat or save it for another use.

2 Melt the butter in a medium-size skillet over medium heat. Add the corn kernels and cook until crisp-tender, about 2 minutes. Add the drained bacon and the tomatoes, and season with pepper to taste. Increase the heat to medium-high and cook until the liquid from the tomatoes partially evaporates, 5 to 7 minutes.

3 Transfer the tomato and corn mixture to a bowl, toss it with the basil, and serve.

SWEET POTATO PANCAKES
with Bacon

Serves 4

This recipe came out of our frustration with attempting to make a better potato latke by incorporating bacon into the traditional batter. But, though we tried several variations, the result wasn't spectacular, just ho-hum. Sometimes you just have to keep searching for a solution and we think this is it. Sweet potatoes, with their natural sugar, proved to be a wonderful taste counterpoint to bacon's saltiness. And because sweet potatoes are much drier and denser than white potatoes, it's not necessary to wring out the potato liquid before frying the pancakes. We added chopped scallions, instead of the more traditional grated onion, and found them to contribute a spark more color and flavor. These pancakes are lovely eaten on their own with sour cream and applesauce or served as a side for roasted pork or chicken.

8 slices bacon, cut into ½-inch pieces

1 pound sweet potatoes, peeled

3 scallions, both white and green parts,
trimmed and finely chopped

2 large eggs, lightly beaten

½ cup unbleached all-purpose flour

½ teaspoon ground ginger (optional)

⅛ teaspoon salt, or more to taste

Freshly ground black pepper

½ to ¾ cup canola or other vegetable oil

Sour cream and applesauce (optional),
for serving

1 Position a rack in the center of the oven and preheat the oven to 250°F. Line a large rimmed baking sheet with paper towels.

2 Cook the bacon in a large skillet over medium heat until lightly browned and most of the fat is rendered, 5 to 8 minutes, stirring often and adjusting the heat as necessary. Using a slotted spoon, transfer the bacon to a paper towel-lined plate to drain. Pour the bacon fat from the skillet into a wire-mesh strainer set over a small bowl. Set the bacon fat aside. Using a paper towel, wipe the skillet clean; you will use it to cook the pancakes.

3 Using the large holes of a box grater, coarsely grate the sweet potatoes. Transfer the grated sweet potatoes to a large mixing bowl. Add the drained bacon and the scallions, eggs, flour, ginger, if using, and salt and stir until thoroughly combined. Season with pepper to taste.

4 Using a ¼-cup measure, divide the potato mixture into 12 to 14 equal portions, setting each portion on a baking sheet. Using the back of a metal spatula, flatten each mound into a ¾-inch-thick pancake.

5 Add the strained bacon fat and ½ cup of the oil to the large skillet. Heat the fats over medium heat until they shimmer, about 1 minute. Using a metal spatula, carefully transfer 3 or 4 pancakes to the skillet and, using the back of the spatula, gently flatten them so that each is about ½ inch thick. Do not crowd the pancakes in the pan; a large skillet will hold 3 to 4 pancakes at a time.

6 Cook the potato pancakes until golden brown, 3 to 5 minutes per side, adjusting the heat as necessary to prevent them from browning too quickly. Transfer the cooked pancakes to the paper towel-lined baking sheet and keep warm in the oven. Repeat with the remaining pancakes, adding more oil to the skillet, if necessary. Serve the potato pancakes hot with sour cream and applesauce, if desired.

GRILLED TOMATOES
Stuffed with Bacon, Basil, and Blue Cheese

Serves 6

Bacon, tomatoes, and blue cheese are, to our way of thinking, wicked great on a cheeseburger. So we thought, why not make them the star of their own recipe? The tomatoes stand alone as a light main course, as a side to grilled meat, or as the fillings of a sandwich. With a rib eye or a fish fry, they are heaven. Make this dish using only locally grown summer tomatoes. There is no way to substitute for a tomato in season.

2 tablespoons extra-virgin olive oil, plus more for oiling the grill grate

5 slices bacon, diced

⅔ cup diced red onion

1 large clove garlic, diced

¾ cup coarsely ground homemade whole-wheat bread crumbs (see page 32)

¼ cup coarsely chopped fresh basil leaves

½ cup loosely packed, coarsely crumbled blue cheese

6 large ripe tomatoes (6 to 7 ounces each)

1 tablespoon red wine vinegar

Salt and freshly ground black pepper

1 Lightly oil the grill grate. Preheat a gas grill to medium or prepare a medium-hot fire in a charcoal grill.

2 Cook the bacon in a large skillet over medium heat until lightly browned and most of the fat is rendered, 5 to 8 minutes, stirring often and adjusting the heat as necessary. Using a slotted spoon, transfer the bacon to a paper towel-lined plate to drain, reserving 1½ tablespoons of bacon fat in the skillet.

3 Add the red onion to the skillet and cook over medium heat until it begins to soften, 2 to 3 minutes, stirring often. Add the garlic and cook until fragrant and the onion is softened, about 1 minute. Add the bread crumbs and basil and

stir until well combined. Transfer the onion mixture to a medium-size bowl. Add the blue cheese and the drained bacon and set aside.

4 Cut about a ½-inch-thick slice off the stem end of each tomato. Using a paring knife, remove the cores of the tomatoes by cutting a cone-shaped piece about 2 inches deep and 1½ inches wide in each. Cut a very thin sliver off the bottom of each tomato to help stabilize it as it grills.

5 Whisk together the olive oil and wine vinegar and drizzle about 1 teaspoon of the dressing over each tomato. Sprinkle the tops of the tomatoes lightly with salt and pepper to taste. Divide the bacon and blue cheese

mixture evenly among the tomatoes, filling the cores and patting the mixture firmly in place to cover the top of each tomato.

6 Place the tomatoes on the oiled grill grate, cover the grill, and grill the tomatoes until they have softened and the stuffing is warmed through, 10 to 15 minutes. If you are using a charcoal grill, check the tomatoes after about 5 minutes and if the fire is too hot, causing the tomatoes to burn or cook too quickly, move them to the edge of the grill to continue cooking. If you need the center of the grill for cooking other foods, such as chicken or steak, the tomatoes can be cooked on the outer edge of the grill or on the grill's top shelf over the main cooking grate; the cooking time will be longer. You can also bake the tomatoes in a shallow oiled baking dish in an oven preheated to 400°F. After baking the tomatoes for about 12 minutes, place them under the broiler for about 1 minute to lightly brown the stuffing.

BACON BREAD CRUMBS

Makes about ¾ cup

T his bread crumb garnish takes just a few minutes to put together and adds crunchy bacony flavor to grilled, sautéed, or roasted vegetables.

Sprinkle it on grilled asparagus or portobello mushrooms, grilled tomatoes, sautéed broccoli florets, baked acorn squash, or pasta tossed in olive oil and garlic. We served the bacon crumb topping over thick wedges of buttered oven-roasted cauliflower—delicious.

3 slices bacon, diced

½ cup coarsely ground homemade bread crumbs (see page 32)

¼ cup pine nuts or coarsely chopped cashews

2 medium-size cloves garlic, minced

Generous pinch of cayenne pepper or curry powder

Cook the bacon in a medium-size skillet over medium heat until the bacon is lightly browned and most of the fat is rendered, 5 to 8 minutes, stirring often and adjusting the heat as necessary. Using a slotted spoon, transfer the bacon to a paper towel-lined plate to drain, reserving 1 tablespoon of bacon fat in the skillet. Add the bread crumbs, pine nuts or cashews, and garlic to the skillet and cook, stirring occasionally, until the bread crumbs are lightly toasted, about 4 minutes. Add the drained bacon and the cayenne pepper or curry powder to the bread crumb mixture and toss to mix well before using.

VARIATION: Add a handful of toasted, coarsely chopped walnuts or pine nuts to the stuffing. Substitute goat cheese for the blue cheese. Use 2 large shallots in place of the red onion.

CHAPTER 10

MUFFINS, BREADS & STUFFINGS

Downside-Up
Apple-Bacon-Pecan Muffins,
page 229

IN THIS CHAPTER...

Our thrifty American ancestors

understood that bacon fat, while different from butter fat, is an equally delicious addition to batters for muffins, breads, pancakes, and biscuits. And the fact that it could be produced, without extra cost or time, from the simple frying and rendering of raw bacon slices made the bacon fat-filled coffee can ubiquitous on the back stove for many generations of Americans. From hardy pioneers to the refined homes of our Founding Fathers, cooks conserved bacon fat. There are few things in this world that can be said to be the equal in flavor to butter: bacon can.

Here we offer muffins, biscuits, flatbreads, and stuffings that make it a crime—or at least a minor sin—to even think about discarding bacon fat once you know you can put it to such good use. For instance, we flat-out love an Herbed Bacon Flatbread with the texture of a crisp, thin cracker that's excellent as a base for creamy spreads or a soft goat cheese. In our Downside-Up Apple-Bacon-Pecan Muffins, a moist mixture of apple, bacon, pecans, brown sugar, and butter is added to the muffin tin to become a gooey, glistening muffin top. In the Bacon Crumble–Topped Bran Muffins, a mix of bran, whole-wheat and white flours, yogurt, molasses, raisins, and bacon puts some fun back into healthy food equations whether for breakfast or served as an afternoon, after-school snack. The Cheddar Cheese and Bacon Biscuits are our personal affirmation of our deep faith that "every dish is delish" when these two flavor-filled ingredients are joined in culinary matrimony. Make and serve them just out of the oven with any kind of meat, fish, or poultry.

You'll also find a recipe that calls for using stone-ground yellow cornmeal to make a shortbread and three different corn breads that balance sweetness and savoriness with the substantial rough flavor and texture of cornmeal, another early-American favorite. You will love the Bacon and Rosemary Shortbread with roasted pork or on its own as a light dessert with tea or coffee. And then, there's everyone's favorite—stuffing: Oyster and Corn Bread Stuffing with Bacon; and Bacon, Sweet Potato, and Greens Stuffing with Jalapeño Corn Bread. If no one had invented the idea of seconds prior to this, these recipes alone would have kick-started the practice of going back for refills.

So save the fat, because as Tina Turner said: "Ain't nothin' no good without the grease." To which we add a reverent amen.

DOWNSIDE-UP APPLE-BACON-PECAN MUFFINS

Makes 12 muffins

E at one of these muffins and you don't need anything else to satisfy you for breakfast. It's not an everyday breakfast, though, because it's sweet and gooey—the kind of thing you want for a treat, not a diet. Kids love to eat muffins and they love to help make them. It never fails to delight them when you remove these muffins from the tin and get a first look and sniff of the beautiful, irresistible topping—or is the proper word *bottoming*? Traditional cookbook titles often use the term *upside-down,* but we prefer *downside-up* because that is where the magic happens, when a plain-looking muffin is flipped over to reveal a treasure trove of flavor.

FOR THE APPLE-BACON-PECAN TOPPING

6 tablespoons (¾ stick) unsalted butter, or as necessary, plus butter for greasing the muffin tin

6 slices maple-flavored bacon, trimmed of excess fat and cut into ½-inch pieces

2 large Granny Smith apples (about 1 pound)

½ cup packed dark brown sugar

Pinch of kosher salt

½ cup toasted pecans (see page 264), coarsely chopped

FOR THE MUFFINS

2 cups unbleached all-purpose flour

¾ cup packed dark brown sugar

1 tablespoon baking powder

¾ teaspoon ground cinnamon

¼ teaspoon kosher salt

8 tablespoons (1 stick) unsalted butter, melted

2 large eggs, lightly beaten

¾ cup sour cream

2 tablespoons milk

1 teaspoon maple extract or pure vanilla extract

1 Position a rack in the center of the oven and preheat the oven to 375°F. Generously butter a 12-cup nonstick muffin tin. (Or you can use two 6-cup muffin tins.)

2 Prepare the apple-bacon-pecan topping: Cook the bacon in a large skillet over medium heat until lightly browned and most of the fat is rendered, 5 to 8 minutes, stirring often and adjusting the heat as necessary. Using a slotted spoon, transfer the bacon to a paper towel-lined plate to drain, reserving the bacon fat in the skillet. Set the skillet aside.

3 Peel and core the apples. Slice the apples lengthwise into wedges that are approximately ¼ inch thick. Cut the wedges in half crosswise into pieces that are 1 to 2 inches long so that they will fit in the bottom of the muffin tin cups.

4 Place the skillet with the reserved bacon fat over medium heat and add enough of the butter to measure a total of 8 tablespoons of melted fat. Add the apples, ½ cup of brown sugar, and pinch of salt and cook until the apples are tender and the brown sugar has caramelized, 8 to 10 minutes. Distribute the drained bacon evenly among the muffin cups, followed by the apple pieces, including the pan syrup. Sprinkle the pecans over the apple slices.

5 Prepare the muffins: Combine the flour, ¾ cup of brown sugar, baking powder, cinnamon, and ¼ teaspoon of salt in a large bowl.

6 Place the 8 tablespoons of melted butter and the eggs, sour cream, milk, and maple or vanilla extract in another large bowl and whisk to mix. Pour the wet ingredients into the dry, folding them together until smooth. Evenly distribute the batter over the layer of bacon, apple, and pecans in the muffin cups. Bake the muffins until they are slightly puffed and lightly browned, 20 to 22 minutes. When the muffins are done a cake tester or toothpick inserted into the center of one will come out clean.

7 Let the muffins cool partly in the muffin tin, then turn the muffin tin over onto a platter, releasing the muffins. Serve the muffins warm or at room temperature. If some of the topping remains in the bottom of the muffin tin cups, gently remove it and place it on top of the muffins. The muffins can be stored in an airtight container at room temperature for up to 3 days.

BACON CRUMBLE-TOPPED BRAN MUFFINS

Makes 9 muffins

W e set out to create a muffin that could be breakfast with the easy addition of a cup of coffee and a glass of juice. It includes bacon and eggs and super-healthful bran. Fifteen or twenty years ago bran muffins were flavorless and so gummy that people who felt guilty about their eating habits could take solace in the "penance" of a chewy, tasteless bran muffin. But bran is powerful and assertive, just the thing to stand up to the bacon in these muffins. And adding yogurt is like adding the fountain of youth—just look at all those yogurt-eating Bulgarians who live to be a hundred. With all that healthiness going for these muffins, why not finish them off with a sweet, crumbly, bacony topping?

Here's to health and fun!

FOR THE BACON CRUMBLE TOPPING

2 slices thick-cut bacon, cut into
¼-inch pieces

Unsalted butter

6 tablespoons unbleached all-purpose
flour

2 tablespoons granulated sugar

2 tablespoons packed light or
dark brown sugar (see Note)

¼ teaspoon ground cinnamon

FOR THE BACON BRAN MUFFINS

3 slices thick-cut bacon, cut into
¼- to ½-inch pieces

¾ cup unbleached all-purpose flour

¼ cup whole-wheat flour

1 teaspoon baking soda

½ teaspoon ground cinnamon

¼ teaspoon salt

1 cup Kellogg's All-Bran cereal

2 large eggs

⅓ cup packed light or dark brown sugar

1 tablespoon molasses

3 tablespoons canola oil

1 cup plain whole-milk yogurt

1¼ teaspoons pure vanilla extract

½ cup golden raisins

1 Prepare the bacon crumble topping: Cook the 2 slices of bacon in a medium-size skillet over medium heat until lightly browned and most of the fat is rendered, 5 to 8 minutes, stirring often and adjusting the heat as necessary. Using a slotted spoon, transfer the bacon to a paper towel-lined plate to drain, reserving 1 tablespoon of bacon fat in the skillet. If necessary, add enough butter to the skillet to measure 1 tablespoon.

2 Combine the 6 tablespoons of flour, the granulated sugar, 2 tablespoons of brown sugar, and ¼ teaspoon of cinnamon in a small bowl. Add 2 tablespoons of butter to the skillet with the bacon fat and heat over medium heat until the butter melts, about 30 seconds. Drizzle the butter and bacon fat mixture over the sugar and flour mixture in the bowl, taking

care to include any browned bacon bits from the bottom of the skillet. Add the drained bacon and toss with a fork until evenly moistened. Set the bacon crumble topping aside.

3 Prepare the bacon bran muffins: Position a rack in the center of the oven and preheat the oven to 400°F.

4 Cook the 3 slices of bacon pieces in a medium-size skillet over medium heat until lightly browned and most of the fat is rendered, 5 to 8 minutes, stirring often and adjusting the heat as necessary. Using a slotted spoon, transfer the bacon to a paper towel-lined plate to drain, reserving the bacon fat in the skillet. Using a pastry brush, grease 9 muffin tin cups (a nonstick muffin tin works best) with the bacon fat from the skillet.

5 Combine the ¾ cup of all-purpose flour and the whole-wheat flour, baking soda, ½ teaspoon of cinnamon, and the salt in a medium-size mixing bowl.

6 Add ½ cup of the bran cereal to the bowl of a mini food processor and pulse until finely ground. Set the ground bran cereal aside. Place the eggs in a second medium-size mixing bowl and whisk until lightly colored, then whisk in the ⅓ cup of brown sugar and the molasses. Add the oil, yogurt, and vanilla and whisk well to combine. Stir in the remaining ½ cup of bran cereal and the ground bran cereal, raisins, and drained bacon and let the bran mixture sit for about 5 minutes.

7 Add the flour mixture to the bran mixture and mix with a rubber spatula until the batter is combined and evenly moistened. The batter will be a little stiff; do not overmix it. Using a ⅓ cup measure, divide the batter evenly among the 9 greased muffin cups. Top each muffin with about 2 tablespoons of the bacon crumble topping.

8 Bake the muffins until a cake tester or toothpick inserted into the center of one comes out clean, 16 to 18 minutes. Let the muffins cool in the muffin tin for about 5 minutes, then transfer the muffins to a wire rack and let cool for about 5 minutes longer before serving. The bran muffins can be stored in an airtight container for 3 to 4 days.

NOTE: You can use either light or dark brown sugar in the muffins, whatever you have on hand. But because dark brown sugar has more molasses it is better for the bacon crumble topping.

CHEDDAR CHEESE AND BACON BISCUITS

Makes 8 biscuits

About twenty years ago, when the famed Union Square Greenmarket was just getting started, a new restaurant opened with the unspecial name of Coffee Shop. The waitstaff all looked like supermodels. The food was mostly Brazilian fare. One of the most popular breakfasts was fresh-squeezed orange juice, espresso with steamed milk, and cheese biscuits. Throw in some high-decibel samba music for a sound track and it was a great way to kick-start the day. We hadn't thought of adding bacon to everything back then, but when putting together the recipes for this book, we were talking about Coffee Shop and figured, "Why not?" Serve the biscuits with a green salad and call it lunch or dinner.

4 slices thick-cut bacon, cut into ¼-inch pieces

2½ cups unbleached all-purpose flour, plus flour for dusting your hands

2¼ teaspoons baking powder

½ teaspoon baking soda

¾ teaspoon salt

8 tablespoons (1 stick) chilled unsalted butter, cut into ½-inch-thick pieces, plus about ⅓ cup melted unsalted butter, for brushing the biscuits

1 cup packed coarsely grated sharp cheddar cheese

2 teaspoons chopped fresh tarragon

Freshly ground black pepper

1 cup well-shaken buttermilk, chilled

1 Line a large heavy baking sheet with parchment paper.

2 Cook the bacon in a medium-size skillet over medium heat until browned and the fat is rendered, 6 to 9 minutes, stirring often and adjusting the heat as necessary. Using a slotted spoon, transfer the bacon to a paper towel-lined plate to drain, reserving 1 tablespoon of the bacon fat in the skillet.

3 Combine the flour, baking powder, baking soda, and salt in a large bowl. Add the chilled butter and, using a pastry blender or 2 knives, cut the butter into the flour until the mixture is the size of peas. (Or, combine ingredients in food processor bowl and process until the mixture is coarsely blended to about the size of peas. If you use a food processor, after processing the flour and butter mixture transfer it to a large bowl.)

4 Add the cheddar cheese, tarragon, drained bacon, and the 1 tablespoon of bacon fat reserved in the skillet to the flour and butter mixture and stir to mix well. Season with 2 to 3 generous grinds of pepper or to taste. Gradually add the buttermilk, stirring to moisten the ingredients evenly (the batter will be a little sticky).

5 Scoop out a generous ½ cup of batter for each biscuit and, using lightly floured hands, drop them onto the prepared baking sheet, spacing the mounds about 2 inches apart (you will have 8 large biscuits). Place the biscuits on the baking sheet in the freezer for about 30 minutes (see Note).

6 Position a rack in the center of the oven and preheat the oven to 425°F.

7 Bake the chilled biscuits until they are golden and a cake tester or toothpick inserted in the center of one comes out clean, 18 to 22 minutes. Remove the biscuits from the oven, brush them lightly with the melted butter, and let them cool on the baking sheet for about 5 minutes. Serve the biscuits warm or at room temperature; the biscuits are best eaten when freshly baked.

NOTE: You can make the dough ahead of time and freeze the unbaked biscuits on a baking sheet in a single layer. Then, transfer the frozen biscuits to a resealable plastic bag and store them in the freezer for up to 1 month. When ready to serve, bake the biscuits as directed in Steps 6 and 7.

BACON AND ROSEMARY SHORTBREAD

Makes sixteen 2-inch squares

This is a very simple tweak to a standard shortbread recipe, and the result is a powerful flavor transformation. If you ever want to demonstrate the magic of ingredients to your friends, try this shortbread side by side with a traditional shortbread (that is to say, follow the recipe but leave out the bacon and rosemary).

4 to 5 slices applewood- or hickory-smoked bacon, cut into ½-inch pieces (see Note)

1½ cups unbleached all-purpose flour

½ cup stone-ground yellow cornmeal

⅓ cup granulated sugar

⅓ cup packed dark brown sugar

1 tablespoon finely chopped fresh rosemary leaves

Scant ½ teaspoon coarse salt

1 cup (2 sticks) cold unsalted butter, cut into ¼-inch-thick pieces

2 teaspoons dark or full-flavored honey

1 Cook the bacon in a medium skillet over medium heat until lightly browned and most of the fat is rendered, 5 to 8 minutes, stirring often and adjusting the heat as necessary. Using a slotted spoon, transfer the bacon to a paper towel-lined plate to drain, reserving 1 tablespoon of the bacon fat in the bowl of a food processor.

2 Position a rack in the center of the oven and preheat the oven to 325°F.

3 Add the drained bacon and the flour, cornmeal, granulated sugar, brown sugar, rosemary, and salt to the food processor and pulse to combine, 6 to 8 seconds. Add the butter and honey and pulse to make a mixture of crumbs, 8 to 10 seconds. Then pulse again until some of the crumbs start to come together, about 5 seconds longer. Don't overprocess the dough; it should be somewhat crumbly, not smooth.

4 Press the dough into an ungreased 8-inch-square baking pan. Pierce it all over with the tines of a fork and bake until golden brown, 45 to 50 minutes. Transfer the baking pan to a wire rack to cool for about 15 minutes, then cut the shortbread into sixteen 2-inch squares. Serve the shortbread warm or at room temperature. The shortbread is best served the day it's made but it will keep in an airtight container for up to 5 days or can be frozen in an airtight container for a couple months.

NOTE: The thickness of bacon slices can vary from one manufacturer to the next. When you open a package of bacon, take a look at the individual slices to gauge their thickness and alter the amount you use, increasing or decreasing the number of slices called for by a slice or two, as you think necessary.

HERBED BACON FLATBREAD

Makes three 9- to 10-inch-round flatbreads

Rosemary is one of the most meat-friendly herbs. When the oil within each little leaf comes into contact with heat—say, from hot meat—it is released into the air, or in this case into the flatbread dough, with an appetizing perfume that says, "Good food here." While rosemary works admirably with steaks, veal chops, and leg of lamb, you'll find when it joins with the intense flavor of bacon the alchemy rises to a new level. Serve the flatbread as an appetizer with a vegetable dip or a platter of assorted cheeses.

4 slices bacon cut into ¼- to ½-inch
pieces

1¾ cups unbleached all-purpose flour,
plus flour for rolling out the flatbread

1 teaspoon baking powder

¾ teaspoon salt

1 tablespoon chopped fresh rosemary
leaves

⅓ cup olive oil, plus olive oil for brushing
on the dough

1 Place a heavy baking sheet on an oven rack positioned in the center of the oven and preheat the oven to 450°F.

2 Cook the bacon in a medium-size skillet over medium heat until lightly browned and most of the fat is rendered, 5 to 8 minutes, stirring often and adjusting the heat as necessary. Using a slotted spoon, transfer the bacon to a paper towel-lined plate to drain.

3 Place the flour, baking powder, salt, rosemary, and drained bacon in large mixing bowl and stir to mix. Make a well in the center of the flour mixture, add the olive oil and ½ cup of water, and stir with a wooden spoon until a dough forms. Knead the dough gently 4 to 5 times in the bowl or on a work surface.

4 Divide the dough into 3 pieces, shaping each piece into a ball. Place 1 piece of dough on a piece of parchment paper about 12 inches square. Using a lightly floured rolling pin, roll out the dough into a 9- to 10-inch round about ¼ inch thick (it doesn't need to be a perfect round). Keep the remaining pieces of dough covered with plastic wrap as you work to prevent them from drying out.

5 Brush the rolled-out round of dough lightly with olive oil. Slide the round, still on the piece of parchment paper, onto the preheated baking sheet in the oven. Bake the flatbread until it is mostly golden and lightly browned in some spots, 8 to 10 minutes. Transfer the flatbread to a wire rack to cool, discarding the piece of parchment paper. Repeat with the remaining pieces of dough, working with one at a time and using a fresh piece of parchment paper for each round of dough.

6 After the flatbread has cooled, it will be crackerlike in texture. Break the rounds into pieces for serving or storing. The flatbread can be stored in an airtight container at room temperature for several days. After a day or two, the rosemary and bacon flavors will become richer.

BACON AND CRANBERRY CORN BREAD

Makes 2 loaves

For some Southern cooks, corn bread is the staff of life and a heavenly gift. Those in the know say cooking authentic corn bread requires the use of stone-ground yellow cornmeal because it is rough-textured, with the flavorful hull and germ intact. Some recipes call for sugar, others rail against it. Some corn bread cognoscenti swear that buttermilk is essential to the texture of the final bread, others recommend 100 percent whole milk. Most recipes agree that a little bacon fat added to the batter is a given. We've taken a few liberties of our own with our down-home quick bread.

Sweet, savory, and floral, this variation on a classic adds depth and complexity of flavor to the straight-ahead simplicity of corn bread. It is the perfect complement to a simple green salad and more than holds its own as a full-tasting foil for pork chops, fried chicken, or fish. Toast a couple of slices, spread on some butter and jam, and you've got breakfast. It's a simple food with endless possibilities; we all can agree that a steaming pan of corn bread fresh from the oven and a pot of Slow-Cooker Pulled Bacon and Bourbon Beans (page 198) is a king's dinner.

3 tablespoons unsalted butter, melted and cooled to room temperature, plus butter for greasing the loaf pans

1 cup unbleached all-purpose flour, plus flour for dusting the loaf pans

4 slices bacon, diced

1 cup stone-ground yellow cornmeal

¼ cup sugar

1½ teaspoons baking powder

¾ teaspoon baking soda

¼ teaspoon salt

1½ cups well-shaken buttermilk

2 large eggs

½ cup dried cranberries, coarsely chopped

4 teaspoons fennel seeds, coarsely crushed in a mortar using a pestle or pulsed in an electric spice grinder or mini food processor

1 Position a rack in the center of the oven and preheat the oven to 375°F. Butter two 8- by 4- by 3-inch metal loaf pans and dust them with flour, knocking out the excess.

2 Cook the bacon in a medium-size skillet over medium heat until lightly browned and most of the fat is rendered, 5 to 8 minutes, stirring often and adjusting the heat as necessary.

Using a slotted spoon, transfer the bacon to a paper towel-lined plate to drain, reserving the bacon fat in the skillet.

3 Place the flour, cornmeal, sugar, baking powder, baking soda, and salt in a large mixing bowl and stir to mix. Place the buttermilk, eggs, butter, and the bacon fat from the skillet in a medium-size mixing bowl and whisk to mix. Make a well in the center of the dry ingredients. Pour the buttermilk mixture into the well and, using a rubber spatula, fold the dry ingredients into the buttermilk mixture until just moistened. Stir in the cranberries, crushed fennel seeds, and drained bacon.

4 Divide the batter evenly between the 2 prepared loaf pans and let stand for 10 minutes. Bake the corn bread until the tops of the loaves are pale and a cake tester or toothpick comes out clean when inserted into the center of each loaf, 30 to 35 minutes. Transfer the loaves to wire racks and let them cool in the pans for about 10 minutes. Then, invert the loaves onto wire racks so that they are right side up and let them cool completely, about 20 minutes, before serving. The corn bread can be stored in an airtight container for 4 to 5 days.

VARIATION:

Make corn bread muffins: Butter and flour 12 muffin tin cups and divide the cranberry corn bread batter evenly among them. Bake the muffins in a 375°F oven until a cake tester or toothpick comes out clean, 20 to 25 minutes.

OYSTER AND CORN BREAD
STUFFING with Bacon

Serves 10 to 12 (see Note)

Everyone loves stuffing yet too few people make their own from scratch. However, many of the preseasoned bread cube and stuffing mixes, while powerful in taste, also share the unmistakable flavor of freeze-dried, chemically enhanced food. When sampled side by side with a stuffing that starts with whole ingredients, homemade wins every time. In our oyster and corn bread stuffing, you can easily pick out the textures and flavors of bacon, tarragon, oysters, and corn bread: ingredients that make for a smooth, extremely satisfying mouthful. Not one of these strongly flavored ingredients overpowers the others, so this stuffing works well served alongside chicken, turkey, pork, or even as a side dish for a fish like sea bass.

All corn bread is naturally crumbly, so to help it retain some shape and structure, we cool the freshly baked bread in the pan, then cut it into bite-size pieces, and dry it in a warm oven before mixing it with the other stuffing ingredients. Lest you think we are totally anticonvenience, our advice is to buy your oysters shucked. Trying to do it yourself is messy and, in many cases, leads to nicks and nasty cuts. If you insist, though, and you have a suit of medieval armor lying around, we advise using one of the steel gloves to hold the oysters as you shuck them.

12 cups ½- to 1-inch cubes Corn Bread with Bacon Drippings (recipe follows)

1½ cups oysters, drained, ½ cup of the oyster liquor set aside

2 cups homemade turkey giblet stock or store-bought low-sodium chicken stock, or more as necessary

2 large eggs

8 slices bacon, cut into ¼- to ½-inch dice, plus 4 slices cooked bacon, reserved from the Corn Bread with Bacon Drippings

About 8 tablespoons (1 stick) unsalted butter, plus butter for greasing the baking dishes

2½ cups diced fennel

2 cups finely chopped shallots (4 to 5 large shallots)

¾ cup chopped fresh flat-leaf parsley

2 tablespoons chopped fresh tarragon leaves

3 medium-size garlic cloves, minced

Salt and freshly ground black pepper

1 Place racks in the upper-middle and lower-middle positions in the oven and preheat the oven to 250°F.

2 Spread out the cubes of corn bread and any crumbs in a single layer on 2 rimmed baking sheets. Bake the corn bread cubes until dried but not browned, 40 to 45 minutes, switching the positions of the baking sheets on the oven racks after about 20 minutes. Let the cubes of corn bread cool on the baking sheets for about 10 minutes then place them in a very large bowl.

3 Chop the oysters into 1-inch pieces and set them aside. Pour the reserved ½ cup of oyster liquor into a medium-size mixing bowl (see Note). Add the stock and eggs to the bowl and whisk to combine. Pour the stock mixture over the cooled corn bread cubes and toss very gently and thoroughly to coat (as much as possible, avoid breaking the corn bread into smaller pieces). Set the corn bread mixture aside.

4 Cook the diced bacon in a large skillet over medium heat until lightly browned and most of the fat is rendered, 7 to 9 minutes, stirring often and adjusting the heat as necessary. Using a slotted spoon, transfer the bacon to a paper towel-lined plate to drain, reserving the bacon fat in the skillet. When cool, transfer the bacon to a small bowl. Add the cooked bacon pieces reserved from the Corn Bread with Bacon Drippings to the bowl, as well.

5 Place the skillet over medium-high heat. Set aside 2 tablespoons of butter for dotting the stuffing, then add enough butter to the bacon drippings to measure $1/2$ cup of fat. When the fats start to shimmer, add the fennel and shallots and cook, stirring occasionally, until the vegetables are softened, 5 to 8 minutes. Add the parsley, tarragon, and garlic and cook, stirring, until the garlic is fragrant, about 2 minutes.

6 Add the fennel mixture, the oysters, and the bacon to the corn bread mixture in the large bowl. Stir gently to combine (again, try to avoid breaking the corn bread into small pieces). Season the stuffing with salt and pepper to taste, salting it lightly if at all, as the oysters and bacon add salt. When you squeeze a small portion of the stuffing in your hand, the stuffing should hold together. If necessary, add more stock to moisten it sufficiently.

7 Position a rack in the center of the oven and preheat the oven to 375°F. Generously butter 2 large (2½- to 3-quart) deep baking dishes.

8 Transfer the stuffing mixture to the prepared baking dishes, dividing it evenly between them. Dot each casserole with 1 tablespoon of the reserved butter cut into small pieces. Cover the baking dishes with aluminum foil and bake the stuffing for 25 to 30 minutes. Remove the foil and continue baking the stuffing until the tops are golden brown and crusty and the centers are warmed through, 15 to 20 minutes longer.

NOTE: To make the stuffing in advance, assemble the mixture without the oysters and the oyster liquor; it can be refrigerated for up to 1 day. Let the stuffing sit at room temperature for about 20 minutes to return to room temperature. When ready to bake, carefully mix the oysters and the ½ cup of oyster liquor into the stuffing, then bake as directed.

CORN BREAD WITH BACON DRIPPINGS

Makes 1 loaf of corn bread

This corn bread has a firm top and a rich, moist texture from the combination of butter and bacon fat. And don't think you need to save it for stuffing. It's delicious to eat on its own.

4 slices thick-cut bacon, cut into ½-inch pieces

Unsalted butter for greasing the baking pan

3 large eggs

1 cup well-shaken buttermilk

1 cup milk

1½ teaspoons your choice of hot sauce

1½ cups stone-ground yellow cornmeal

1½ cups unbleached all-purpose flour

1 tablespoon baking powder

¾ teaspoon baking soda

1 tablespoon sugar

½ teaspoon salt

1 Cook the bacon in a large skillet over medium heat until browned and crisp and the fat is mostly rendered, 6 to 8 minutes, stirring often and adjusting the heat as necessary. Using a slotted spoon, transfer the bacon to a paper towel-lined plate, reserving 3 tablespoons of bacon fat in the skillet. If necessary, add enough butter to the skillet to measure 3 tablespoons. When cooled, wrap and refrigerate the cooked bacon to add to the Oyster and Corn Bread Stuffing with Bacon.

2 Position a rack in the center of the oven and preheat the oven to 375°F. Butter a 13- by 9-inch baking pan.

3 Beat the eggs in a medium-size mixing bowl. Whisk in the buttermilk, milk, and hot sauce.

4 Place the cornmeal, flour, baking powder, baking soda, sugar, and salt in a large mixing bowl and whisk to mix. Make a well in the center of the dry ingredients. Pour the egg and milk mixture into the well. Add the 3 tablespoons of reserved fat and whisk until just combined.

5 Pour the batter into the prepared baking pan, spreading it evenly and into all of the corners. Bake the corn bread until the top is golden brown and a cake tester or toothpick inserted into the center of the bread comes out clean, 25 to 30 minutes. Set the baking pan on a wire rack and let the corn bread cool for at least 1 hour before serving or slicing it into $1/2$- to 1-inch cubes for the Oyster and Corn Bread Stuffing with Bacon.

BACON, SWEET POTATO, AND GREENS STUFFING
with Jalapeño Corn Bread

Serves 8 to 10

We were inspired by the combination of greens, sweet potatoes, and bacon that go so well alongside many traditional Southern meals. So, we thought, why not put them all together in a stuffing and why not bind it with a zingy jalapeño corn bread? The result was so good we felt like having it for lunch—which is exactly what we did . . . for three days running.

Jalapeño Corn Bread (recipe follows)

5 slices thick-cut bacon, cut into ½-inch pieces

2 tablespoons (¼ stick) unsalted butter, cut into small pieces, plus more as necessary

2 medium-size onions, chopped (about 2 cups)

3 tablespoons chopped fresh flat-leaf parsley

2 tablespoons fresh thyme leaves

1¼ pounds sweet potatoes, peeled and cut into ½-inch cubes

2 large cloves garlic, chopped

10 ounces kale, tough stems and ribs removed and discarded, leaves coarsely chopped and rinsed but not patted dry

10 ounces red Swiss chard, tough stems and ribs removed and discarded, leaves coarsely chopped and rinsed but not patted dry

2 tablespoons apple cider vinegar

2 tablespoons plus 1½ teaspoons packed light brown sugar

½ teaspoon coarse sea salt

¼ teaspoon ground ginger

¼ teaspoon dry mustard

Freshly ground black pepper

1½ cups lightly toasted pecans (see page 264), coarsely chopped

2 large eggs, beaten

¾ to 1¼ cups homemade giblet turkey stock or store-bought low-sodium chicken stock

1 Position a rack in the center of the oven and preheat the oven to 300°F.

2 Cut the corn bread into 2-inch chunks and place the chunks in a single layer on a large rimmed baking sheet. Bake the corn bread chunks until lightly toasted, about 35 minutes, turning the chunks once after about 15 minutes. Let the corn bread chunks cool on the baking sheet until cool enough to handle, 5 to 10 minutes. Crumble as much of the corn bread as needed to make 5 cups coarsely crumbled bread and set it aside (save any remaining corn bread chunks for a snack or breakfast treat).

3 Increase the oven temperature to 350°F.

4 Place the bacon in a large deep pot and cook over medium heat until lightly browned and most of the fat is rendered, 6 to 9 minutes, stirring often and adjusting the heat as necessary. Using a slotted spoon, transfer the bacon to a paper towel-lined plate to drain, reserving the bacon fat in the pot. If necessary, add enough butter to the skillet to measure at least 3 tablespoons of fat.

5 Add the onions, parsley, and thyme to the pot and stir to coat with the bacon fat. Cook over medium heat, stirring occasionally, until the onions start to soften, 2 to 3 minutes. Add the sweet potatoes and cook until the potatoes are just tender but still firm, 5 to 6 minutes. Stir in the garlic and add the kale and Swiss chard, including the water still clinging to the leaves after rinsing. Cover the pot, reduce the heat to medium-low, and cook until the greens are just wilted, about 5 minutes, using metal tongs to turn the greens over in the onion and sweet potato mixture once or twice. Remove the pot from the heat.

6 Place the cider vinegar, brown sugar, salt, ginger, and mustard in a small bowl and whisk

until blended. Season the dressing with pepper to taste.

7 Drizzle the dressing over the mixture of sweet potatoes and greens. Add the drained bacon and the pecans and stir to combine. Stir in the crumbled corn bread. Beat the eggs with ¾ cup of the stock and pour over the stuffing mixture, stirring to combine. The stuffing should be moist and hold together easily when pressed gently in the palm of your hand. If it seems dry, add more stock, as necessary, to moisten it sufficiently. (Stuffings baked outside of a turkey, like this one, don't benefit from the turkey's roasting juices, so moisten the stuffing well.)

8 Generously butter a deep 3-quart baking dish. Spoon the stuffing into the buttered dish and dot it with the 2 tablespoons of butter. Cover the baking dish with aluminum foil and bake the stuffing until heated through, 30 to 40 minutes. Remove the foil and continue baking the stuffing until the top is slightly crisp, about 10 minutes longer.

JALAPENO CORN BREAD

Makes 1 loaf of corn bread

We love corn bread rather than white bread as a base for stuffing and made this corn bread for the Bacon, Sweet Potato, and Greens Stuffing a little sweeter and a little richer than the corn bread for the Oyster and Corn Bread Stuffing with Bacon on page 240. With some more sugar, it nicely complements the natural sugars in the sweet potatoes. Along with the sweet-savory dressing of brown sugar and cider vinegar, the corn bread offsets the slight bitterness of the hearty greens. Don't think you need to save this corn bread recipe only for making the stuffing. Like the corn bread for the oyster stuffing, it's a standout all on its own.

8 tablespoons (1 stick) unsalted butter, melted and slightly cooled, plus butter for greasing the baking pan

1½ cups stone-ground yellow cornmeal

1 cup unbleached all-purpose flour

¼ cup sugar

2 teaspoons baking powder

¼ teaspoon baking soda

¼ teaspoon salt

1 medium-size jalapeño pepper, seeded and minced

1 cup well-shaken buttermilk

2 large eggs

1 Position a rack in the center of the oven and preheat the oven to 400°F. Generously butter a 9-inch-square baking pan.

2 Place the cornmeal, flour, sugar, baking powder, baking soda, salt, and jalapeño pepper in a medium-size mixing bowl and stir to combine. Set the cornmeal mixture aside. Place the buttermilk and eggs in another medium-size mixing bowl and whisk until well combined.

3 Make a well in the center of the dry ingredients. Pour the buttermilk mixture into the well and, using a rubber spatula, fold the dry ingredients into the wet, using only a few turns to combine. Add the melted butter and mix just until the dry ingredients are moistened.

4 Pour the corn bread batter into the prepared baking pan and bake until a cake tester or toothpick inserted into the center comes out clean, 25 to 30 minutes.

5 Let the corn bread cool in the baking pan on a wire rack. The corn bread will keep in the baking pan, covered with aluminum foil, at room temperature, for 2 to 3 days.

CHAPTER 11

BREAKFAST
MEANS BACON

French Toast Bread Pudding
with Bacon and Cinnamon,
page 262

IN THIS CHAPTER...

Ask someone about memories of

childhood breakfast and you can almost smell the aroma of bacon wafting over them. For most of us, this is where bacon memories begin: waking up on Sunday morning to the heavenly scent of bacon that found its way into your room, even with the door closed! All moms know a whiff of cooking bacon is a surefire kiddie alarm clock. It wakes you from a dead sleep and, like a magnet, draws you to the kitchen table.

The foundation for each of our breakfast/brunch recipes is the winning combination of bacon and eggs, but with lots of twists and turns. Our Nuevos Huevos Rancheros are eggs gently poached in a mixture of black beans, bacon, and salsa. We add bacon to the traditional pairing of eggs and spinach in Spinach and Bacon Soufflé or Baked Eggs with Spinach, Bacon, and Salsa. The benefits of bacon grace a classic Spanish *tortilla* and a Sicilian asparagus frittata.

We're hoping that for you, as it has for us, French Toast Bread Pudding with Bacon and Cinnamon becomes one of your Sunday morning family faves. And Candied Bacon Slices, caramelized with a brown sugar and spice coating, are like eating bacon candy—the perfect side for pancakes, French toast, or scrambled eggs.

NUEVOS HUEVOS RANCHEROS

Serves 4

From the American Southwest down to the highlands of Chiapas, Mexico, huevos rancheros are as common a breakfast item as waffles or bacon and eggs are in the United States. Ours adds bacon to the traditional ingredients and, rather than frying the eggs, we poach them in the hot, bacony, bean, and salsa mixture. For a fancier serving idea, divide the salsa among four half cup lightly greased ramekins, add an egg to each, sprinkle on the salt, pepper, and remaining bacon, and bake on a baking sheet in a 400°F oven for about 20 minutes. Garnish with cilantro and serve.

6 slices thick-cut bacon, coarsely chopped

1 can (about 15 ounces) black beans, rinsed and drained

½ teaspoon ground cumin

Roasted Tomato and Pepper Salsa (recipe follows), or 1½ cups store-bought salsa

4 large eggs

Salt and freshly ground pepper

1 to 2 tablespoons chopped fresh cilantro leaves, for garnish

4 small flour or corn tortillas, warmed

1 Cook the bacon in a large skillet over medium heat until lightly browned and most of the fat is rendered, 6 to 9 minutes, stirring often and adjusting the heat as necessary. Using a slotted spoon, transfer the bacon to a paper towel-lined plate to drain. Remove and discard all but 4½ teaspoons of bacon fat from the skillet.

2 Reheat the bacon fat in the skillet over medium heat until it shimmers, about 1 minute, then add the black beans, cumin, and two thirds of the cooked bacon. Cook until the mixture is heated through, 3 to 4 minutes, stirring occasionally and scraping up any brown bits from the bottom of the skillet. Add the salsa and let the mixture come to a simmer.

3 Using the back of a spoon, make 4 wells in the salsa, each about 2 inches across. Crack an egg into a small bowl and slide it gently into one of the wells without breaking the yolk (don't be concerned if some of the egg white runs out of the well). Repeat with the remaining eggs. Season the eggs with salt and pepper to taste. Sprinkle the remaining bacon around the eggs. Cover the skillet and cook over medium heat, 4 to 6 minutes for slightly runny yolks, or as desired. Sprinkle cilantro over the huevos rancheros, divide it among 4 small bowls, and serve with warm tortillas.

ROASTED TOMATO AND PEPPER SALSA

Makes about 1½ cups

Salsa is most often a fresh uncooked mix of vegetables. For this one, however, we wanted to concentrate and intensify the flavor; slow roasting and caramelization does just that. The salsa is good with white-fleshed fish, chicken breasts, and grilled meats.

1¼ pounds ripe plum tomatoes (about 5 large), cored and cut in half lengthwise

2 serrano peppers, or 3 jalapeño peppers, cut in half lengthwise, stems, seeds, and ribs removed (see Note)

1 medium-size onion, cut into wedges

3 medium-size cloves garlic, peeled

2 tablespoons extra-virgin olive oil

2 to 3 tablespoons minced fresh cilantro leaves

2 teaspoons fresh lime juice (from about half a lime)

Salt and freshly ground black pepper

Your choice of hot sauce

1 Preheat the oven to 375°F.

2 Place the tomatoes, serrano or jalapeño peppers, onion, and garlic on a large rimmed baking sheet. Drizzle the olive oil over the vegetables and toss to coat them with the oil. Turn the tomatoes and peppers cut side down on the baking sheet.

3 Bake the tomato mixture for 15 minutes, then rotate the baking sheet 180 degrees so the back of the baking sheet faces the front of the oven. Continue baking until the tomatoes are tender and their skins start to brown and shrivel, 20 to 25 minutes longer. Let the tomato mixture cool on the baking sheet for about 10 minutes.

4 Transfer the tomatoes to a small bowl. Using a spatula, scrape the peppers, onion, garlic, and any juices in the baking sheet into a food processor. Process until smooth, about 10 seconds, stopping to scrape down the side of the processor bowl. Add the tomatoes and their juices and pulse until the salsa is slightly chunky, 4 to 5 pulses. Transfer the salsa to a bowl and stir in the cilantro and lime juice. Season the salsa with salt, black pepper, and hot sauce to taste.

NOTE: Serrano peppers are hotter than jalapeño peppers. Make your choice depending on how much heat you want in the salsa. Or, use a combination of the two.

BAKED EGGS
with Spinach, Bacon, and Salsa

Serves 4

S ome recipes cry out for a particular kind of bacon. We first tried this with streaky supermarket bacon, but it was really blah. Then we made it with Benton's country bacon. We knew we were on to something good as we nibbled our way through half the bacon before we even began to make the recipe. The tantalizing smokiness as it sizzled in the skillet awoke memories of great cuts of meat on the charcoal grill. With this, as with many recipes in this book, experiment with different bacons until you find the one you like best. Picking the right bacon is like wine pairing, though nowhere near as complicated.

In the summertime, when tomatoes are at their flavorful best, take the time to make the Roasted Tomato and Pepper Salsa on the facing page. As for the rest of the year, a really good store-bought salsa is the way to go.

6 slices thick-cut bacon, cut crosswise into ½-inch-wide pieces

5 to 6 packed cups (5 to 6 ounces) spinach, rinsed, tough stems removed and discarded

1 cup Roasted Tomato and Pepper Salsa (see facing page), or your favorite store-bought salsa

4 large eggs

Salt and freshly ground black pepper

4 whole-wheat English muffins, or 4 slices multigrain bread

Butter, for the toasted muffins or bread

1 Position a rack in the center of the oven and preheat the oven to 400°F.

2 Cook the bacon in a large skillet over medium heat until browned and most of the fat is rendered, 6 to 9 minutes, stirring often and adjusting the heat as necessary. Using a slotted spoon, transfer the bacon to a paper towel-lined plate to drain. Pour all but 1 tablespoon of the bacon fat into a small bowl, then set aside the skillet with the 1 tablespoon of fat.

3 Chop the spinach coarsely. (If you use baby spinach, don't bother with this step.) Place the skillet over medium heat and heat the 1 tablespoon of bacon fat. Add the spinach to the skillet and cook it for a few

seconds, using tongs to turn the spinach over in the fat, until the spinach is just wilted.

4 Place four ½ cup ramekins on a rimmed baking sheet. Using a pastry brush, brush the inside of each ramekin lightly with the reserved bacon fat.

5 Layer the drained bacon and then the wilted spinach in the ramekins, dividing them evenly among the ramekins. Add ¼ cup of salsa to each ramekin. Using the back of a spoon, make an indentation in the center of the salsa in each ramekin. Gently crack 1 egg, without breaking the yolk, into the indentation in each ramekin. Season the eggs with salt and pepper to taste.

6 Bake eggs until the whites are just set and the yolks are still runny, 18 to 20 minutes. Remove the ramekins from the oven and let them sit on the baking sheet for 1 to 2 minutes; the eggs will continue to cook. As the eggs set, toast and butter the whole-wheat English muffins or multigrain bread and then serve them with the baked eggs.

SPINACH AND BACON SOUFFLE

Serves 4

Although we are firm believers that almost everything is better with bacon—hence this book—few vegetables are better paired with bacon than spinach. As everyone who has stopped by a salad bar knows, bacon and spinach is a favorite combo. The same goes for cooked spinach and bacon: The slight bitterness of spinach is a great counterpoint to the deep powerful taste of bacon. Even better, cooked baby spinach has an ethereal creaminess that blends in so well with the light custardy texture and melty, slightly tart taste of the Gruyère in this soufflé. Parmesan also works well, so if you want, substitute an aged Parmesan cheese for about one third of the Gruyère.

5 slices bacon, cut into ¼-inch pieces

Extra-virgin olive oil, if necessary

1 large onion, chopped

1 medium-size clove garlic, minced

1 package (9 ounces) baby spinach, rinsed and well drained

½ teaspoon ground nutmeg

Salt and freshly ground black pepper

6 large eggs, separated

1½ cups (6 ounces) grated Gruyère cheese

2 to 3 drops of your choice of hot sauce

1 Cook the bacon in a large skillet over medium heat until lightly browned and most of the fat is rendered, 5 to 8 minutes, stirring often and adjusting the heat as necessary. Using a slotted spoon, transfer the bacon to a paper towel-lined plate to drain, reserving the bacon fat in the skillet.

2 Using a pastry brush, brush the inside of the ramekins or the soufflé dish with some of the bacon fat that has been reserved in the skillet. Set the ramekins or soufflé dish aside.

3 Position a rack in the center of the oven and preheat the oven to 325°F (see Note).

4 If necessary, add enough olive oil to the remaining bacon fat in the skillet to make 2 tablespoons of fat. Place the skillet over medium heat, and when the fat is hot and shimmers, after about 1 minute, add the onion and cook until the onion is softened, about 5 minutes, stirring occasionally. Add the garlic and cook until fragrant, about 1 minute. Add the spinach, reduce the heat to low, cover the skillet, and cook until the spinach is wilted, 2 to 3 minutes. Remove the skillet from the heat. Add the nutmeg and season the spinach mixture with salt and pepper to taste (or don't salt it at all as the bacon will add salt). Stir to combine. Set the spinach mixture aside to cool.

5 Place the egg yolks in a large bowl and beat until well blended. Add the Gruyère cheese, a pinch of salt, a couple of grindings of black pepper, and the hot sauce and stir well to combine. Add the spinach mixture and stir well. Add the bacon and stir again until well combined.

6 Place the egg whites in a clean, dry bowl (stainless steel is best) and beat them until they just hold a stiff peak. Gently fold about a third of the beaten whites into the yolk and spinach mixture to lighten it. Then, using a rubber spatula, gently fold in the remaining whites. Don't overmix or you will deflate the whites.

7 Pour the soufflé mixture into the greased ramekins or the soufflé dish, dividing it evenly among the ramekins, if using. Bake the soufflé(s) until golden and puffy, about 30 minutes if you are using individual ramekins and about 35 minutes if you are using a soufflé dish. Serve the soufflé(s) immediately.

NOTE: If you are baking the soufflés in individual ramekins, place a large, rimmed baking sheet on the oven rack before preheating the oven. Preheat the oven. Fill the ramekins with the soufflé mixture, then place them on the baking sheet. This will enable you to remove the ramekins from the oven all at once when the soufflés are done.

BACON, GRITS, AND LEEK SOUFFLE

Serves 4 to 5 as a main dish, 6 to 8 as a side dish

Grits and bacon, often served with a calories-be-damned side of biscuits and sausage gravy, is a classic American breakfast. This is our "spa version." It's not exactly as cloudlike as a dessert soufflé—the grits give it a puddinglike body—but it is elegant and delicate in its own way. The soufflé is great for breakfast, naturally, but also as a light lunch. With a roast beef dinner or a Thanksgiving turkey, it's a nice change from your standard Yorkshire pudding or stuffing. Be sure to use a good-quality cheddar, one that's been aged for eight to twelve months. You'll taste the difference.

1 to 2 tablespoons unsalted butter, at room temperature, plus butter for greasing the soufflé dish

2 cups low-sodium chicken stock

½ cup half-and-half or light cream

¾ teaspoon salt

1 cup white grits (old-fashioned or quick cooking, but not instant)

1½ cups (6 ounces) grated sharp aged yellow or white cheddar cheese

1½ teaspoons your choice of hot sauce, or more to taste

Freshly ground black pepper

5 slices bacon, cut in ¼-inch pieces

1 large leek, white part only, well rinsed and thinly sliced (about 1 cup)

2 large cloves garlic, minced

5 large eggs, separated

1 Butter the soufflé dish.

2 Place the chicken stock, half-and-half or light cream, salt, and 1½ cups of water in a large heavy-bottomed saucepan and let come to a boil over medium-high heat. Slowly stir in the grits. Reduce the heat to medium-low and let simmer gently, partially covered, stirring often, until the mixture is smooth, thick, and creamy, 10 to 12 minutes for old-fashioned grits, less time for quick-cooking grits. Stir in the cheddar

cheese and hot sauce and season with pepper to taste. Set the grits mixture aside to cool.

3 Cook the bacon in a large skillet over medium heat until lightly browned and most of the fat is rendered, 5 to 8 minutes, stirring often and adjusting the heat as necessary. Using a slotted spoon, transfer the bacon to a paper towel-lined plate to drain. Pour off and discard all but 2 tablespoons of the bacon fat in the skillet. If necessary, add enough butter

to measure 2 tablespoons. Add the leek to the bacon fat and cook over medium heat, stirring occasionally, until the leek softens, about 4 minutes. Add the garlic and cook until fragrant, about 1 minute, stirring often. Remove the skillet from the heat, stir in the drained bacon and 1 tablespoon of the butter into the leek mixture, and set the skillet aside.

4 Position a rack in the center of the oven and preheat the oven to 375°F.

5 Beat the egg yolks in a small bowl until lemon colored. Stir a heaping tablespoon of grits into the yolks, then stir all of the yolks into the grits. Add the leek mixture and stir well to combine. Set aside.

6 Place the egg whites in a clean dry bowl (stainless steel is best) and beat them until they form stiff peaks. Using a rubber spatula, gently fold about one third of the beaten whites into the grits mixture to lighten it. Then fold in the remaining whites.

7 Transfer the soufflé mixture to the buttered soufflé dish. Bake the soufflé until the mixture is set, the soufflé has risen, and the top is a golden brown, 45 to 50 minutes. If the soufflé browns too quickly as it bakes, cover the top loosely with aluminum foil. Serve the soufflé immediately.

POTATO BACON TORTILLA

Serves 4 as a main dish, 8 as an appetizer

Right up there with a plate of ham, a dish of olives, or Marcona almonds, the egg and potato *tortilla* (a kind of spanish omelet) is probably the most common item in Spanish restaurants that serve tapas (which includes every bar in Spain). The Basque people from the north of Spain and the southwest of France have their own variation; they cube the potatoes instead of slicing them and cook them in olive oil before combining them with the eggs. Adding sweet potatoes to the *tortilla* makes for a honeylike creaminess. We pep our *tortilla* up with jalapeño pepper. It contributes the kind of powerful accent that can stand up to the bacon that we added to the traditional recipe. Since we use bacon drippings to sauté all the vegetables and also to cook the eggs, very little extra oil and no butterfat is required. Serve the *tortilla* either warm or at room temperature.

6 slices thick-cut bacon, coarsely chopped

Extra-virgin olive oil, as necessary

½ pound Yukon Gold or russet potatoes, peeled and cut into ½-inch cubes

½ pound sweet potatoes, peeled and cut into ½-inch cubes

Salt and freshly ground black pepper

1 small onion, chopped

1 tablespoon diced jalapeño pepper (optional)

1 ripe plum tomato, cored and chopped

1 large clove garlic, finely chopped

9 large eggs

1 Cook the bacon in a 12-inch cast-iron or other large ovenproof skillet over medium heat until lightly browned and most of the fat is rendered, 6 to 9 minutes, stirring often and adjusting the heat as necessary. Using a slotted spoon, transfer the bacon to a paper towel-lined plate to drain. Pour all but 2 tablespoons of the bacon fat into a small bowl, leaving the 2 tablespoons of fat in the skillet. If necessary, add enough olive oil to the skillet to measure 2 tablespoons.

2 Add the potatoes and sweet potatoes to the skillet, tossing them in the bacon fat to coat. Season the potatoes lightly with salt and black pepper and then spread them in a single layer in the skillet. Cook the potatoes over medium heat until you can easily pierce them with the tip of a knife, 15 to 20 minutes, turning them over with a metal spatula every 4 to 5 minutes to facilitate browning. Transfer the potatoes to a medium-size bowl.

3 Add 1 tablespoon of the reserved bacon fat to the skillet, using additional olive oil, if necessary, to measure 1 tablespoon. Add the onion and jalapeño, if using, and cook over medium heat until the onion is softened and lightly browned, 4 to 5 minutes. Add the tomato and garlic and cook, stirring occasionally, until the tomato is softened, about 2 minutes. Transfer

the tomato mixture to the bowl with the potatoes and toss gently to mix. If necessary, wipe the skillet clean with a paper towel to remove any brown bits.

4 Position a broiler rack about 6 inches from the broiler and preheat the broiler.

5 Place the eggs in a large bowl and beat them with salt and pepper to taste. Add the potato mixture to the eggs.

6 Add any remaining reserved bacon fat to the skillet, then add as much olive oil as necessary to measure a total of 2 tablespoons of fat. Place the skillet over medium-high heat and heat the fat until it shimmers, less than a minute, then add the egg and potato mixture to the skillet. Scatter the drained bacon evenly over the eggs. Immediately reduce the heat to medium and let the eggs cook without disturbing them for about 3 minutes. Once the bottom of the *tortilla* starts to firm up, use a thin plastic spatula to lift the edge of the *tortilla* closest to you. Tilt the skillet slightly toward you, allowing the uncooked eggs to run underneath the *tortilla* onto the hot skillet. Return the skillet to a level position. Repeat the process 2 to 3 times until the eggs on top are no longer runny. Reduce the heat to low and cook the *tortilla*, covered, until the top is nearly set, 8 to

10 minutes (watch carefully so as not to let the bottom of the *tortilla* burn). When the *tortilla* is ready to place under the broiler the center will appear slightly wet and a little loose.

7 Uncover the skillet, place it under the broiler, and cook the *tortilla* until the top is set, checking it after each minute of cooking. If your broiler is very hot, it should take only 1 to 2 minutes. Watch carefully as the *tortilla* will cook quickly. When done, let the *tortilla* set for a few minutes before cutting it into wedges to serve. Or let the *tortilla* cool completely and serve it at room temperature.

FRITTATA
with Asparagus, Shallots, and Bacon

Serves 3 to 4

talian frittatas are like quiches without the complications and the extra work of a crust. They are first cooked gently on top of the stove in a heavy, ovenproof skillet and then finished in the oven, sometimes using the broiler, to set the top, puff it up, and give it a gorgeous brown color. Once you've mastered the technique, a frittata is something you can throw together with whatever you have on hand in your fridge or pantry. Eggs and bacon (of course) are our only must-have ingredients. Served with a mug of coffee with steamed milk and toasted bread with strawberry jam, a frittata makes for an amazing breakfast. With a salad of delicate greens, such as Bibb lettuce and a shallot vinaigrette, this is a great lunch. A glass of crisp Albariño adds to the pleasure.

15 thin asparagus stalks
(about ½ pound)

4 slices bacon, cut into ¼- to ½-inch
pieces

1 tablespoon extra-virgin olive oil

2 medium-size shallots, diced

6 large eggs

⅓ cup freshly grated Parmesan cheese

1 tablespoon half-and-half or water

¼ teaspoon your choice of hot sauce, or
more to taste

Pinch of kosher salt

Freshly ground black pepper

1 Position a rack in the center of the oven and preheat the oven to 350°F.

2 Snap the woody ends off the asparagus stalks about 2 inches from the bottom and discard them. Cut the trimmed stalks diagonally into 1-inch pieces.

3 Cook the bacon in a 10-inch ovenproof skillet over medium heat until the bacon is lightly browned and most of the fat is rendered, 5 to 8 minutes, stirring often and adjusting the heat as necessary. Using a slotted spoon, transfer the bacon to a paper towel-lined plate to drain, reserving the bacon fat in the skillet.

4 Add the olive oil to the skillet and place the skillet over medium heat. Add the asparagus, cover the skillet, and cook, stirring occasionally, until the asparagus is lightly browned, 2 to 3 minutes. Add the shallots and cook, uncovered, stirring occasionally, until the shallots are softened and the asparagus is tender, about 3 minutes. Remove the skillet from the heat.

5 Place the eggs, 2 tablespoons of the Parmesan cheese, the half-and-half or water, hot sauce, and salt in a medium-size bowl. Season with pepper to taste and whisk to mix.

6 Place the skillet with the asparagus mixture over medium heat and cook until the oil in the skillet is hot, about 1 minute. Pour the egg mixture over the asparagus. Sprinkle the drained bacon over the egg mixture and cook, covered, just until the eggs start to set, about 2 minutes. Once the bottom of the frittata starts to firm up, use a thin plastic spatula to lift up the edge of the frittata closest to you. Tilt the skillet toward you, allowing the uncooked eggs to run underneath the frittata onto the hot skillet. Return the skillet to a level position. Repeat the process as necessary until the edges are set and the top is still slightly runny.

7 Sprinkle the top of the frittata with the remaining Parmesan cheese and bake the frittata until the top is just set, 2 to 5 minutes. (Some cooks like to brown the frittata slightly by placing it under a hot broiler for about 30 seconds before serving.) To serve, loosen the frittata by running a spatula around the edge and bottom; then cut it into wedges. Serve the frittata hot or at room temperature.

FRENCH TOAST BREAD PUDDING
with Bacon and Cinnamon

Serves 6 to 8

The inspiration for this dish comes from the French dessert *coupétade,* which combines two recipes, French toast and bread pudding, in one. It's less custardy than classic bread pudding but more so than French toast. By adding bacon we've turned this classic dessert into a breakfast that is both savory and sweet. Kids adore it. We especially like maple-flavored bacon for this recipe, but any fruitwood-smoked bacon works nicely.

FOR THE BACON AND FRENCH TOAST

4 to 6 tablespoons (½ to ¾ stick) unsalted butter, plus butter for greasing the baking dish

6 slices thick-cut bacon

4 large eggs

6 tablespoons granulated sugar

¾ cup milk

8 slices (each ½ inch thick, about 10 ounces total) stale brioche or challah (see Note)

½ cup chopped pecans or walnuts, lightly toasted (see page 264)

½ cup moist golden raisins or dried cranberries

4 large eggs

1 egg yolk

¼ cup granulated sugar

1 tablespoon pure vanilla extract

1½ cups milk

1½ cups half-and-half

¼ cup pure maple syrup

¾ teaspoon freshly grated nutmeg

Scant ¼ teaspoon salt, or more to taste

⅛ teaspoon freshly ground black pepper

2 packed tablespoons light or dark
   brown sugar

¾ teaspoon ground cinnamon

1 Position a rack in the center of the oven and preheat the oven to 400°F. Butter a 13- by 9-inch baking dish. (Pyrex or ceramic dishes both work well.)

2 Prepare the bacon and French toast: Line a broiler pan with aluminum foil. Arrange the slices of bacon on a slotted broiler rack set over the foil-lined broiler pan. Bake the bacon for 6 to 7 minutes, then rotate the broiler pan 180 degrees so the back of the broiler pan faces the front of the oven. Continue baking the bacon until it is nicely browned, 5 to 7 minutes longer. Using a slotted spoon, transfer the slices of bacon to a paper towel-lined plate to drain. When the bacon is cool enough to handle, coarsely chop it. Set the chopped bacon aside.

3 Reduce the oven temperature to 325°F.

4 Place the 4 eggs, 6 tablespoons of granulated sugar, and ¾ cup of milk in a large bowl and whisk until well blended. Add 2 to 3 slices of brioche or challah, soaking each side well.

5 As the slices of bread soak, place a large skillet over medium heat and add 2 tablespoons of the butter. When the butter is just hot but not yet browning, add the soaked bread slices to the skillet and then put more slices in the bowl with the egg mixture to soak. Cook the slices of bread until both sides are golden and crusty, 2 to 3 minutes per side. (Watch the slices of bread carefully to prevent them from burning; the sugar in the egg mixture will cause them to brown rapidly.) Transfer the cooked bread slices to a paper towel-lined plate. Repeat with the remaining slices of bread, using a paper towel as necessary to wipe out the skillet to remove any burnt bits and adding more butter to the skillet when needed before adding more slices of soaked bread. Stack the cooked bread slices, separating the slices with pieces of paper towel.

6 Cut each slice of bread in half on the diagonal to make 16 triangles. Arrange enough triangles of bread in the buttered baking dish to cover the bottom. Then, cut any remaining slices into 1-inch cubes. Scatter the bread cubes, nuts, raisins or cranberries, and chopped bacon over the bread slices and set the baking dish aside.

7 Prepare the custard and brown sugar-cinnamon topping: Place the 4 eggs, egg yolk, ¼ cup of granulated sugar, and the vanilla in a large mixing bowl and whisk until well blended. Whisk in the 1½ cups of milk and the half-and-half, maple syrup, nutmeg, salt, and pepper. Pour the custard mixture over the bread mixture in the baking dish. Let the bread pudding stand for 15 minutes.

8 Combine the brown sugar and cinnamon in a small bowl. Sprinkle the cinnamon sugar evenly over the bread pudding. Cover the baking dish with aluminum foil. Bake the bread pudding for 25 minutes, then remove the foil and bake the pudding until the top is a deep golden brown and a toothpick or knife inserted into the center comes out with streaks of slightly wet custard, 20 to 25 minutes longer.

9 Remove the baking dish from the oven, cover it loosely with aluminum foil, and let the bread pudding cool until set but still warm, about 20 minutes. (As it sets, the custard will continue to cook, which is why you take it out before it sets completely.) Cut the pudding into squares to serve. Leftover pudding can be cut into individual servings, covered loosely with paper towels, and refrigerated. Microwave it until warmed through, about 1 minute on high power.

TOASTING NUTS

Toasting nuts before you use them intensifies their rich flavor. Although many recipes say to toast nuts in the oven, we recommend toasting them on top of the stove so you can watch them brown and prevent them from burning. Heat a dry skillet—one that is large enough so all of the nuts will fit in a single layer—over medium-high heat. (Do not use a nonstick skillet for this.) Add the nuts and cook them a few minutes, stirring often. (Pine nuts will take only about 1 minute.) When the nuts are fragrant and lightly browned, remove the skillet from the heat. Let the nuts cool on a heatproof plate or on paper towels before chopping or using them.

NOTE: If the bread is fresh, bake the slices on a large baking sheet in a 200°F oven for 15 to 20 minutes to dry them out.

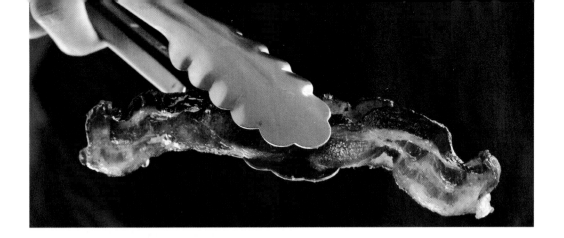

CANDIED BACON SLICES

Makes 7 to 8 slices of bacon

These caramelized slices of bacon are fine snacks on their own or as partners for pancakes and waffles. Or, serve them as finger appetizers by cutting each slice in half and stacking the pieces on a serving plate. Don't think you have to stick strictly to the quantities of sugar and spice in our recipe. Go ahead and have some fun with this by working in your own selection and quantity of spices. Our recipe combines some curry and cinnamon and a little heat from red and black pepper to counter the sweetness of the sugar. Your house will smell like bacon heaven.

7 to 8 slices bacon, preferably
    applewood-smoked

2 packed tablespoons light brown sugar

1 teaspoon yellow curry powder, or more
    to taste

½ teaspoon ground cinnamon

Freshly ground black pepper

Cayenne pepper (optional)

1 Position a rack in the center of the oven and preheat the oven to 400°F.

2 Line a large broiler pan with aluminum foil, shiny side down (this will make cleaning the pan easier). Place the rack of the broiler pan on top of the pan, then arrange the slices of bacon in a single layer on the rack.

3 Mix the brown sugar, curry powder, and cinnamon in a small bowl. Add black pepper and cayenne pepper, if using, to taste. Sprinkle the brown sugar-spice mixture liberally and evenly over each slice of bacon.

4 Bake the bacon until it is crisp and glazed, 10 to 14 minutes; the total baking time will depend on the thickness of the bacon slices. After about 6 minutes, rotate the broiler pan 180 degrees so the back of the broiler pan faces the front of the oven.

5 Let the bacon cool on the broiler rack for about 2 minutes before transferring to a paper towel-lined plate to drain. Serve the bacon warm.

VARIATION: To make praline bacon slices, follow the recipe for Candied Bacon Slices but omit the curry powder and add ¼ to ½ cup finely chopped pecans to the spice mix. Praline bacon slices are terrific for dessert served alone or with vanilla ice cream or alongside French toast.

CHAPTER 12

SWEET'N SAVORY

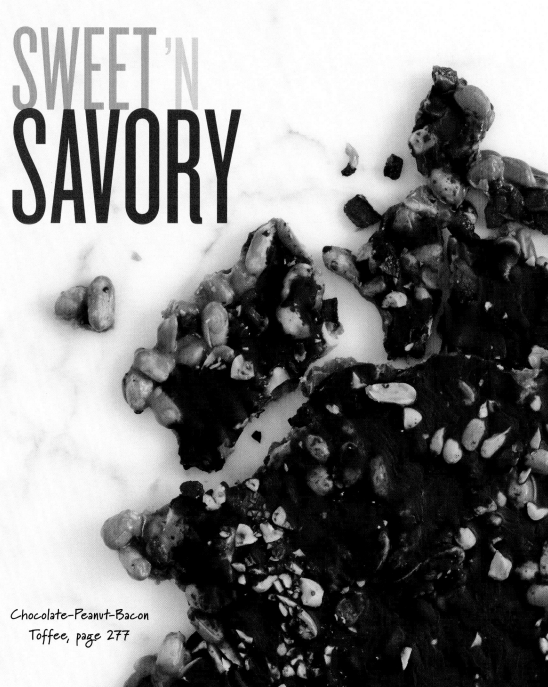

Chocolate-Peanut-Bacon
Toffee, page 277

IN THIS CHAPTER...

We're not the first to discover that

a salty, savory, aged product can help make sublime desserts. Hey, a chocolate chip cookie takes a bitter, fermented product (cacao), adds some salt and sugar, and the result is one of America's great contributions to the world's store of insanely great desserts. These days, with the bacon craze fully upon us, ingenious dessert makers are finding inventive ways to use bacon. Many food blogs and websites offer bacon in doughnuts, ice cream, chocolate chip cookies, and more. We explore our own favorite bacon desserts in this chapter, only scratching the surface of the possibilities. Traditionalists might say, "Bacon doesn't belong in a dessert." But hold off judgment until you make the Peanut Butter Bacon Cookies or the Apple-Bacon Coffe Cake, where bacon shows off its dessert potential.

The Bacon Lace Cookies are delicate, thin, brittle, and savory-sweet with finely chopped peanuts and crisp bacon. The Bacon Granola Bars, with their mix of cranberries, rolled oats, chopped nuts, and bacon, also work well as a breakfast or a trail snack and have just enough honey and brown sugar to satisfy your sweet craving.

Our Chocolate-Peanut-Bacon Toffee, one of our favorite recipes, binds layers of peanuts, bacon, and chocolate with a caramelized butter and sugar mixture. The toffee cools and hardens in the freezer, and then you snap it into uneven pieces of firm, delicious chocolate-peanut-bacon candy.

BACON LACE COOKIES

Makes about 2½ dozen cookies

L ace cookies are sometimes known as florentines although, as best we can tell, they don't come from Florence. They have a unique texture because of the lacy holes that create chewy, slightly crunchy surfaces for your tongue to play over as you munch on them. They are also pretty. We are working with the combination of sweet and salty and the result is paper-thin lacy cookies that never fail to get compliments. They are nice with an afternoon espresso or a scoop of ice cream but are indescribably delicious with ripe strawberries and sweet cream.

⅓ cup diced bacon (about 3 slices)

4 tablespoons (½ stick) unsalted butter, cut into 1-inch-thick pieces

½ cup sugar

3 tablespoons light corn syrup

1 tablespoon heavy (whipping) cream

½ teaspoon pure vanilla extract

½ cup unbleached all-purpose flour

⅓ cup plus 1 tablespoon lightly salted cocktail peanuts, roughly or finely chopped

1 Position a rack in the center of the oven and preheat the oven to 350°F. Line a 13- by 18-inch baking sheet with a nonstick baking liner, such as one made by Silpat.

2 Cook the bacon in a medium-size skillet over medium heat until lightly browned and most of the fat is rendered, 5 to 8 minutes, stirring often and adjusting the heat as necessary. Using a slotted spoon, transfer the bacon to a paper towel-lined plate to drain. Set aside 1 tablespoon of the bacon fat in a heavy 2-quart saucepan. Pat the bacon with paper towels to blot any excess grease.

3 Add the butter, sugar, corn syrup, cream, and vanilla to the reserved bacon fat in the saucepan. Let the mixture come to a boil over

medium heat, stirring constantly. Add the flour and cook, stirring constantly, until the batter is slightly thickened, about 1 minute. Stir in the peanuts and drained bacon.

4 Working in small batches, drop level teaspoons of batter about 3 inches apart on the lined baking sheet. (The batter will spread out into a thin 2- to 3-inch cookie so don't overload the teaspoon.) Bake the cookies until they are golden and bubbly, 5 to 6 minutes.

5 Let the cookies cool on the baking sheet until you can pry up an edge and then gently wedge a metal spatula underneath the cookie to lift it off the baking sheet, 3 to 4 minutes. Transfer the cookies to a wire rack to cool, then stack them between paper towels to absorb any excess grease. Wipe the baking sheet liner with a paper towel and repeat the process with the remaining batter. The cookies can be stored in an airtight container at room temperature for 4 to 5 days; separate each layer of cookies with a piece of waxed paper to prevent the cookies from sticking together. Packed this way, the cookies can be frozen for up to 2 months.

PEANUT BUTTER BACON COOKIES

Makes about 25 cookies

The peanut butter cookie has been a mainstay of the American cookie baker's arsenal since the mid-1930s when they first made their appearance in cookbooks. Our inspiration here was the lifelong love we have always felt for peanut butter and bacon sandwiches. The result is in no way a "shy" cookie. It's all about flavor and crunch: You get the flavors of brown and granulated sugars, peanut butter, and bacon in each bite. The bacon provides a little chewiness as well as saltiness, and the peanut butter enriches the batter with its creaminess. If you have any cookies left over (that's a big if), freeze them in an airtight container.

Vegetable oil cooking spray (optional)

5 slices bacon, cut into ¼-inch pieces

1¼ cups unbleached all-purpose flour

¼ teaspoon baking powder

¼ teaspoon baking soda

¼ teaspoon salt

1 stick (½ cup) unsalted butter, at room temperature

½ cup granulated sugar

½ cup packed light brown sugar

½ cup extra-crunchy peanut butter (not one labeled natural)

1 large egg

1¼ teaspoons pure vanilla extract

1 Position a rack in the upper third of the oven and preheat the oven to 350°F. Line a large baking sheet with parchment paper or spray it with vegetable oil cooking spray.

2 Cook the bacon in a large skillet over medium heat until lightly browned and most of the fat is rendered, 5 to 8 minutes, stirring often and adjusting the heat as necessary.

Using a slotted spoon, transfer the bacon to a paper towel-lined plate to drain.

3 Place the flour, baking powder, baking soda, and salt in a medium-size mixing bowl and stir to combine.

4 Place the butter in a large bowl and, using a standing electric mixer, beat until creamy, 1 to 2 minutes. Add the granulated sugar and brown sugar and beat until very fluffy and well blended, 2 to 3 minutes, stopping the mixer to scrape down the side of the bowl as necessary. Beat in the peanut butter until thoroughly incorporated, about 1 minute. Add the egg and vanilla and beat until just blended.

5 Stir the flour mixture into the peanut butter mixture until well blended. Stir in the drained bacon until just incorporated.

6 Working in batches, roll 1 generous tablespoon of dough between the palms of your hands to form a 1-inch ball (the dough will be soft). Arrange the balls of dough about 2 inches apart on the prepared baking sheet. Use the back of a fork to press each ball into an approximately 1½-inch round and then use the tines of the fork to make a crosshatch pattern on the top of each cookie. It helps to dip the fork into a glass of water after pressing the crosshatch on each cookie. Refrigerate the remaining cookie dough.

7 Bake the cookies until they are slightly browned at the edges, 10 to 12 minutes. To facilitate even browning, after about 6 minutes rotate the baking sheet 180 degrees so the back of the baking sheet faces the front of the oven.

8 Let the cookies cool on the baking sheet until they firm slightly, 1 to 2 minutes. Then, using a wide metal spatula, transfer the cookies to a wire rack to cool completely. Repeat with the remaining cookie dough. The cookies can be stored in an airtight container at room temperature for up to 4 days or frozen for up to 2 months.

BACON GRANOLA BARS

Makes 12 bars

I f you glance at the granola offerings at any mini-mart or newsstand, you'll note that many have strayed from their Age of Aquarius whole-ingredients roots. Too often granola has become a way that we tell ourselves that even when we eat sweets, we are really eating health food. Well, we will just come out and proclaim that while they are not unhealthy, our Bacon Granola Bars are made to satisfy your sweet tooth and your salt tooth and your hint-of-meat tooth. We love them with a freshly brewed cup of good coffee. We love them equally, if not more, with a happy-hour scotch. Keep some in the freezer; you will like the chewy texture and cool mouthfeel.

8 slices apple-wood–smoked or maple-flavored bacon, diced

½ cup dried cranberries

Juice of 1 medium-size orange

3½ cups old-fashioned rolled oats

¼ cup canola oil

¾ cup coarsely chopped almonds

¾ cup coarsely chopped pecans or walnuts

2 teaspoons grated orange zest

1 teaspoon ground cinnamon

Salt

⅓ cup honey

⅓ cup packed dark brown sugar

1½ teaspoons pure vanilla extract

1 Cook the bacon in a large skillet over medium heat until nearly browned but not yet crisp, about 5 minutes, stirring often and adjusting the heat as necessary. Then, using a slotted spoon or a Chinese bamboo skimmer, turn the pieces of bacon over in the fat to render as much fat as possible without over-browning the bacon. Transfer the bacon to a paper towel-lined plate to drain.

2 Combine the cranberries and orange juice in a small saucepan. Cover the pan, let the orange juice come to a simmer over medium-low heat, and cook until the cranberries are very tender and most of the liquid has evaporated, about 8 minutes. Spoon the cranberries into a wire-mesh strainer and, working over the sink, use the bottom of a glass to gently push down on the cranberries to extract and drain off any excess liquid. Let the strained cranberries cool, and discard the liquid.

3 Position a rack in the center of the oven and preheat the oven to 375°F. Line an 8-inch-square baking pan with aluminum foil (see Note).

4 Place the rolled oats and oil in a large bowl and mix until evenly coated. Spread the oats in an even layer in the prepared baking pan and bake until pale golden, 25 to 28 minutes, stirring every 10 minutes. Watch the oats carefully to prevent them from overbrowning toward the end of the baking time.

5 While the oats bake combine all of the nuts in a large mixing bowl. Transfer half of the nuts to a food processor and process them for a few seconds until finely ground. Add the ground nuts to the coarsely chopped nuts. Set aside 2 to 3 tablespoons of the drained bacon and add the remaining bacon and the orange zest, cinnamon, and cooled cranberries to the bowl of nuts. Season the nut mixture with salt to taste.

6 Combine the honey and brown sugar in the small saucepan. Place it over medium-low heat and cook, stirring frequently, until the sugar is fully dissolved, 3 to 4 minutes. Remove the pan from the heat and stir in the vanilla.

7 Remove the baking pan with the oats from the oven and reduce the oven temperature to 300°F. Stir the toasted oats into the nut mixture, setting aside the foil-lined baking pan. Add the honey and brown sugar mixture to the oat and nut mixture and stir with a wooden spoon or rubber spatula until the granola is well blended. Transfer the granola to the foil-lined baking pan. Using the bottom of a glass, pack the granola into a flat, tight layer. Sprinkle the reserved bacon evenly over the packed granola and, using the bottom of the glass, press the bacon into the granola. Bake the granola until golden, 30 to 40 minutes.

8 Place the baking pan on a wire rack and let the granola cool for 20 to 25 minutes. Grasping the foil, remove the granola from the baking pan and transfer it to a cutting board. Using a paring knife or boning knife, cut the granola into bars, each about 1¼- by 4-inches long.

The granola bars can be stored in an airtight container for 4 to 5 days or frozen for up to 2 months.

NOTE: Granola bars have a tendency to stick to the baking pan after they are baked. To make them easy to remove and also prevent the toasted oats from overbrowning, place a piece of aluminum foil, 12 to 16 inches long, in the baking pan, pushing the foil into the corners of the pan (the ends of the foil will hang over the side of the baking pan). After the granola has baked and cooled, pick up the ends of the foil to lift the granola out of the pan in one piece. Then, transfer the granola to a cutting board and cut it into individual bars, removing the foil from the bottom of the bars.

BACON S'MORES

Serves 2

We added pieces of salty, smoky bacon to the layers of graham crackers, chocolate, and melted marshmallow in this campfire classic. It instantly turns what is often considered a child's treat into a dessert more suitable for adult palates. Keep the bacon warm on the edge of the grill and it will help the chocolate square melt a little before you add the toasted marshmallow. Although this recipe serves two, the ingredients can be increased easily to serve any number of lucky diners at the end of a tailgate or backyard picnic, when the grill fire is starting to die and the afternoon sun is starting to fade away. Pass around long-forks, or, better yet, have guests hunt for their own roasting sticks (forsythia branches are perfect).

1 slice applewood- or cherrywood-
    smoked bacon, cooked and cut in half
    crosswise

2 whole graham crackers, broken into 4
    squares

2 thin 2-inch squares milk chocolate

2 large marshmallows (see Note)

1 Prepare a low fire in a charcoal grill or hibachi.

2 When the fire is ready, place the pieces of cooked bacon on the edges of the grill to keep them warm.

3 Just before you toast the marshmallows, lay a piece of bacon on each of 2 graham cracker halves. Then top each piece of bacon with a square of chocolate. Set aside.

4 Place each marshmallow on a thin, long stick or a long-handled fork and toast until they are lightly browned on all sides with a soft, gooey center.

5 Place 1 hot, toasted marshmallow on each of the chocolate squares and cover each with 1 of the remaining graham crackers.

6 Press down on the s'mores lightly to hold the sandwiches together. Let set a few seconds to allow the marshmallow to melt the chocolate, then enjoy!

NOTE: Roasting 2 marshmallows per s'more helps to more fully melt the chocolate.

CHOCOLATE-PEANUT-BACON TOFFEE

Makes about 1½ pounds

t's hard to eat just one piece of bacon, one peanut, or one little square of chocolate. Combine the three and you don't have a chance at moderation, so consider yourself warned: If you make this toffee be prepared to give some away or you will surely eat it all. If you like to make sweets as a holiday gift, add this brittle toffee to your repertoire. While it's delicious at room temperature, the toffee is wonderful to freeze and then break off a piece after dinner when you want something sweet but you don't want to commit to a full-on dessert.

5 slices applewood- or hickory-smoked bacon, cut into ¼-inch pieces

1½ cups lightly salted cocktail peanuts, plus 2 tablespoons chopped lightly salted cocktail peanuts

15 tablespoons (1¾ sticks, plus 1 tablespoon) unsalted butter, cut into ½-inch-thick pieces, plus butter for greasing the baking pan

1 cup sugar

½ teaspoon pure vanilla extract

4 ounces 70 percent cacao dark chocolate, finely chopped

1 Butter a 15- by 10- by 1-inch nonstick baking pan and place it on a heatproof surface.

2 Cook the bacon in a medium-size skillet over medium heat until lightly browned and crisp and most of the fat is rendered, 5 to 8 minutes, stirring often and adjusting the heat as necessary. Using a slotted spoon, transfer the bacon to a paper towel-lined plate to drain, reserving the bacon fat in the skillet.

3 Blot the drained pieces of bacon with paper towels to remove any excess grease. Set aside 3 tablespoons of the bacon pieces.

Combine the remaining bacon pieces with the 1½ cups of peanuts in a medium-size bowl.

4 Pour the bacon fat from the skillet through a wire-mesh strainer set over a small bowl and then place 1 tablespoon of the strained bacon fat in a heavy deep 3- or 4-quart saucepan.

5 Add the butter and sugar to the saucepan and cook over medium-high heat until the butter is almost melted, less than 1 minute. Then whisk constantly until the sugar is incorporated into the butter and the mixture is smooth, 2 to 3 minutes. Add the vanilla. Attach a candy

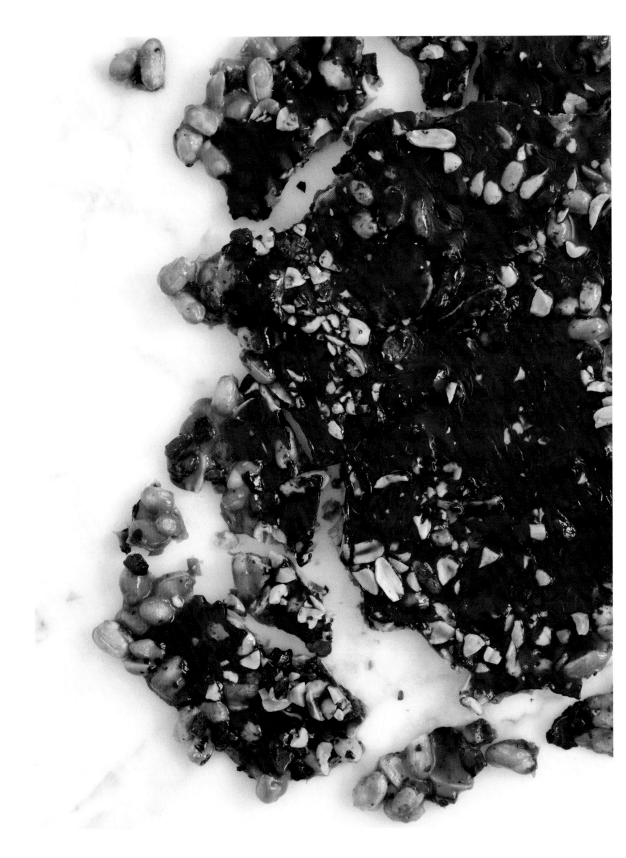

thermometer securely to the side of the saucepan and let the butter and sugar mixture boil, whisking occasionally, until it is a deep golden and registers 300°F on the thermometer.

6 Remove the saucepan from the heat and immediately stir in the bacon and peanut mixture. Pour the hot toffee mixture carefully into the center of the prepared baking pan. Using a butter knife or metal spatula, spread the toffee mixture so that it covers about two thirds of the surface of the pan and is slightly less than 1/2 inch thick. Let the toffee set for about

30 seconds, then sprinkle the chocolate on top, spreading it out with the butter knife or spatula. Sprinkle the remaining 2 tablespoons of chopped peanuts and the reserved bacon evenly over the top of the toffee and then freeze it until firm, about 30 minutes.

7 Slip the spatula under the toffee to loosen it from the pan and then break the toffee into pieces. The toffee can be stored in an airtight container at room temperature for up to 5 days or in the freezer for up to 2 weeks.

CARAMEL SAUCE
with Bacon and Pecans

Makes about 1⅔ cups

More properly a topping rather than a full-fledged dessert, this sauce is like pouring the flavor essence of pecan pie (porked up with bacon) over a scoop of ice cream. Bacon amplifies the distinctive flavors of caramelized sugar and cream. You can also serve this topping over waffles, baked apples, grilled bananas, or pound cake. And do add a snifter of Cognac or brandy to sip beside a nice fire.

1 vanilla bean, or 1 teaspoon pure vanilla
    extract

4 slices bacon, diced

1¼ cups sugar

1 cup heavy (whipping) cream

⅓ cup toasted pecans (see page 264),
    coarsely chopped

1 If you are using a vanilla bean, cut it in half crosswise and set one half aside for another use. Split the remaining half in half lengthwise

and, using the tip of the knife, scrape out the seeds into a small bowl and set aside.

2 Cook the bacon in a medium-size skillet over medium heat until lightly browned and the fat is rendered, 5 to 8 minutes, stirring often and adjusting the heat as necessary. Using a slotted spoon, transfer the bacon to a paper towel-lined plate to drain.

3 Combine the sugar and ⅓ cup of water in a heavy saucepan. Cover the pan and cook over low heat, without stirring, until the sugar dissolves, about 5 minutes. Increase the heat to medium-high and let boil, uncovered, until the sugar turns a rich amber brown, 4 to 5 minutes. If you want a medium-colored caramel, remove the sugar mixture from the heat when it is still a light amber; it will continue to cook and darken off the heat. Watch the sugar mixture carefully as it will change from a rich caramel to a burnt one quickly.

4 Remove the sugar mixture from the heat and, while whisking, gradually pour in the heavy cream. Be careful as you do this as the cream will bubble up wildly. If the sauce hardens, return the saucepan to low heat and whisk until smooth. Add the vanilla bean seeds to the caramel sauce and whisk to blend. Or whisk in the vanilla extract, if using.

5 Place the pan over medium-low heat, stir in the drained bacon and the pecans, and cook, stirring, until the sauce is thick and smooth, 3 to 5 minutes. Serve the caramel sauce warm or at room temperature. The sauce can be refrigerated, covered, for about 1 week and reheated in a microwave oven on high power or on top of the stove in a small pan over very low heat, stirring occasionally until warmed through.

RUM ICE CREAM
with Candied Bacon Chips

Makes about 5½ cups

I n childhood, rum raisin ice cream was a puzzlement. Why would you want to ruin a good sweet with yucky booze? There comes a time, however, when we recognize that a little liquor perks up a dessert (and a dessert eater). Hence, this ice cream. We skipped the raisins (you can toss some in) and went straight for the rum-bacon one-two punch. The result is a dessert with the sweet smoothness of homemade ice cream, the salty sweet savoriness of candied bacon, and the pleasing bite of rum.

A word of thanks is due here to the modern ice-cream maker; it's much less taxing and a good deal more speedy than the eternally arm-wearying hand-cranked rock-salt machine of yore.

4 cups half-and-half (see Note)

⅓ cup packed light or dark brown sugar

5 large egg yolks

⅓ cup granulated sugar

1 teaspoon pure vanilla extract

Candied Bacon Chips
  (recipe follows)

4½ teaspoons dark rum or bourbon

1 Place a medium-size saucepan over medium to medium-low heat, add the half-and-half and brown sugar, and whisk them together. Cook gently just until the mixture comes to a boil, whisking occasionally.

2 Meanwhile, as the half-and-half mixture heats, combine the egg yolks and granulated sugar in a medium-size bowl. Using a wire whisk or a hand-held electric mixer, beat the egg yolk and sugar mixture until it is thick and a pale yellow color, 2 to 3 minutes.

3 When the half-and-half mixture has just come to a boil, whisk about one third of it into the egg yolk and sugar mixture. Whisk another third into the egg yolk mixture and then pour the entire mixture into the saucepan. Using a wooden spoon, stir the custard constantly over low heat until it thickens slightly and coats the back of a spoon. Do *not* let the custard boil or the yolks will overcook and harden.

4 Pour the custard through a wire-mesh strainer set over a large bowl and let come to room temperature. Stir in the vanilla. Cover and refrigerate the custard for 2 hours or as long as overnight. Or, set the custard over an ice bath (a bowl filled with ice water) to chill quickly.

5 Following the manufacturer's instructions, turn on the ice-cream maker and pour the chilled custard into the chilled freezer bowl. Run the machine until the custard is nearly thickened, 15 to 20 minutes (see Note). Add the Candied Bacon Chips to the custard about one third at a time and mix for 30 seconds to 1 minute after each addition, repeating until all of the bacon chips have been incorporated. Add the rum or bourbon and mix just to blend it into the ice cream, about 1 minute.

6 When done, the ice cream will have a soft, creamy texture. If you desire a firmer ice cream, transfer the mixture to an airtight container and freeze it for about 2 hours. Remove the ice cream from the freezer about 5 minutes before serving to allow it to soften slightly.

NOTE: We made this ice cream using half-and-half and found it to be sufficiently rich and creamy. However, if you are a purist, go ahead and substitute up to 4 cups of heavy cream for the half-and-half.

CANDIED BACON CHIPS

Makes about ½ cup of bacon chips

Bacon chips, sweetened with brown sugar, are a good addition not only for the rum ice cream but also for sprinkling into mixed green salads and chocolate chip cookie dough or for adding to batters for pancakes, waffles, quick breads, and corn and fruit muffins. They make for little bits of unexpected crunch, wrapped in a salty-sweet package. We also use bacon chips in our recipe for caramelized pears with ice cream.

5 slices bacon (see Note)

5 teaspoons packed light brown sugar

1 Position a rack in the center of the oven and preheat the oven to 400°F.

2 Line a broiler pan with aluminum foil to make cleaning the pan easier. Set the broiler pan rack on the pan and arrange the slices of bacon on the rack in a single layer so that they do not touch. Sprinkle each slice of bacon evenly with 1 teaspoon of the brown sugar.

3 Bake the bacon until crisp and darkly glazed, 10 to 14 minutes (the baking time will depend on the thickness of the bacon). After the bacon has baked about 6 minutes, to facilitate even browning, rotate the broiler pan 180 degrees so the back of the pan faces the front of the oven.

4 Let the bacon cool for 2 to 3 minutes before using tongs to transfer the slices to a cutting board. When cool, chop the bacon into ¼-inch pieces. Place the bacon chips in a small container, fitted with a lid, and refrigerate or freeze until ready to use. The bacon chips can be refrigerated for 1 week or frozen for up to 2 months. It is not necessary to thaw frozen chips before using.

NOTE: We've found it's best to use a bacon of regular thickness, one that's neither too thin nor too thick, to make bacon chips.

CARAMELIZED PEARS AND CANDIED BACON CHIPS

Serves 4

When you don't have time to make your own ice cream (which, face it, is most of the time), serving your favorite store-bought premium ice cream with this caramelized fruit and bacon topping will dress it up nicely. Pears have a beautifully soft sweet flesh that melts in your mouth, a happy partner to the salty sweet, crunchy bacon topping. When we pulled this from the oven, we were inspired by the taste of Jacques Torres's salted caramel ice cream; so the next time we made it we picked up a pint of dulce de leche ice cream. Jacques would have approved. Superb!

In the interests of complete research, we also tasted it with vanilla, chocolate, and chocolate chip ice cream. Superb again! We have resolved to continue researching this interesting question.

3 slices bacon

2 tablespoons packed light brown sugar

2 ripe Bartlett or Anjou pears, peeled, cored, and cut in quarters lengthwise

4½ teaspoons fresh lemon juice

1 teaspoon pure vanilla extract

2 tablespoons (¼ stick) unsalted butter

2 tablespoons granulated sugar

1 pint vanilla or dulce de leche ice cream

1 Position a rack in the center of the oven and preheat the oven to 400°F.

2 Line a broiler pan with aluminum foil to make cleaning the pan easier. Set the broiler pan rack on the pan and arrange the slices of bacon on the rack in a single layer so that they do not touch. Sprinkle each slice of bacon evenly with 1 teaspoon of the brown sugar.

3 Bake the bacon until crisp and darkly glazed, 10 to 14 minutes (the baking time will depend on the thickness of the bacon).

After the bacon has baked about 6 minutes, to facilitate browning, rotate the broiler pan 180 degrees so the back of the pan faces the front of the oven. Let the bacon cool for 2 to 3 minutes before using tongs to transfer the slices to a cutting board. When cool, chop the bacon into ¼-inch pieces and set them aside.

4 Place the pears in a large bowl, add the lemon juice and vanilla, and toss to combine.

5 Melt the butter in a medium-size skillet set over medium to medium-low heat. Add the

remaining 1 tablespoon of brown sugar and the granulated sugar and, using a long-handled wooden spoon, stir constantly until the sugars are dissolved and the syrup turns a deep golden color, 2 to 3 minutes. Adjust the heat as necessary and watch that the syrup doesn't get too dark or too hot or it will smoke and burn.

6 Place the pears, with a cut side down, in the syrup. Add the pears carefully as the syrup will be very hot; it helps to use a pair of long-handled tongs. Pour any remaining lemon juice and vanilla mixture from the bowl over the pears. Cover the skillet and cook the pears until just fork-tender, 2 to 3 minutes, turning the pears over in the syrup once or twice.

7 Divide the pears among 4 plates. Scoop a portion of ice cream onto each plate. Sprinkle each serving evenly with the candied bacon chips and drizzle the skillet sauce over all.

VARIATION: You can substitute 2 bananas for the pears in this recipe. Cut each banana in half crosswise and then again in half lengthwise, so that you have 8 pieces in all. Then proceed with the recipe, sprinkling the bananas with the lemon juice and vanilla and making the caramelized syrup in the skillet. When the syrup reaches a golden color, add the bananas and cook them until just slightly softened, about 1 minute. Place 2 pieces of banana on each dessert plate and serve them with the ice cream, bacon chips, and skillet sauce as directed in Step 7.

APPLE-BACON COFFEE CAKE
with Bourbon-Pecan Glaze

Makes sixteen 2-inch cake squares

Here's a cake that's a family reunion of many delicious ingredients—apple, cinnamon, bourbon, and maple or vanilla. We use bacon twice as a flavoring agent, once in the cake batter and again sprinkled on top of the baked cake before it's glazed. We recommend a lean, meaty cut of bacon. If you find that the bacon is very fatty, simply trim off most of the fatty ends of each slice and use another meaty slice or two to supplement what you've trimmed away. We used five slices of bacon in this recipe, but if you want to push the bacon flavor a little more, add another slice of bacon to the cake batter and one more to the pecan and bacon topping.

8 tablespoons (1 stick) unsalted butter, at room temperature, cut into 1-inch pieces, plus butter for greasing the baking pan

2 cups unbleached all-purpose flour, plus flour for dusting the baking pan

5 slices maple-flavored or applewood-smoked bacon, diced

2 teaspoons baking soda

1 teaspoon ground cinnamon

Pinch of salt

½ cup granulated sugar

¼ cup packed light brown sugar

2 large eggs

2 tablespoons bourbon

1½ teaspoons maple or pure vanilla extract

¾ cup well-shaken buttermilk

1 medium-size Granny Smith apple, peeled, cored, and diced (about 1 cup)

½ cup confectioners' sugar

2 teaspoons heavy (whipping) cream or half-and-half

¼ cup lightly toasted coarsely chopped pecans (see page 264)

1 Position a rack in the center of the oven and preheat the oven to 350°F. Butter an 8-inch-square baking pan and dust it with flour, knocking out the excess flour.

2 Cook the bacon in a medium-size skillet over medium heat until lightly browned and most of the fat is rendered, 5 to 8 minutes, stirring often and adjusting the heat as necessary. Using a slotted spoon, transfer the bacon to a paper towel-lined plate to drain.

3 Combine the flour, baking soda, cinnamon, and salt in a large mixing bowl. Place the butter, granulated sugar, and brown sugar in the bowl of a standing mixer or in a large mixing bowl and beat with a standing mixer or a hand-held mixer at medium speed until well creamed, 2 to 3 minutes. Add the eggs, 1 tablespoon of the bourbon, and the maple or vanilla extract and beat on medium speed until well combined, 2 to 3 minutes. Add the buttermilk and beat until well blended, 1 to 2 minutes, stopping the mixer occasionally to scrape down the side of the bowl. The butter-milk mixture will appear curdled.

4 Add the dry ingredients to the buttermilk mixture, one half at a time, beating on low speed until just incorporated. Stir the apple and all but 2 to 3 tablespoons of the drained bacon into the batter, setting aside the remaining bacon for topping the coffee cake.

5 Transfer the batter to the prepared baking pan. Bake the coffee cake until a cake tester or toothpick inserted into the center comes out clean, 35 to 40 minutes. Transfer the coffee cake to a wire rack and let it cool in the pan for about 10 minutes. Then, invert the coffee cake onto the rack so that it is right side up and let it cool to room temperature before glazing it.

6 While the coffee cake cools, place the confectioners' sugar, heavy cream or half-and-half, and the remaining 1 tablespoon of bourbon in a medium-size mixing bowl and whisk until smooth. Place the cooled cake on a serving platter and sprinkle the pecans and the remaining bacon over it. Using a spoon, drizzle the glaze back and forth over the pecans and bacon. Let the glaze set for about 30 minutes before cutting the coffee cake into 2-inch squares. The coffee cake can be stored in a covered container for 2 to 3 days.

Conversion Tables

Please note that all conversions are approximate but close enough to be useful when converting from one system to another.

OVEN TEMPERATURES

FAHRENHEIT	GAS MARK	CELSIUS
250	½	120
275	1	140
300	2	150
325	3	160
350	4	180
375	5	190
400	6	200
425	7	220
450	8	230
475	9	240
500	10	260

NOTE: *Reduce the temperature by 20°C (68°F) for fan-assisted ovens.*

APPROXIMATE EQUIVALENTS

1 stick butter = 8 tbs = 4 oz = ½ cup = 115 g

1 cup all-purpose presifted flour = 4.7 oz

1 cup granulated sugar = 8 oz = 220 g

1 cup (firmly packed) brown sugar = 6 oz = 220 g to 230 g

1 cup confectioners' sugar = 4½ oz = 115 g

1 cup honey or syrup = 12 oz

1 cup grated cheese = 4 oz

1 cup dried beans = 6 oz

1 large egg = about 2 oz or about 3 tbs

1 egg yolk = about 1 tbs

1 egg white = about 2 tbs

LIQUID CONVERSIONS

U.S.	IMPERIAL	METRIC
2 tbs	1 fl oz	30 ml
3 tbs	1½ fl oz	45 ml
¼ cup	2 fl oz	60 ml
⅓ cup	2½ fl oz	75 ml
⅓ cup + 1 tbs	3 fl oz	90 ml
⅓ cup + 2 tbs	3½ fl oz	100 ml
½ cup	4 fl oz	125 ml
⅔ cup	5 fl oz	150 ml
¾ cup	6 fl oz	175 ml
¾ cup + 2 tbs	7 fl oz	200 ml
1 cup	8 fl oz	250 ml
1 cup + 2 tbs	9 fl oz	275 ml
1¼ cups	10 fl oz	300 ml
1⅓ cups	11 fl oz	325 ml
1½ cups	12 fl oz	350 ml
1⅔ cups	13 fl oz	375 ml
1¾ cups	14 fl oz	400 ml
1¾ cups + 2 tbs	15 fl oz	450 ml
2 cups (1 pint)	16 fl oz	500 ml
2½ cups	20 fl oz (1 pint)	600 ml
3¾ cups	1½ pints	900 ml
4 cups	1¾ pints	1 liter

WEIGHT CONVERSIONS

US/UK	METRIC	US/UK	METRIC
½ oz	15 g	7 oz	200 g
1 oz	30 g	8 oz	250 g
1½ oz	45 g	9 oz	275 g
2 oz	60 g	10 oz	300 g
2½ oz	75 g	11 oz	325 g
3 oz	90 g	12 oz	350 g
3½ oz	100 g	13 oz	375 g
4 oz	125 g	14 oz	400 g
5 oz	150 g	15 oz	450 g
6 oz	175 g	1 lb	500 g

Really Good Bacon

Here are a few of the more than twenty-five brands of bacons we used when testing our recipes. Those that aren't available in major supermarkets almost always have websites where you can place an order and have their wonderful bacon delivered right to your door. You may expect to pay a premium for these super bacons and a minimum order is sometimes required, but to our way of thinking, it's worth it.

BENTON'S SMOKY MOUNTAIN COUNTRY HAMS

2603 Highway 4ll North
Madisonville, Tennessee 37354-6356
(423) 442-5003
bentonscountryhams2.com

Allan Benton says that the book *Pig Perfect* (full disclosure: written by Peter Kaminsky) changed his farming life. Benton's bacon, made from heritage-breed pigs, has more of the intramuscular fat that's needed when smoking so that the pork meat doesn't become overly dry and tough. Allan sent us several packages of bacon for testing and tasting, and before we opened a package we could smell the smoke. His bacon is mostly made with hickory with a touch of applewood, and Allan says chefs love to pair it with all kinds of foods. Because of its intensity you need only a small piece to make a big impression in a dish. Allan recommends not cooking the bacon too crisply. He says packages can be refrigerated for several months without freezing.

Allan's bacon is one of our favorites. We made Bucatini all'Amatriciana (page 183); Baked Eggs with Spinach, Bacon, and Salsa (page 253); and Bacon, Sweet Potato, and Greens Stuffing with Jalapeño Corn Bread (page 244) with Benton's bacon.

BROADBENT'S

257 Mary Blue Road
Kuttawa, Kentucky 42055
(800) 841-2202
broadbenthams.com

While the company was founded in 1909, Broadbent's current owners have been in charge since 1999. Its bacon has a deep red meat color and a little more fat in proportion to the meat than the average bacon. It is also a little thicker than commercially produced bacons. In flavor its salty hamminess brings to mind English or Irish bacon, made from the loin. For us the strong saltiness meant less of this bacon was needed for some recipes. However, the amount of salt varies from one kind of bacon to another. Broadbent's applewood-smoked, dry-cured country bacon, cured with salt, sugar, and sodium nitrate, was not as salty. The flavor was very good, quite intense. We love this bacon and used it to make a cauliflower-onion-tomato bake (page 206).

Broadbent's offers a variety of bacons featuring such flavor-boosting ingredients as cinnamon or sun-dried tomatoes. It makes a dry-cured nitrate-free bacon with salt and sugar and also hickory-smoked, applewood-smoked, and maple-flavored bacons.

Our favorite is Broadbent's hickory-smoked pepper bacon, made with salt, sugar, sodium nitrite, and pepper. It's fantastic, with a strong smoky taste. Throw it in a pan with a little olive oil and then sauté a bunch of fresh vegetables. Or microwave it until it just begins to crisp, then chop it into $\frac{1}{2}$-inch pieces and toss these with greens, chopped fennel, ripe tomatoes, and red onion. In both of these dishes the bacon adds an element of fat, salt, smokiness, and a distinctive peppery taste—four strong seasoners in one ingredient. You can't beat that. Try it with Broccoli Rabe with Bacon and Garlic (page 201) or Garlicky Rosemary Bacon and Kale (page 211).

CAW CAW CREEK

709 Woodrow Street #220
Columbia, South Carolina 29205
(803) 255-0112
cawcawcreek@gmail.com

Emile DeFelice, owner of Caw Caw Creek, was a major character in *Pig Perfect* (by Peter Kaminsky) and is known for his pastured pork. He is one of the pioneers of the artisanal food and farming movement in his native South Carolina. Many of his hogs roam the woods of his South Carolina farm, foraging for acorns just like the famed Ibérico hogs of Spain. This produces a most succulent, flavorful fat. Emile's thick-cut bacon is dry-cured in sugar and salt and smoked; he uses no preservatives. The bacon is simple, straightforward, old-fashioned, and a testament to the truth that if you use the best ingredients you will get a superior product. Try it in our Butternut Squash Soup (page 53). Emile's bacon and full line of pork products are available online.

DREYMILLER AND KRAY

140 South State Street
Hampshire, Illinois 60140
(847) 683-2271
dreymillerandkray.com

A small company in Hampshire, Illinois, with a big reputation, Dreymiller and Kray has been making great hickory-smoked bacon since 1929. In 2011 it launched the supernal Goose Island Matilda Beer bacon. Dreymiller and Kray start with pork bellies that are massaged and tumbled in a beer brine (which doesn't sound half bad for anybody's belly). Then the pork bellies are brick-house-smoked over mild, fruity applewood. "You can smell the applewood smoke and the beer together in the smokehouse," says owner and president Ed Reiser. We found Dreymiller and Kray's to be more heavily salted than other bacons. You can purchase the bacon online or at the retail store Dreymiller and Kray. Try this bacon in our Bacon Brisket and Beer Chili (page 107).

FLYING PIGS FARM

246 Sutherland Road
Shushan, New York 12873
(518) 854-3844
flyingpigsfarm.com

One of the pioneers raising free-range heritage-breed pigs, Flying Pigs Farm, in upstate New York, is one of the favorite purveyors at New York City farmers' markets. It's the type of local supplier that you will find at farmers' markets around the country, and we urge you to try the meats from these farms. They can be your best source for bacon. While you're at it, also try the fresh pork and smoked hams they sell. Flying Pigs Farm's bacon was delicious in our Warm Spinach Salad with Bacon, Shrimp, and Bell Peppers (page 96).

HERITAGE FOODS USA

Box 198
402 Graham Avenue
Brooklyn, New York 11211
(718) 389-0985
heritagefoodsusa.com

Founded by Patrick Martins, who was also the moving force behind Slow Food USA, this outpost of heritage breeds in Williamsburg, Brooklyn, supports some of America's premier sustainable farmers of heritage breeds. You can buy pork, beef, and turkey from Heritage Foods USA, and we love its bacon program, which delivers a selection of six different bacon varieties every two months. A true bacon treat!

HORMEL NATURAL CHOICE

hormelnatural.com

Hormel Natural Choice bacon is free of added colors, flavors, and preservatives and has a winning proportion of meat to fat. The bacon is available at supermarkets nationally. We loved it in our Bacon Bolognese with Saffron (page 191).

JONES DAIRY FARM

601 Jones Avenue
Fort Atkinson, Wisconsin 53538
(800) 563-1004 or (920) 563-2963
jonesdairyfarm.com

A family-owned and -operated business that is more than a century old, Jones Dairy Farm was established in Fort Atkinson, Wisconsin, in 1889. The current president and sixth generation owner, Philip Jones, went to Paris for his culinary expertise and worked as an executive chef for thirteen years before his relatives would allow him to even think about coming home to work in the family business. Jones Dairy Farm makes a pure cherrywood-smoked bacon that has a perfectly balanced salty, sweet, smoky flavor and is wonderful served with eggs for breakfast or when making our Paella with Chicken and Bacon (page 146). Its regular thinner-cut bacon is also good for making our Crusted Salmon with Avocado and Red Onion Green Salad (page 159) or delicious in our Rum Ice Cream with Candied Bacon Chips (page 281). Jones Dairy Farm sells its bacon in such specialty food shops as Harris Teeter and Wegmans and through its website.

NATURE'S PROMISE

Stop & Shop

(800) 767-7772

stopandshop.com

Uncured hickory-smoked bacon—no antibiotics, no hormones, no nitrates, no growth stimulants or added hormones, no preservatives, and vegetarian fed with no animal by-products: That's a lot of nos and we like that. Nature's Promise is the organic house brand for Stop & Shop. Like a number of supermarket chains around the country, Stop & Shop has started to offer organic food. Three cheers! Nature's Promise is a little more thinly sliced than other artisanal bacons. Four slices produced about two tablespoons of bacon fat. It fries up with a lovely mix of sweet-salty-smoky flavors. Use it as an everyday bacon or in the Sweet Potato Pancakes with Bacon (page 219); Non-Suffering Succotash (page 215); or Frittata with Asparagus, Shallots, and Bacon (page 260).

NIMAN RANCH

1600 Harbor Bay Parkway

Suite 250

Alameda, California 94502

(510) 808-0340

nimanranch.com

"We let pigs be pigs" is the simple philosophy of Paul Willis, founder of Niman Ranch. Among devotees of sustainably, humanely raised pigs and of pork farmer-owned cooperatives, Niman Ranch is known as the industry leader. It produces truly beautiful bacon. Thick-sliced, both cured and uncured, the bacon from free-range animals has really good-tasting fat, and because the meat comes from well-exercised animals it also has more flavor than the average bacon. This is what farm-raised bacon tasted like fifty years ago—simple, to the point, and fabulous. We found this bacon to work in so many of our recipes. You will like it with Chicken Tagine with Bacon, Butternut Squash, and Prunes (page 136), Chicken Marsala with Bacon and Sage (page 138), or our Chocolate-Peanut-Bacon Toffee (page 277).

Many Whole Foods Markets and specialty food shops all across the country stock Niman Ranch products, which are also available through its website.

SMOKEHOUSE OF THE CATSKILLS

724 Route 212

Saugerties, New York 12477

(845) 246-8767

smokehouseofthecatskills.com

We've been patronizing this Catskill institution just outside Saugerties, New York, for years. Smokehouse of the Catskills' double-smoked bacon has a beautiful color, a good proportion of meat to fat, and killer flavor. We asked the owner what the secret of double smoking is and his answer was as instructive as a politician's when he wants to duck a question about a former mistress. Oh well, what did we expect? The point is, if you ever drive by a smokehouse, stop in and check it out. You may find some great bacon as well as sausages and other smoked meats that you've never tried before.

By the way, Saugerties is the town where the house known as Big Pink is, made famous by The Band in *Music from Big Pink*, revered by music aficionados as one of the two or three great albums of the rock-and-roll era. Don't limit yourself to our choices, but Smokehouse of the Catskills' bacon worked for us when we tested Bacon and Butternut Squash Galette (page 43) and Nuevos Huevos Rancheros (page 250).

S. WALLACE EDWARDS & SONS, INC.

P.O. Box 25

Surry, Virginia 23883

(800) 222-4267

virginiatraditions.com

Affable Sam Edwards is a poster boy for sustainable American products. He uses only heritage breeds and says he can't get enough of them, completely selling out all the bacon he makes. He produces three different bacons: hickory smoked; pepper coated; and brown sugar, cinnamon, and apple rubbed. According to Sam his bacon loses about 10 percent of its weight after curing, giving it a more intense flavor and a more stable shelf life. Sam adds that chefs really like using his bacon with poultry and fish dishes. We liked his bacon in Flaky Cod Fillets with Bacon and Wine-Braised Fennel (page 156).

SWISS MEAT & SAUSAGE CO.

2056 South Highway 19

Hermann, Missouri 65041

(800) 793-7947

swissmeats.com

The four Sloan sisters are justly proud of their bacon recipe, which was handed down from their parents, Bill and Margie. Their hickory wood-smoked bacon is sugar cured, hardwood smoked, and tumbler dried to tenderize and season it. We've tasted Swiss Meat & Sausage Co.'s very good pepper-rubbed, honey-cured, and cinnamon- and applewood-smoked bacons, as well as their cottage bacon, made from a boneless pork shoulder, which tastes something like English or Canadian bacon. Try the hickorywood-smoked bacon with Bacon, Grits, and Leek Soufflé (page 256) or the cinnamon and applewood-smoked bacon with French Toast Bread Pudding with Bacon and Cinnamon (page 262).

THIELEN MEATS OF PIERZ

310 North Main Street

Pierz, Minnesota 56364

(877) 377-6256 or (320) 468-6616

thielen-meats.com

A family business since 1922, Thielen Meats works with pork bellies that are leaner than those many producers use, resulting in an exceptionally high ratio of meat to fat. Thielen Meats clings to a traditional long-smoking recipe, which is almost double the hours of present-day methods and produces a very smoky bacon. Breathe in the aroma when you open the package. It smells like a campfire the morning after.

We tested our Spiced Nuts with Bacon (page 22) with Thielen Meats' bacon. The high meat-to-fat ratio produced bite-size nuggets with just the right amount of mouth-filling crunch to go with the nuts. But don't expect much fat when the bacon is fried; this is a bacon that presents itself when cooked like small, thin pieces of delicious smoked ham. For one of its specialty bacons, Thielen Meats uses minced garlic in the marinating and curing process and then leaves the garlic sitting on the bacon while it smokes. It's delicious and mighty powerful, but you need to be a garlic lover. We used it to sauté broccoli rabe and onions for a quick tomatoless pasta sauce and it was also lean but superb in our Osso Buco with Orange and Lemon Gremolata (page 110).

Thielen Meats' bacon is not available online but you can call directly and someone will take your order and explain the shipping and handling policy.

VANDE ROSE FARMS

P.O. Box 160

305 Main Street, Suite #1

Iowa Falls, Iowa 50126

(866) 522-4448

vanderosefarms.com

We have only good things to say about Vande Rose Farms' great bacon, definitely one of our favorites. With its deep, vibrant reddish-brown color this bacon proudly wears its old-fashioned brown sugar cure and applewood smoke. Equally old-fashioned, the heritage-breed Duroc hogs are raised without growth hormones, antibiotics, or phosphates. The bacon has a nice proportion of meat to fat and there is minimal shrinkage when cooked. Three slices yielded 3 tablespoons of bacon fat and still left us with generously thick slices. It hit the spot with Linguine with Fresh Clams, Bacon, and Basil (and a Touch of Cream) (page 193) and our Bacon Bread Crumbs (page 224).

Granted, it's not the cheapest bacon, but it's worth every penny. Unless you live in Iowa, where Vande Rose Farms sells its bacon at Hy-Vee stores, you can only purchase it through the website.

VERMONT SMOKE AND CURE

P.O. Box 278

South Barre, Vermont

(802) 476-4666

vtsmokeandcure.com

We tested our Bacon-Flavored Stock (page 54) and our Slow-Cooker Pulled Bacon and Bourbon Beans (page 198) with the wonderful Vermont Smoke and Cure slab bacon, which is brined in Vermont maple syrup and smoked using corncobs and maplewood. It is not overly salty and has a slight sweetness from the Vermont maple syrup brine. The company is committed to the local farming industry and buys its hogs, syrup, and wood for smoking from Vermont suppliers. We found Vermont Smoke and Cure bacon, made from certified humanely raised hogs, at Whole Foods. It's sold in the Boston area at Roche Bros., but it's also available by mail order online.

ZINGERMAN'S

422 Detroit Street

Ann Arbor, Michigan 48104

(888) 636-8162

zingermans.com

Zingerman's is probably the best mail-order house for the full range of artisanal, sustainable, and every other good thing you can think of in terms of food. If you are looking for an easy way to try some of the best bacons, Zingerman's Bacon Club is the place to start. *Zingerman's Guide to Better Bacon* by Zingerman's founder Ari Weinzweig is a super introduction to baconology. In addition to his own book, Weinzweig also sells the completely charming, authoritative, and wacky *Adventures of a Bacon Curer* by Maynard Davies.

INDEX